HUNDREDS OF TIPS, TRICKS,
AND TECHNIQUES FROM
TOP ILLUSTRATOR ARTISTS

The Adobe® Illustrator® CS5

WOW!
Book

Sharon Steuer
AND THE ILLUSTRATOR WOW! TEAM

**Peachpit
Press**

The Adobe Illustrator CS5 WOW! Book

Sharon Steuer

Peachpit Press

1249 Eighth Street

Berkeley, CA 94710

510/524-2178

Find us on the Web at: www.peachpit.com

To report errors, please send a note to errata@peachpit.com

Peachpit Press is a division of Pearson Education.

Real World Adobe Illustrator CS5 excerpted content is ©2011 Mordy Golding

Used with permission of Pearson Education, Inc. and Peachpit Press.

Contributing Writers & Consultants to this edition: Cristen Gillespie, Steven H. Gordon, Lisa Jackmore, Aaron McGarry, Ryan Putnam, Chris Leavens, and Pete Maric
Technical Editor: Jean-Claude Tremblay
Line Editor: Eric Schumacher-Rasmussen
Cover Designer: Mimi Heft
Cover Illustrator: Lance Jackson
Indexer: Jack Lewis
Proofreaders: Darren Meiss and Peg Maskell Korn
First edition Illustrator **WOW! Book** designer: Barbara Sudick
WOW! Series Editor: Linnea Dayton

ISBN 13: 978-0-321-71244-8

ISBN 10: 0-321-71244-7

9 8 7 6 5 4 3 2 1

Printed and bound in the United States of America.

WOW!
Contents
at a
Glance...

Contents

1

Your Creative Workspace

Introduction

2

Designing Type & Layout

Introduction

3

Rethinking Construction

Introduction

Advanced Techniques:

6 Reshaping Dimensions

7 Mastering Complexity

Creatively Combining Apps

pull-out card, inside back cover:

Windows WOW! Glossary/Windows Fingerdance

Mac WOW! Glossary/Mac Fingerdance

The Adobe Illustrator CS5 WOW! Book
Team of Contributing Writers and Editors

Sharon Steuer has been teaching, exhibiting, and writing in the digital art world since 1983. Sharon is the originator and lead author of **The Illustrator WOW! Book** series, and author of **Creative Thinking in Photoshop: A New Approach to Digital Art**, and the soon to be released **Zen of Illustrator** (info@zenofillustrator.com). In between books, Sharon is a full-time artist working in traditional and digital media (www.ssteuer.com). She lives with her cats and her audio professor husband, Jeff Jacoby (jeffjacoby.net). As always, she is extremely grateful to **WOW!** team members (past and present), Peachpit, Adobe, and of course the amazing **WOW!** artists for constant inspiration, and for making this book possible.

Jean-Claude Tremblay is the owner of Proficiografik, a consulting and training service for the graphic and print community, designed to help clients work efficiently. He is an Adobe Certified Expert Design Master and an Adobe Community Professionals member. He acts as an Adobe Community Help Moderator for Illustrator help and co-representative for the newly created InDesign User Group in Montréal. After serving as a magnificent **WOW!** tester, Jean-Claude returns for his third mandate as the **WOW!** technical editor, chief advisor, software collector, and resident magician. He lives in the greater Montréal area with his wife Suzanne and his wonderful daughter Judith.

Cristen Gillespie has contributed to other **WOW!** books, including coauthoring the current edition of **The Photoshop WOW! Book**. She has also coauthored articles for *Photoshop User* magazine. Recently armed with a broadband connection, Cristen creatively tackles step-by-step Techniques, Galleries, and Introductions with equal strength and commitment. She is a wonderful writer and a fabulous collaborator, and we hope she'll stay with **Illustrator WOW!** for many years to come.

Steven H. Gordon is a returning coauthor for step-by-step Techniques and Galleries. Steven has been an ace member of the team since **The Illustrator 9 WOW! Book.** He has too many boys to stay sane and pays way too much college tuition. Steven runs Cartagram (www.cartagram.com), a custom cartography company located in Madison, Alabama. He thanks Sharon and the rest of the **WOW!** team for their inspiration and professionalism.

Lisa Jackmore is a contributing writer for Galleries, as well as for step-by-step Techniques. She is an artist both on and off the computer, creating miniatures to murals. Lisa continues to share her talent, evident throughout this book, as a writer and a digital fine artist. She would like to thank the sources of distraction—her family and friends—as they are so often the inspiration for her artwork.

Aaron McGarry is a San Diego-based writer and illustrator who spends time in Ireland, where he is from. While writing provides his bread, commercial illustration supplements the bread with butter. He paints and draws to escape and relax, but finds his greatest source of joy with his wife Shannon, a glass artist, and their resplendent 5-year-old daughter Fiona. Please visit: www.amcgarry.com.

Ryan Putnam (rypearts.com), a designer, illustrator, and blogger, and also known as Rype, Putnam runs Vectips (vectips.com), a blog dedicated to Illustrator tips, tricks, and tutorials. In addition to Vectips, Putnam does client-based projects, and creates stock vector illustrations, but he couldn't do it all without the support of his wife Carmen.

Pete Maric has been working independently as an architectural illustrator and designer since 2001 and is based in Cleveland, Ohio. His multimedia style of illustration mixes hand-drawn techniques with digital renderings. Recently, he has become immersed in learning 3D modeling and animation and incorporating this skill set into his daily work. His client list includes Adidas, Nintendo, Go Media, and Everlast among others. To view work samples, please visit www.petemaric.com.

Chris Leavens is an illustrator with a penchant for drawing mustaches and cyclopes, residing in the foothills of Los Angeles with his wife, Adriana, and their daughter Sonja. His vector artwork appears in computer games, educational materials, magazines, art galleries, and more (chrisleavens.com).

Additional contributing writers and editors: **Eric Schumacher-Rasmussen** has been writing and editing copy since long before it was his job. He's currently a freelance writer and editor, as well as editor of *Streaming Media* magazine (www.streamingmedia.com). **Peg Maskell Korn** is a woman of many hats. After rescuing Sharon in the last hours of the first edition, she has transformed into the master proofer of the visuals and text in the entire book. Please see the **Acknowledgments** for a thorough listing of the **WOW!** team contributors.

Important: Read me first!

Beginners are of course most welcome to find inspiration in this book. However, be aware that the assumed user level for this book is intermediate through professional. If you're a beginning Illustrator user, please supplement this book with basic, beginning Illustrator instruction and training materials. In addition, don't miss the free Illustrator training videos from the Adobe TV website: **http://tv.adobe.com/#pd+Illustrator**.

ZenLessons folder on the DVD

Once you understand the concepts of how the tools work, if you still find Illustrator cryptic, see the "ZenLessons" folder on the **WOW! DVD**. These lessons walk you through some of the basics of working with the Pen tool, Bézier curves, layers, and stacking order, helping you to learn to "think in Illustrator." You'll also find the "Zen of the Pen" PDF (by Sharon Steuer and Pattie Belle Hastings); these lessons include QuickTime movies to help you with the Pen tool and Bézier curves. To be notified when **Zen of Illustrator** books and videos become available, please send an email with the subject "Zen" to: **info@zenofillustrator.com**.

First of all, it is important for you to know that this 11th edition in the **Illustrator WOW!** series has become a truly collaborative project. In order to provide you with the most thoroughly updated information in a timely manner (and as close as possible to the shipping of the new version of Adobe Illustrator), this book evolved into a project that involves a large team of international experts working simultaneously. The process begins with Steven Gordon and myself acting as co-curators; Steven surfs web and print sources and collects potential artists and artwork we'd like to feature, then posts samples of these, along with submissions sent by readers and artists we've covered in the past, to a website where we can see the works and take notes about the art. I work with each co-writer to determine which sections they want to concentrate on, based on their expertise in Illustrator. For the artists/writers that often means asking them to focus on integrating new tools and functions into their current projects so they can share that knowledge with you.

Our technical editor, Jean-Claude Tremblay, marks up the last edition in PDF, and then he and I continue to oversee every page of the book as it progresses. In addition to Jean-Claude and myself, the entire team of writers, as well as our stellar team of **WOW!** testers, test and critique each section as it develops. What this all means is that this book is the collaborative result of this amazing group of experts scattered around the globe, coming together by email, iChat, and PDF, and acrobat.com, to deliver the best book possible to you, the reader.

With the skyrocketing price of printing in full-color, and the fragile state of the economy for most of us, I looked for ways to bring down the cover price of the book. After consultations with the team, colleagues in the field, and Peachpit, we settled on a total rethinking of the focus of this book, which we've nicknamed "the leaner, meaner" **Illustrator WOW! Book**. With a renewed focus on creating art and design with Adobe Illustrator, we now leave the more basic and most technical aspects of the program, to books such as Mordy Golding's *Real World Adobe Illustrator CS5* (look for two chapters from this book in PDF format on the **WOW! DVD**).

It's always sad to delete favorite artworks from previous editions, but it's also inspiring and exciting to add dozens of new gorgeous examples of art, essential production techniques, and time-saving tips—all generously shared by **Illustrator WOW!** artists worldwide. In addition to the contributing artists and coauthors, our amazing team of **WOW!** testers sets this book apart from all others. This team thoroughly tests every lesson and gallery to make sure everything actually works. We deliberately keep all lessons short to allow you to squeeze in a lesson or two between clients, and to encourage the use of this book within the confines of supervised classrooms.

The user level for this book is "intermediate through professional," which means that we not only assume that the reader has a reasonable level of competence with Mac and Windows concepts (such as opening and saving files, launching applications, copying objects to the Clipboard, and clicking-and-dragging), but also that you have a familiarity with most of Illustrator's tools and functions. In addition, please see the pull-out card at the back of the book for a thorough summary of the shortcuts and conventions that we'll refer to regularly in the book (please see the "How to use this book…" section, following).

After you've read this book, I encourage you to read it again—you'll undoubtedly learn something you missed the first time. The more experienced you become with Adobe Illustrator, the easier it is to assimilate all the new information and inspiration you'll find in this book. I'm immensely proud of and grateful to everyone who works with me on this project. And I welcome you to the team.

Sharon Steuer

How to use this book...

If the Welcome Screen is unwelcome, hide it by enabling "Don't show again"

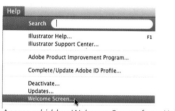

Access a hidden Welcome Screen from Help

While everyone is welcome to be inspired by the fabulous work showcased in this book, please keep in mind that this **Adobe Illustrator CS5 WOW! Book** has been designed and tested for intermediate through professional-level users of Adobe Illustrator. That means that you'll need to be familiar enough with the basics of Illustrator to be able to create your own art to follow along with the lessons. Unlike some books that do all the work for you, this book encourages experiential learning; as you follow along with the lessons, you'll not only be mastering the techniques, but you'll be creating your own art along the way. And to help you figure things out and inspire you further, this icon ⊙ tells you to look for the featured artwork within that chapter's folder on **The Adobe Illustrator CS5 WOW! DVD** (referred to hereafter as the **WOW! DVD**).

Shortcuts and keystrokes

Please start by looking at the **WOW! Glossary** on the pull-out quick reference card at the back of the book for a thorough list of power-user shortcuts that you'll want to become familiar with. The **WOW! Glossary** provides definitions for the terms used throughout this book, always starting with Macintosh shortcuts first, then the Windows equivalent (⌘-Z/Ctrl-Z). Conventions covered range from simple general things such as the ⌘ symbol for the Mac's Command or Apple key, and the Cut, Copy, Paste, and Undo shortcuts, to important Illustrator-specific conventions, such as ⌘-G/Ctrl-G for grouping objects, and Paste In Front (⌘-F/Ctrl-F)/Paste In Back (⌘-B/Ctrl-B) to paste items copied to the Clipboard directly in front/back of the selected object, and in perfect registration. Because you can now customize keyboard shortcuts, we're restricting the keystrokes references in the book to those instances when it's so standard that we assume you'll keep the default, or when there is no other way to achieve that function (such as Lock All Unselected Objects).

Setting up your panels

In terms of following along with the lessons in this book, if you want your panels to look like most of our panels, you'll want to sort swatches by name. Choose "Sort by Name" and "List View" from the Swatches pop-up menu. (Hold Option/Alt when you choose a view to set this as the default for all swatch kinds in the Swatches panel.)

In addition, Illustrator initially launches with an application default that could inhibit the way Illustrator experts work. One of the most powerful features of Illustrator is that, when properly set, you can easily style your next object and choose where it will be in the stacking order, by merely selecting a similar object. But in order for your currently selected object to set all the styling attributes for the next object you draw (including brush strokes, live effects, transparency, etc.), you must first disable the New Art Has Basic Appearance setting from the pop-up menu in the Appearance panel (✓ shows if it's enabled). Your new setting sticks even after you've quit, but needs to be reset if you reinstall Illustrator or trash the preferences.

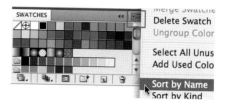

With the All Swatches icon selected, choose "Sort by Name" and then "List View" from the Swatches pop-up menu

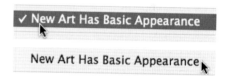

The Swatches panel viewed with "Sort by Name" and "List View" selected

If you want your currently selected object to set all styling attributes for the next object, disable New Art Has Basic Appearance by choosing it from the pop-up menu in the Appearance panel

HOW THIS BOOK IS ORGANIZED...

You'll find a number of different kinds of information woven throughout this book—all of it up-to-date for Illustrator CS5: **Introductions, Tips, Techniques, Galleries,** and **References.** The book progresses in difficulty both within each chapter, and from chapter to chapter.

1 Introductions. Every chapter starts with a brief, general introduction. In these intros you'll find a quick overview of the features referred to in the chapter Techniques and Galleries that follow, as well as a robust collection of tips and tricks that should help you get started.

2 Tips. Look to the information in the gray and red boxes for hands-on Tips that can help you work more efficiently. Usually you can find Tips alongside related text, but if you're in an impatient mood, you might just want to flip through, looking for interesting or relevant Tips. The red

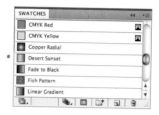

The Introduction sections begin every chapter with overviews of features

2 **Tip boxes**
Look for these gray boxes to find Tips about Adobe Illustrator.

Red Tip boxes
Red Tip boxes contain warnings or other essential information.

3

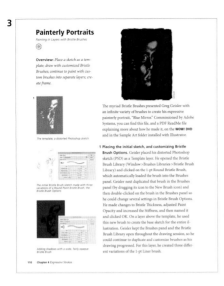

Painterly Portraits
Painting in Layers with Bristle Brushes

Overview: *Place a sketch as a template; draw with customized Bristle Brushes; continue to paint with custom brushes on separate layers; create frame.*

The template, a distorted Photoshop sketch

The initial Bristle Brush sketch made with three variations of a Round Point Bristle Brush; the Bristle Brush Options

Adding shadows with a wide, fairly opaque Bristle Brush

The myriad Bristle Brushes presented Greg Geisler with an infinite variety of brushes to create his expressive painterly portrait, "Blue Mirror." Commissioned by Adobe Systems, you can find this file, and a PDF ReadMe file explaining more about how he made it, on the **WOW! DVD** and in the Sample Art folder installed with Illustrator.

1 Placing the initial sketch, and customizing Bristle Brush Options. Geisler placed his distorted Photoshop sketch (PSD) as a Template layer. He opened the Bristle Brush Library (Window > Brushes Libraries > Bristle Brush Library) and clicked on the 1 pt Round Bristle Brush, which automatically loaded the brush into the Brushes panel. Geisler next duplicated that brush in the Brushes panel (by dragging its icon to the New Brush icon) and then double-clicked on the brush in the Brushes panel to open the Bristle Brush Options. He made changes to Bristle Thickness, adjusted Paint Opacity and increased the Stiffness, and then named it and clicked OK. On a layer above the template, he used this new brush to create the base sketch for the entire illustration. Geisler kept the Brushes panel and the Bristle Library open throughout the drawing session, so he could continue to duplicate and customize brushes as his drawing progressed. For this layer, he created three different variations of the 1-pt Liner brush.

110 Chapter 4 *Expressive Strokes*

4

G A L L E R Y

Ann Paidrick

Ann Paidrick enhanced her vase illustration from the previous lesson by adding the patterned pear wallpaper to the background. Paidrick locked all the layers of the finished vase and, on a new layer beneath these locked layers, placed a photograph of the wallpaper (saved as a .jpg) as the background. With the Pen tool, she drew rough outlines where the distorted pears would be, and then turned these outlines into guides (⌘-5 /Ctrl-5). On a separate layer above the background wallpaper, she placed another photo of the wallpaper, this time one that she had cropped in Photoshop to fit between the top and bottom of the clear glass. In order to use an Illustrator envelope to distort the cropped part of the photo, she had to first embed the photo by selecting the Embed icon in the Control panel. Paidrick then chose Object > Envelope Distort > Make with Mesh (6 rows, 8 columns). She used

the Direct Selection tool to adjust the envelope mesh object into the shape of the interior of the glass. To add more rows and columns, Paidrick clicked with the Gradient Mesh tool and added additional mesh points with the Add Anchor Point tool. She continued to adjust the mesh points, referring to her guides until she was satisfied with the distortion results. To make the envelope mesh object fit into the vase shape, on a new layer above, she drew a closed path with the Pen tool, selected the envelope mesh object, then chose Object > Clipping Mask > Make.

136 Chapter 5 *Color Transitions*

5

Access Illustrator Help from the Help menu

Everything's under Window...

Almost every panel in Illustrator is accessible through the Window menu. If we don't tell you where to find a panel, look for it in the Window menu!

---

arrows ——➤, red outlines, and **red text** found in tips (and sometimes with artwork) have been added to emphasize or further explain a concept or technique.

3 Techniques. In these lesson-oriented sections, you'll find step-by-step techniques gathered from artists and designers around the world. Most **WOW!** techniques focus on one aspect of how an image was created, though we'll sometimes refer you to different **WOW!** chapters (or to a specific step-by-step Technique, Tip, or Gallery where a technique is introduced) to give you the opportunity to explore a briefly covered feature more thoroughly. Feel free to start with almost any chapter, but be aware that each technique builds on those previously explained, so you should try to follow the techniques within each chapter sequentially. Some chapters include **Advanced Technique** lessons, which assume that you have assimilated all of the techniques found throughout the chapter. The *Mastering Complexity* chapter is packed with lessons dedicated to advanced tips, tricks, and techniques.

4 Galleries. The Gallery pages consist of images related to techniques demonstrated nearby. Each Gallery piece is accompanied by a description of how the artist created that image, and may include steps showing the progression of a technique detailed elsewhere.

5 References. At the back of the book, you'll find one appendix listing the artists featured in this book, and another listing the resources we've referred to, most of whom have included a demo or additional information for you on the **WOW! DVD**. In addition to these sections, you'll also find a *General Index*, and a pull-out quick reference card containing Mac and Windows versions of a **WOW! Glossary** and **Finger Dance** shortcut sequences. Finally, within the text you'll occasionally be directed to *Illustrator Help* to find specific information that's well-documented in the Adobe Help Viewer. To access this, choose Help > Illustrator Help.

Acknowledgments

As always, my most heartfelt gratitude goes to the many artists and Illustrator experts who generously allowed us to include their work and divulge their techniques.

Special thanks to Jean-Claude Tremblay, our amazing technical editor; we are so lucky to have JC advising us on every technical detail of this project, collecting all the software demos, and even producing our press-ready PDFs! Thanks to Mordy Golding, who, as author of *Real World Adobe Illustrator CS5*, continues to champion this book and to share his expertise with the **WOW!** team. And thanks to the folks at Adobe, especially David Macy, Terry Hemphill, Brenda Sutherland, Ian Giblin, Teri Pettit, Michael Ninness (now at Lynda.com), Jane Brady, and John Nack.

This revision is the result of a major team effort by an amazing group of friends and collaborators. Thankfully Cristen Gillespie somehow had just enough time (again) between *Photoshop Wow!* work to help with almost everything, including contributing the vast majority of new lessons, galleries, and introductions. Also blessedly returning were veteran **WOW!** artist/writer Lisa Jackmore (who did a great job with Galleries, lessons, and the **Adobe Illustrator CS5 WOW! Course Outline**), and cartographer/writer Steven Gordon (who returned to create and update important lessons and Galleries, join me on curatorial duties, and continue to contribute dry wit when needed). Also returning were artist/writers Aaron McGarry (who focused on the new perspective features for intros, lessons, and Galleries), and Ryan Putnam (aka rypearts.com) who gave us a critical Width tool lesson. Joining us for the first time as **WOW!** writers were the wonderful artists Chris Leavens and Pete Maric. Thank you Eric Schumacher-Rasmussen for stepping in (with kindness and humor) as the master juggler of so many edits from so many of us. A special thanks goes to our stellar team of testers: Nini Tjäder, Federico Platón, Bob Geib, Nicholas van der Walle, Darren Winder, David Lindblad, Brian Stoppee, Janet Stoppee, Scott Weichert, Chris Nielsen, Chris Leavens, Greg Maxson, Franck Payen, Frederick Jansen, Kevin Stohlmeyer, Michel Bozgounov, Stéphane Nahmani, and Adam Z Lein (who also helped set up and trouble-shoot the Sharepoint database that tracks who's doing what). Thanks to Sandee Cohen who continues to act as our official kibitzer, and for introducing me to Jim Birkenseer and Peter Truskier who as Premedia Systems wrote a batch of essential scripts for InDesign and Illustrator that helped us produce the book, and improve our lessons. Thanks to Jack Lewis for being so flexible with the index deadlines, and to Darren Meiss for providing the best proofing we've ever had. And heartfelt thanks to Peg Maskell Korn, for being involved since the beginning and putting up with me on a moment-to-moment basis.

Thank you to CDS for the fabulous printing job. Thank you Doug Little (and Erin and Wes) at Wacom for helping us to get situated with the new CS5 tablet features. And thanks to everyone at Peachpit Press for everything you do to make sure this book happens, *especially* Nancy Peterson, Tracey Croom, Nancy Davis, Nancy Ruenzel, Gary-Paul Prince, Sara Jane Todd, Rebecca Freed, Mimi Heft (for the gorgeous cover design again), Glenn Bisignani, and Eric Geoffroy (who, with Jay Payne, was our patient media producer). Thank you Linnea Dayton for being **WOW!** series editor, and for sharing Cristen. And last but *not* least, thanks to all my wonderful family and friends.

ILLUSTRATOR WOW! BOOK PRODUCTION NOTES:

Interior Book Design and Production

This book was produced in InDesign CS4 using primarily Adobe's Minion Pro and Frutiger LT Std OpenType fonts. Barbara Sudick is the artist behind the original **Illustrator WOW!** design and typography, using Jill Davis's QuarkXPress layout of **The Photoshop WOW! Book** as a starting point. Cary Norsworthy and Mimi Heft contributed to new page-design specs. Victor Von Salza led the porting of our templates from QuarkXpress to InDesign CS. Jean-Claude Tremblay is our technical editor; his company Proficiografik also produces (and troubleshoots) the press-ready PDFs for the book and cover. Computer Documentation Services (CDS) printed this book.

Additional Hardware and Software

Although most of the **WOW!** team uses Macintosh computers, we now have testers and writers who do Windows (or both Mac and Win). In addition to Adobe InDesign CS5, we used Adobe Illlustrator CS5 (of course!), Adobe Photoshop CS4, and Ambrosia Software's Snapz Pro X for the screenshots. We used acrobat.com and Adobe Acrobat 9 for distribution of the book pages to each other, to testers, the editor, the indexer, Peachpit, and the proofreaders. Premedia Systems wrote a number of custom scripts to help us update and sync the many InDesign files. Many of us use Wacom tablets and Art Pens. Adam Z Lein created (and does emergency maintenence on) an online **WOW!** database so the team can track the daily details of the book production.

How to contact the author

If you've created artwork using Illustrator's new features and would like to submit for consideration for inclusion in future **Illustrator WOW!** books, please send printed samples to Sharon Steuer, c/o Peachpit Press, 1249 Eighth Street, Berkeley, CA 94710. Or email a link to a web address containing samples of your work (no files please!) to **wowartist@ssteuer.com**.

1

Your Creative Workspace

Your Creative Workspace

Tabbed docs & the App Frame

- Change whether documents are tabbed (the default) or not through Preferences > User Interface.
- If more documents are open than are visible on tabs, a double-arrow at the tab bar's right will list them.
- Drag documents away from the tab to make them free-floating.
- Drag object layers from one document into another by dragging over that document's tab. The tab will spring open to let you drop the object in place.
- On a Mac, you can also turn on the Application Frame (disabled by default) from the Window menu. The frame contains all the panels and documents, and everything you can do in AI takes place within the frame.

Note: *You should turn off the Application Frame in an extended monitor setup (or video projection).*

Magically appearing panels

If you have used Tab or Shift-tab to hide your panels, mouse carefully over the narrow strip just before the very edge of the monitor where the panels were and they'll reappear, then hide themselves again when you move away.

OK, this might not seem like sexy **WOW!** stuff, but to save time and stay focused on being creative, you need to work efficiently. In this chapter you'll find tons of things you might have missed or overlooked. You'll find tips for customizing your workspace and in-depth coverage of newer organizational features such as working with multiple artboards and the multi-functional Appearance panel, which can take the place of several panels.

ORGANIZING YOUR WORKSPACE

You can save time and frustration in the long run if you spend a few minutes setting up custom workspaces and creating your own document profiles. The work you do to create the elements for a Flash animation is probably different from what you do to create a technical illustration or the layout for a series of brochures. Not all panels are needed for every job, but by organizing all that you definitely need—eliminating all you won't need or might only rarely need—you'll be able to locate quickly just what you need when you need it. In addition, the Control and Appearance panels often contain the same information found in the special purpose panels, permitting you to close some of those panels and streamline your interface even more than you might think possible (see the "Using the Appearance Panel" section later in this chapter).

In deciding which panels you want on your desktop for any given project, you'll probably first want to cluster panels that you will frequently use in sequence, such as Paragraph and Character Styles or Transform and Align. You'll also decide where each panel or group of panels should live, and whether, when you collapse them to get them out of your way, you want them to collapse to their icon and label, or all the way down to their icon. When you have everything arranged to your liking, choose Save Workspace from either the pop-up menu in the Application bar, or from Window > Workspace. Once you've created and saved a custom workspace, its name will show up in the Window>Workspace submenu and on the Application Bar (by default at the top of your working area). Switch between different workspaces by choosing a name. Note that any changes to a workspace, such as a panel opened or moved, are temporarily saved when you quit Illustrator so that you can always open Illustrator right where you left off. To restore a workspace to its original configuration, open the list of workspaces and reselect it. Following are some tips for arranging your panels:

- **Dock panels** to the edges of your screen or, if you want them closer to your work, drag them around freely. (The Control panel docks to the top or bottom of the screen.)

- **Resize most panels** once they're open. Look for the double-headed arrow when hovering over an edge to see if the panel can be dragged in that direction.

- **Collapse and expand free-floating and fully expanded columns to their title bar** by double-clicking the dark gray bar next to the panel name. (If the open panel is one in a column of icons that has been temporarily opened by itself, it can't be reduced to its title bar.) Double-click on the name of any open panel to reduce it to its smallest size while still allowing it to remain open. Experiment with expanding and minimizing open panels in your workspace to get used to how the panels work, and you'll save time and frustration later when you want to get a panel out of your way quickly.

- **If you need multiple panels open at once**, place each panel you want open in a separate column (drag to the side of an existing column until you see the vertical blue bar). Only one item in a column of panel icons can be open, but one from each column can be open simultaneously and will remain open until you manually close it by clicking on its double arrow in the upper right corner. The exception is if you have enabled Auto Collapse Icon Panels in Preferences>User Interface. In that case, clicking anywhere outside a panel that was opened from an icon will close it for you. Since panels are "spring-loaded," you can still drag items into them even when they're closed.

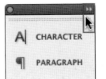

When you click the double arrow in the upper right, open panels will cycle through contracted and expanded states, which will vary depending on how you've customized the panel; customize the width manually when the cursor turns into a double-headed arrow, allowing you to click-drag to resize the panel

Dock and stack panels with different results by watching where the blue highlight shows up

A double-headed arrow in the upper left (next to the panel name), indicating that you can display more, or fewer, options in the panel; the fewest options will be shown by default

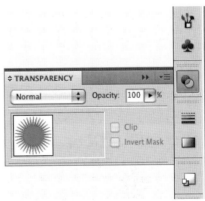

To minimize a panel opened from a column of panels that have been reduced to icons, click the double arrow in the upper right (you can't minimize it by double-clicking the dark gray bar)

Cool Extras—templates & more

Choose File > New from Template and navigate to the Templates folder, which is within the Cool Extras folder (which is within the Adobe Illustrator application folder). Here in Cool Extras you'll find more templates, store your own custom templates, and find sample art with PDFs explaining how the art was created.

Changing measurement units

Control-click/Right-click on a ruler to change units of measurement, or cycle through ruler units with ⌘-Option-Shift-U/Ctrl-Alt-Shift-U. Set default units of measurement in Preferences > Units & Display Performance.

Scripting the coordinates

To ensure that legacy scripts will still work, scripts themselves maintain the internal origin point in the lower left corner. If you write new scripts, you have to take into account that a move of 25 pt on the Y axis using the current coordinate system needs to be scripted as a move of –25 pt.

Patterns and rulers

Pattern fills will not shift when you move the origin point while using Artboard rulers, but patterns will shift if you change the origin point for a Global ruler.

Using New Document Profiles

When you create a New Document Profile, you can establish not only the size, color mode, and resolution of your document, but also whether or not that document includes specific swatches, symbols, graphic styles, brushes, and even the default font that is selected. By saving this to the New Document Profiles preset folder along with your other user presets, the document appears in the New Document dialog, and also on the Welcome Screen, if you keep that enabled. Pressing the Option/Alt key when clicking on a New Document Profile in the Welcome Screen bypasses opening the New dialog.

Rulers, Guides, Smart Guides, and Grids

Now that Illustrator offers multiple artboards, you can choose to display the ruler (⌘-R/Ctrl-R) as a Global ruler that extends across all your artboards, or as an Artboard ruler, one for each artboard with its own x,y coordinate system. The rulers look the same, but if you Control-click/Right-click on a ruler, or press ⌘-Option-R/Ctrl-Alt-R, the Change to (Global/Artboard ruler) command reveals which ruler is active, and you can switch rulers here. In order to be consistent with other Adobe programs, new documents by default use Artboard rulers and set the origin point at the upper left corner, instead of the lower left. Documents created in older versions will still open with Artboard rulers active and the origin point in the upper left, but if you switch to the Global Ruler, the origin point will be at the legacy lower left corner, as it was when the document was originally created. If you need to work with legacy positioning, switch to Global Rulers with your legacy documents to see the old X,Y coordinates. You can still change the location of the origin point by dragging from the upper left corner of the rulers to the desired location, but you can give each artboard its own origin point when you choose Artboard Rulers.

You can apply guides globally or to individual artboards. To place a non-global guide with the Artboard tool selected (Shift-O), drag a guide from the ruler to the active artboard, being careful to drag right over the board, not between it and another. If you drag a guide in between the artboards, it will place the guide across all artboards.

If you intend to use more than a couple of guides in a project, you should probably create separate layers for specific sets of guides. By keeping guides on named layers, you'll not only be able to easily control which guides are visible at any time, but also how the global locking, visibility, and clearing of guides is applied.

You can also create guides by selecting an object and defining it as a guide by choosing Object > Make Guides (⌘-5/Ctrl-5, or via View > Guides). By default, guides are unlocked, but you can lock them using the Lock/Unlock toggle (in the context-sensitive or View menus); the Lock/Unlock Guides toggle is global, and affects all guides in all documents. Any unlocked guide can be changed into a regular, editable path by targeting the guide and, again in the context-sensitive menu, choosing Release Guides. Guides not targeted will not be converted.

Smart Guides, which can be powerful aids for constructing and aligning objects as you draw, are now helpful enough to become an essential part of your workflow. Try keeping them on (the toggle is ⌘-U/ Ctrl-U). Enable or disable viewing options in Preferences > Smart Guides.

MASTERING OBJECT MANAGEMENT

Take control of the stacking order of objects right from the beginning, and become familiar with the different ways to focus on just the necessary objects at one time.

Although probably the easiest and most important thing that you can do to keep your file organized is to name your layers as you create them, it's easy to get lazy and just click the New Layer icon. To avoid amassing a stack of ambiguously numbered layers, try to get in the habit of holding Option/Alt when you click the New Layer icon so you can easily name your layer as you go. (Of course you can double-click the layer name at any time to access Layer Options to edit the name or other settings.) Both the Layers and the Appearance panel are designed

Changing Constrain Angle

If you adjust the X and Y axes in Preferences > General > Constrain Angle, it will affect the drawn objects and transformations of your grid, as they will follow the adjusted angle when you create a new object. This can be helpful if you're working in isometrics or another layout requiring alignment of objects at an angle.

Hide/Show Edges

The shortcut for Hide/Show Edges is ⌘-H/Ctrl-H (or choose View > Hide/Show Edges). Once you hide the selection edges (paths and anchor points), all path edges in that file will remain hidden until you show them again—and that hidden state is saved with your file! Get in the habit of toggling it off when you're done with the task at hand. And, if you open a file and can't decode the mystery of why things don't appear selected, remember to try ⌘-H/Ctrl-H.

Three grids

View Illustrator's automatic grid using View > Show Grid (⌘-"/Ctrl-"). Illustrator also offers a Perspective Grid and a Pixel Grid that serve special functions. For details on the Perspective Grid, see the *Reshaping Dimensions* chapter, and for information on using the Pixel Grid, see the *Creatively Combining Apps* chapter.

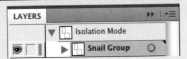
primarily to help you locate, select, and modify your artwork objects, so you want to take full advantage of Illustrator's changing interface to know just where you are and what you'll be affecting.

Using Isolation Mode

Isolation mode is a feature that has evolved considerably over the last few versions of Illustrator. Although isolation mode was once somewhat cryptic—even annoying—improvements have made it an essential part of the power-user workflow. The next time you want to edit an object, group, or layer without accidentally selecting or altering any other nearby objects, use isolation mode instead of locking or hiding things that are in the way.

See the Tip at left for a summary of how to enter and exit isolation mode. Once you enter, a gray bar appears at the top of your document window, indicating that you're now in isolation mode, and the gray bar displays the hierarchy that contains the isolated object. Everything on your artboard *except* the object(s) you've just isolated will be dimmed, indicating that those other objects are temporarily locked. If you have isolated an object or group, you can expand the isolation to the sublayer or layer that the object is on by clicking on the word for that layer in the gray bar. As long as isolation mode is active, anything you add to your artboard will automatically become part of the isolated group. (Disable "Double-click to Isolate" in General Preferences to prevent a double-click from putting you in isolation mode.)

Isolation mode isn't limited to objects you've grouped yourself. Remember that other types of objects—such as blends, envelopes, or Live Paint objects—exist as groups and isolation mode works for them, too. In addition to groups, you can also use isolation mode on almost anything—layers, symbols, clipping masks, compound paths, opacity masks, images, gradient meshes, and even a single path. The next time you think you have to enter Outline mode, or lock or hide objects to avoid grabbing other objects, try isolation mode instead.

Select Behind

To select objects from the document window that are hidden by other objects without first having to lock or hide those objects, you can enable ⌘-click/Ctrl-click to Select Object Behind, found in Preferences > Selection and Anchor Display. The first click brings up the Select Behind cursor and selects the topmost object, and each subsequent ⌘-click/Ctrl-click targets the Fill for the next objects in the stacking order. You can't target Strokes in this manner, but if the object has a Fill, you can target the object and use the Appearance panel to change the Stroke.

Selecting & Targeting Indicators in the Layers Panel

Many seasoned Illustrator artists have missed the introduction of targeting versus selecting. When you simply select objects and apply effects or adjust opacity, the effects might not be applied as you expected, and in order to remove or edit the effects you'll have to carefully reproduce this level of selection (see Tips "Can't target a layer?" and "Decoding appearances" nearby). If instead you apply an effect to a targeted group, layer, or sublayer, then the effects are easy to remove (simply target that level again).

To know for sure whether you have successfully targeted a layer, in the Layers panel you should see the double-circle as the target indicator for that layer, and a large square box indicating that you've selected all objects within that layer (a small square means you have only some objects on that level selected). In addition, in the Appearance panel you should see the word "Layer" listed first as the thumbnail name (as opposed to "Group," "Path", or "Mixed Objects"). When a group, layer, or sublayer has an effect applied to it, any new objects placed into that level will immediately acquire those effects.

Copy and Paste techniques

When you copy an object, Illustrator offers a number of power options for how the objects are pasted, including Paste in Front, Paste in Back, Paste in Place, and Paste on All Artboards. Note that none of these are affected by the

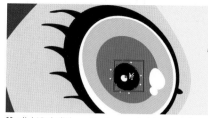

⌘-click/Ctrl-click on the topmost object to bring up the Select Behind cursor

Selection and target indicators (from left to right): 1) target indicator for any layer or subcomponent, 2) selection is also currently targeted, 3) target indicator for any targeted component with effect applied, 4) selection indicator for a container layer, 5) selection indicator when all objects are selected

Can't target a layer?

No matter how carefully you click on a layer's target icon, it's possible that you're really only *selecting* the objects on that layer. If your layer contains empty sublayers, Illustrator thinks it can only partially select the whole layer, and instead it selects the individual objects. If your effects aren't applied as expected, check that you see the double circle target, and the big square icon next to your layer in the Layers panel. If you don't see both, then show or delete empty sublayers.

(Left) Tribet by Michael Cressy; (center) after selecting all objects and applying an effect (the effect applies to each object separately); (right) after targeting the layer and applying the effect (effect applies to the layer as a unit, and not to individual objects)

A basic appearance does not include multiple fills or strokes, transparency, effects, or brush strokes. More complex appearances are indicated by a gradient-filled circle in the Layers panel. When you need to modify artwork created by others (or open artwork you created earlier), it's essential to have both the Appearance and Layers panels visible. Unless an effect is applied at the level of a layer or a group, you might not see the filled circle icon until you expand your view of the layer to locate the object that has the effect applied.

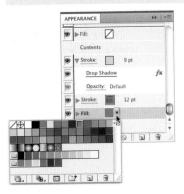

Perform many functions in the Appearance panel

Duplicating fills/strokes/effects

To duplicate a fill or stroke: select the object and click on the Add New Stroke or Add New Fill icon at the bottom of the Appearance panel, from the panel menu, or select one or more strokes, fills, and effects in the panel and drag them to the Duplicate Selected Item icon at the bottom of the panel.

ruler origin, but are positioned in the same relative position to the upper left corner of the artboard. Some of the distinctions include:

- **If you choose Paste in Front or Paste in Back with nothing selected,** Illustrator pastes the cut or copied object at the extreme front or back of the current layer.
- **If you choose Paste in Front or Paste in Back with an object selected,** Illustrator pastes the object directly on top of or behind the selected object in the stacking order.
- **Paste in Place** is the same as Paste in Front with nothing selected, but it pastes to any selected artboard.
- **Paste on All Artboards** pastes the object in the same relative position onto each artboard.

Using the Appearance panel

You probably know by now that many functions can be handled in the Control panel instead of individual panels. The Appearance panel takes this even further, and can replace a number of separate panels. Instead of opening and locating many panels, the Appearance panel contains most of the information you need, as well as many of the options, for everyday creating and editing, making it an indispensable hub for a productive and efficient workflow. Here you can view or edit a selected object's stroke, fill, or transparency; check to see if it's part of a Group; or adjust an effect or named graphic style applied to it. With a group or layer targeted, double-clicking on Contents reveals object-level attributes. With a text object, double-click on Characters to see the basic text attributes. In the Appearance panel you can also add additional strokes or fills to the object, apply effects, choose whether or not the next object you draw will have the same appearance, or construct a new graphic style to save for future objects. Important concepts for using the Appearance panel include the following:

- **The Basic Appearance** consists of a stroke and fill (even if set to None), and its transparency (0%–100% Opacity).
- **Apply an Appearance** to any path, object, group, layer or sublayer.

- **The stacking order of attributes** affects the final appearance, and can be changed simply by dragging the attribute up or down in the list.
- **The visibility of attributes** can be toggled on or off by clicking the Eye icon, and multiple selected items can be unhidden with Show All Hidden Attributes from the panel menu. The visibility of thumbnails can be toggled on or off with Show/Hide Thumbnail in the panel menu.
- **Click on underlined words**, such as Stroke, Opacity, or Drop Shadow to open their respective panels; Shift-click on a swatch icon to open the Color panel.

Graphic Styles and the Appearance panel

A Graphic Style consists of all the attributes applied to an object, group, or layer, and can be saved by dragging the thumbnail from the Appearance panel to the Graphic Styles panel, or by dragging the object to the Graphic Styles panel. Option-drag/Alt-drag the thumbnail over on top of an existing Graphic Style in the Graphic Style's panel to replace it.

To add a Graphic Style to an object that already has a Graphic Style without removing any of the existing attributes, Option-click/Alt-click on the Graphic Style in the Graphic Styles panel. When you look at the Appearance panel, you'll see the new attributes stacked on top of the original attributes.

MANAGING MULTIPLE ARTBOARDS

Having multiple artboards allows you to organize work within and across projects in a single document, whether you need to create multi-panel storyboards, set up elaborate character stagings for animations, organize many elements within a single complex project, or even keep multi-sized, collateral business material (such as cards, stationery, envelopes, postcards, and brochures) within one document. And then, of course, you can print or export to PDF any combination of the artboards that you want into one multi-page PDF, even one with multi-sized pages. To help you set up, organize, and work with

Great layers feature...

With Paste Remembers Layers enabled (it's off by default in the Layers panel menu), pasted objects retain their layer order, and if the layers don't exist, Paste Remembers Layers makes them for you! If you paste, and it pastes flattened (because it was disabled), Undo, change the toggle, then paste again.

Drawing with Appearances

Whether or not your new object will have the same attributes as your last-drawn object depends upon settings in the Appearance panel menu.

- **If New Art Has Basic Appearance is enabled,** you'll be drawing with only the current Stroke, Fill, and Opacity. Any other attributes from your last-drawn object are ignored.
- **If you have disabled New Art Has Basic Appearance,** your new art will have the exact same Appearance as your last object, but you can choose Reduce to Basic Appearance in the panel menu to remove all attributes except the Stroke, Fill, and Opacity.
- **To eliminate even the Basic Appearance,** click on the Clear Appearance icon at the bottom of the panel, which reduces the selected object to None for Stroke and Fill, and the Default (100%) Opacity.

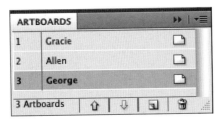

Artboards panel showing reorder arrows, icon for Artboard Options dialogs, and New Artboard and Delete Artboard icons

artboards, both the Artboards panel and the Control panel options with the Artboard tool selected provide the access and features you'll need. To manage the artboards themselves, make sure you're familiar with basic artboard functions:

- **Set up artboards** when you're configuring a new document, or later through the Artboards panel or the Control panel with the Artboard tool active. Artboard configurations can be saved as part of a New Document Profile.

- **To add an artboard** using the same properties as the currently highlighted artboard, Click on the New Artboard icon. It will be added to the same row as the current artboard, but you can rearrange the artboards later.

- **Modify artboard settings in the Artboard Options dialog** by choosing Artboard Options from the Artboards menu; double-clicking on the artboard layer's icon in the Artboards panel (single-click if the artboard is already active); double-clicking on the Artboard tool; or clicking the Artboard Options icon on the Control panel when the Artboard tool is active.

- **Create and manage artboards manually** and interactively by selecting the Artboard tool (Shift-O) instead of invoking the dialog, dragging artboards to scale and position them, and using the Control panel options. Enabling Smart Guides can help with precise manual alignment.

- **Name your active artboard** by selecting the Artboard tool and changing its name in the Control panel, or in the Artboards Options dialog. The name is listed in the Artboards panel and in the list of artboard panels in the status bar (Artboard Navigation, located at the bottom right of the document window).

- **Rearrange artboards** through the Artboards panel menu or Object > Artboards > Rearrange, choosing rows, columns and spacing. The last-used settings persist, and you can choose whether or not to move your artwork with the artboard.

- **Reorder the list of artboards** in the Artboards panel using the up and down arrow icons. Perhaps in your document window you have arranged a storyboard sequence, but now you want to work just with those artboards where a particular character appears. If you place those artboards together in the Artboards panel, you won't disturb your sequence in the document window, but you can easily target the artboards in the panel without scrolling through the entire list.

- **Use Shift-Page Up or Shift-Page Down to navigate** the Artboard panel layers, which will fill the window with your selected artboard as you navigate.
- **Artboards have a reference point**. In the Position area of Artboard Options, choose the reference point from which artboards get resized.
- **Overlapping art across multiple artboards, or overlapping artboards onto one piece of art,** allows you to develop multiple versions of the same image without duplicating elements. Each artboard will print only those portions of the art wholly contained within its borders, allowing you to print or export duplicates, and/or portions of an art piece, from the one instance of the art (this is a useful technique for storyboarding and comic strips).
- **Convert a non-rotated rectangle** to an artboard by choosing Object > Artboards > Convert to Artboard.
- **Use Fit to Artwork Bounds and Fit to Selected Art** commands (in the Preset list on the Control panel when the Artboard tool is selected, or under Object > Artboards), for resizing artboards according to their contents.
- **To locate an artboard visually** when another artboard fills your view, choose View > Fit All in Window (⌘-Option-0/Ctrl-Alt-0). To activate it, click on the artboard with the Selection tool or click on its name in the Artboards panel.
- **When zooming,** the commands Fit Artboard in Window (⌘-0/Ctrl-0) and Actual Size (⌘-1/Ctrl-1) affect the active artboard. Double-clicking on an inactive artboard's name (single-click if it's active) in the Artboards panel also zooms that artboard to Fit Artboard in Window size.
- **Export artboards as separate TIFF, JPEG, PSD, or PNG files** when you need a rasterized version of every artboard in your document.

Copying art between artboards

Working productively and maintaining consistency within a project often means duplicating elements from one document to another, and with multiple artboards you have a variety of methods to accomplish this task, depending upon your needs:

- With the "Move/Copy Artwork with Artboard" icon enabled in the Control panel (Artboard tool selected), hold down the Option/Alt key while dragging an active artboard to a new location in order to duplicate the artboard and all its contents.
- Use Edit > Paste (⌘-Option-Shift-V/Ctrl-Alt-Shift-V) on all artboards to copy artwork from one artboard to the same position on all artboards of any size.
- Turn artwork created on one artboard into a symbol, then drag that symbol from the shared Symbols panel to any other artboard. Now just update the symbol to update all instances of it used on any artboards.
- Using the Measure tool, measure the distance between the artwork and where you want it on another artboard, and use Transform > Move to move or copy the artwork.
- Apply the Transform Effect on a layer to copy "instances" of artwork to another artboard in the same relative position.

Digitizing a Logo

Learning to Use a Template Layer

Overview: *Create a scan and place it on a template layer in Illustrator; hand-trace the template; modify the paths with the Direct Selection tool; refine lines with the Pencil tool; use basic objects for ease and speed.*

1

A clean, high-contrast scan of the sketch

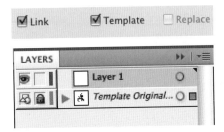

Creating the template and a drawing layer

2

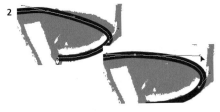

Using the Direct Selection tool and dragging on the direction handles to adjust the path to better fit the sketch

Beginning with his scanned sketch imported as a template layer, Jack Tom used Illustrator's basic drawing tools to create this logo for the Bertz Design Group. Illustrator's Pen, Pencil and basic geometric tools, such as the Rectangle and Ellipse tools, can handle any object you need to make, creating a polished logo for any occasion.

1 Placing a scanned image as a template. Create a high-contrast copy of your sketch for the logo by scanning the image at a high resolution to provide the detail you need for hand-tracing. If you have an image-editing program such as Photoshop, you can increase contrast first, thus making your sketched lines more distinct, before placing the file in Illustrator. Save your scan as a PSD or TIFF and choose File > Open to select your scan. From the Layers panel pop-up menu, choose Template, and then create a new, empty layer for your tracing. Or create your Illustrator document first, choose File > Place, and enable Template in the Open dialog. A Template layer is placed beneath the original layer. Template layers are automatically set to be non-printing and dimmed layers.

2 Hand-tracing the template. With the template as an on-screen tracing guide, begin using the Pen tool on the empty layer for tracing the straight lines and smooth curves. Don't worry too much about the tracing being a bit off at first. You'll adjust the paths to fit the sketch more closely next. As you trace, remember to click for corners, click-drag for curves, and to hold down the Option/Alt key when dragging out a direction handle in order to create a hinged curve in the path. (See the *Zen lessons* on the **WOW! DVD** for help with Bézier curves.) Once you've drawn a basic path, zoom in close and use the Direct Selection tool to adjust anchor points and direction handles. Use the Convert Anchor Point tool to switch between corners and curves, if necessary. You can simplify your view of an object by entering Outline mode. You can toggle between Outline and Preview modes for that object's layer by holding down the ⌘/Ctrl key and clicking on the visibility icon. Use ⌘-Y/Ctrl-Y to toggle the entire image between Outline and Preview modes.

Using Option/Alt with the Pen tool to "scallop" (make a hinged curve) while you draw

Toggling between Outline and Preview mode on a single layer by holding down ⌘/Ctrl as you click on the layer's visibility icon

3 Drawing, and redrawing, irregular lines with the Pencil tool. Using the mouse or a graphic tablet (such as a Wacom tablet), draw as you would with an actual pencil. Double-click the Pencil tool icon to customize settings. Create smoother lines by setting higher Fidelity and Smoothness numbers, or zoom in closer on the path while editing with the Pencil or Smooth tools. You can also select any path and start drawing close to or overlapping that path in order to redraw it (in Options specify the pixel distance from the selected path so that you can edit it instead of starting a new one). Use the Pencil tool with low settings to transform Pen tool paths into jagged lines. That will help you to express natural elements, such as the mountains in this logo.

3

Using the Pen tool for a quick path (top), then using the Pencil tool to add a stroke expressing jagged, rough elements

4

Constructing elements quickly from geometric objects

4 Using basic objects to help build your logo. To speed up drawing, use Illustrator's ready-made objects rectangles, ellipses, and even stars (or the sun, as in this logo). Add paths and filled objects with the Pen or Pencil tools, or use the Shape Builder tool to combine objects (see the *Rethinking Construction* chapter for more about this tool), to finish converting your sketch to a clean illustration.

Vector logos adapt well to B&W or color printing

Basic to Complex

Starting Simple for Creative Composition

Overview: *Start with simple elements to build complexity; create layers to keep elements separated for easy modifications; use a Live Paint group to organize many small details.*

1

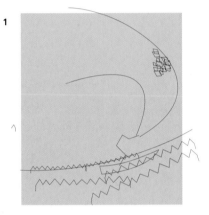

Rudmann's initial sketch to organize placement of his forms and their proportions, cropped to the artboard

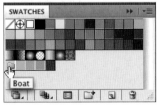

Creating diamonds and the color group

When Andrew Rudmann set out to create the art piece "And Then I Swam," he began with a simple outline and a very few basic elements. He defined a color group, created clusters along with the basic elements, and then layered all of them to form more complex imagery. He also created a Live Paint group in order to draw forms without having to draw each path as a closed object. By slowly building complexity from very simple beginnings, he was able to control the results he sought to capture his vision.

1 Beginning with a simple sketch and simple objects.
Rudmann began with the Pen tool (P), sketching the structure that would tell the story. Since he was going to create the water from a single diamond shape he would modify, he only needed to sketch the proportions and placement of his elements. He used the Artboard tool (Shift-O) to adjust the artboard to fit the composition.

He next auditioned his basic elements, coloring them, and combining some of them into larger elements. To determine the colors for the piece, he first chose the background color: "My base color is usually very obnoxious, acidic, or uncomfortable so I tend to dull down the other colors in the piece," he said. He selected his final choice of four colors and saved them as a color group (Boat) by clicking the New Color Group icon in the Swatches panel.

To keep the process of building up the art from basic elements as fluid as possible, he found a method that minimized working with panels, and allowed him to keep his attention on the artboard. Selecting a diamond (or cluster of diamonds) that he wanted to duplicate and modify, he copied, used Paste in Front (or Back), and then used the Free Transform tool (E). He often ungrouped his clusters to freely modify and randomize a cluster by transforming some of the individual diamonds.

2 **Using layers to organize complex objects.** Despite working freely, Rudmann needed to be able to access portions of the image for modifications. The illusion of organic chaos and randomly placed elements requires some control, and separating sections with just a few layers, descriptively named, made all the difference as he worked. He could lock all the layers to prevent moving artwork already in place, and turn off visibility for some layers in order to concentrate on just one region without distraction. He created the illusion of depth and distance by placing small waves behind the big waves, yet kept each set of waves accessible by putting the smaller waves on a layer beneath the big waves. Rudmann sandwiched the man and his boat on a layer between the large and small diamond-shaped waves, and the big splash came last.

3 **Using Live Paint to quickly fill the man with dripping water.** After Rudmann drew the outlines for the boat and the man, he used the Pen tool to freely draw open paths for the dripping water on the man, and a few stripes to signify his bucket. These he selected and turned into a Live Paint Group because it helped him to work with the outlines as flat coloring book forms. He didn't have to draw fully enclosed objects before filling them, since outlines and overlaps enclosed the areas. (See the *Rethinking Construction* chapter for more on using Live Paint.)

2
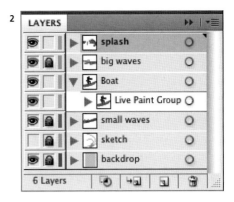
Using layers to lock and hide areas in the artwork in order to concentrate on a single area

3

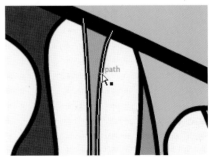
A Live Paint Group allows for coloring objects without having to draw each of them as separate objects made from closed paths.

Guides for Arcs

Designing with Guides, Arc, and Pen Tools

Overview: *Create guides on one side of the artboard; reflect and copy guides to the other side; create an arc with the Arc tool; cut and extend the arc with the Pen tool; reflect and copy the arc and join with the two arcs using the Pen tool; print templates using the Tile option.*

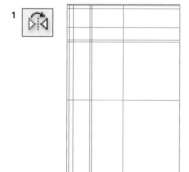

Reflect tool icon on the left; on the right, selected guides (colored magenta) that will be reflected and copied to the other side of the artboard

Tasked with building a garden gate as a functional sculpture for an outdoor exhibition on the grounds of the Norman Rockwell Museum, artist Stephen Klema sat down with Illustrator to create life-sized drawings that would serve as templates for cutting the sculpture's wood pieces.

1 Creating the document and positioning guides. To start, Klema made a new document with the same dimensions as those of the constructed gate (80" tall by 44" wide). Next, he turned on rulers (⌘-R/Ctrl-R) and dragged guides from the rulers. To position a guide more precisely, first make sure that guides are unlocked (go to View > Guides and choose Lock Guides if it has a check mark before its name), select the guide and use the Control Panel's Transform fields to enter values for the X or Y position of the guide on the artboard.

If your artwork will be symmetrical, like Klema's, you can create guides on one side of the document and then select and copy them to the other side. Start by creating a guide in the exact middle of the document. An easy way to do this is to drag a new guide from the ruler and, making sure that Guides are still unlocked, click the Horizontal Align Center icon in the Control panel to center it horizontally on the artboard (be sure that you've chosen Align to Artboard in the Control panel). Next, activate

Smart Guides from the View menu (this will help position the cursor over the exact middle of the document). Finally, select all of the guides you've created, choose the Reflect tool (it's hidden under the Rotate tool icon) and Option-click/Alt-click on the guide you created in the middle of the document. From the Reflect dialog, choose Vertical as the Axis and click on the Copy button.

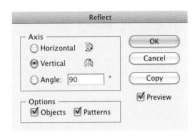

The Reflect tool dialog

2 **Drawing an arch.** Klema turned to the Rectangle, Arc, Ellipse, and Pen tools to draw the different objects in his illustration. For the inner arch, Klema selected the Arc tool (hidden under the Line Segment tool) and double-clicked its icon to bring up the Arc Segment Tool Options dialog. Because he planned on drawing from the center guide outward to the left, Klema clicked on the dialog's Base Along menu and selected the Y Axis option. Next, he clicked on the center guide and dragged down and to the left until the arc was shaped the way he wanted. Depending on the shape of the arc you need, you may have to draw it wider or longer. If that's the case, you'll need to cut the arc with the Scissors tool as Klema did so that it fits the width of the arch shape you want. Next, extend the arc downward as a straight line by selecting the Pen tool, clicking the bottom endpoint of the arc, and then Shift-clicking below to complete the straight line. Duplicate the extended arc using the Reflect tool and the center guide, just as you did in the previous step with the guides. Klema connected the bottom endpoints of the two extended arcs with the Pen tool, creating a single object.

On the left, the Arc tool icon; on the right, the Arc Segment Tool Options dialog

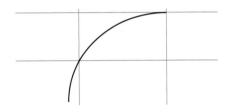

The arc and the guides

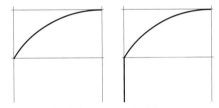

The arc after being cut with the Scissors tool on the left; on the right, the arc extended after drawing a vertical path with the Pen tool

3 **Printing templates for construction.** After drawing all the objects in his design, Klema printed the full illustration and separate illustrations of each of the gate parts (he used the Tile option in the Print dialog because the pieces were bigger than his printer paper). The prints served as templates that he traced on the wood so that he could precisely cut out the individual pieces of the gate. He used the full-sized illustration as a guide for assembling the gate parts into the finished sculpture.

Printed template pages assembled on wood

Nested Layers

Organizing with Layers and Sublayers

Overview: *Plan a layer structure; create layers and sublayers; refine the structure by rearranging layers and sublayers in the Layers panel's hierarchy; hide and lock layers; change the Layers panel display.*

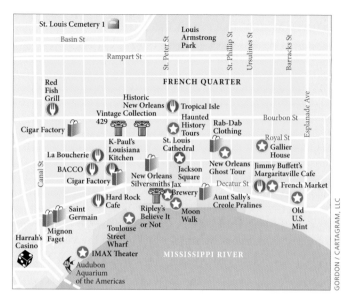

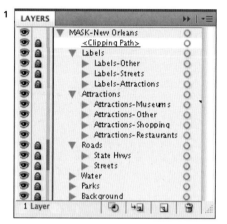

The completed layer structure for the map showing layers and two levels of sublayers (with Thumbnails disabled via Panel Options from the Layers panel's pop-up menu)

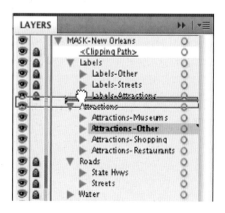

Selecting and dragging the Attractions-Other sublayer up and out of the Attractions sublayer, then placing the Attractions-Other sublayer on the same level in the hierarchy as Attractions

Layers have always been a great way of organizing artwork. With Illustrator, you can organize your Layers panel as a nested hierarchy, making it easier to navigate and manipulate. For this map of New Orleans, created for the Metairie Hampton Inn, Steven Gordon relied on layers and sublayers to organize the map artwork.

1 Planning, then creating and moving layers and sublayers. Gordon began by planning a layer structure for the map in which layers with similar information would be nested within several "master" layers, so he could easily navigate the Layers panel and manipulate the layers and sublayers. After planning the organization of your layered artwork, open the Layers panel and begin creating layers and sublayers. (When you start a new document Illustrator automatically creates a Layer 1; it's a good habit to double-click Layer 1 to rename it.) To name a new layer or sublayer as you create it, hold Option/Alt and in the bottom of the Layers panel click on the Create New Layer icon or the Create New Sublayer icon (this creates a sublayer nested within a currently selected layer).

As you continue working, you may need to refine your organization by changing the nesting of a current layer or sublayer. To do this, drag the layer name in the Layers panel and release it over a boundary between layers. To convert a sublayer to a layer, drag its name and release it above its master layer or below the last sublayer of the master layer (watch the sublayer's bar icon to ensure that it aligns with the left side of the names field in the Layers panel before releasing it). Don't forget that if you move a layer in the Layers panel, any sublayer, group, or path it contains will move with it, affecting the hierarchy of artwork in your illustration.

2 Hiding and locking layers. As you draw, hide or lock sublayers of artwork by simply clicking on the visibility (Eye) icon or edit (Lock) icon of their master layer. Gordon organized his map so that related artwork, such as different kinds of labels, were placed on separate sublayers nested within the Names layer, and thus could be hidden or locked by hiding or locking the master Names layer.

If you click on the visibility or edit icon of a master layer, Illustrator remembers the visibility and edit status of each sublayer before locking or hiding the master layer. When Gordon clicked the visibility icon of the Names layer, sublayers that had been hidden before he hid the master layer remained hidden after he made the Names layer visible again. To make the contents of all layers and sublayers visible, Option-click/Alt-click on a visibility icon. To unlock the content of all layers and sublayers, Option-click/Alt-click on an edit icon. If you have layers hidden or locked you can also choose Show All Layers, or Unlock All Layers from the Layers panel's pop-up menu.

3 Changing the Layers panel display. You can change the Layers panel display to make the panel easier to navigate. In Layers Panel Options (from the panel pop-up) you can set custom rows and thumbnails sizes, or choose no icons at all. Double-click a layer name and change its layer color using the Color menu. Or do as Gordon did: Shift-click to select contiguous related layers (⌘-click/Ctrl-click for non-contiguous layers) to set the same layer color in order to help identify them in the Layers panel.

Top, the Labels "master" layer with three sub-layers locked; bottom, after the master layer is locked, the three sublayers' edit icons are not dimmed, indicating that they will remain locked when the layer is unlocked

Changing the Color for the layer using the Layer Options dialog

Another way to unlock layers

A quick way to unlock all the contents of a layer: Make sure the layer itself is unlocked (the lock icon is gone) and then choose Unlock All from the Object menu.

Let Illustrator do the walking

Illustrator can automatically expand the Layers panel and scroll to a sublayer that's hidden within a collapsed layer. Just click on an object in your artwork and choose Locate Layer or Locate Object from the Layers panel's menu.

Basic Appearances

Making and Applying Appearances

Overview: *Create appearance attributes for an object; build a three-stroke appearance, save it as a style, and then draw paths and apply the style; target a layer with a drop shadow effect, create symbols in the layer, and then edit layer appearance if needed.*

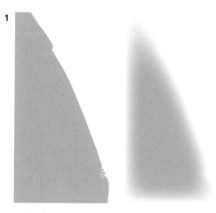

(Left) The ocean with blue fill; (right) the water with the Inner Glow added to the appearance attribute set

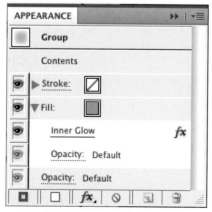

Appearance panel displaying the finished set of attributes with an Inner Glow effect applied

Complexity and simplicity come together when you use Illustrator's Appearance panel to design intricate effects, develop reusable styles, and simplify production workflow. In this location map of the California coastline, cartographer Steven Gordon relied on the Appearance panel to easily build appearances and apply them to objects, groups, and layers.

1 Building an appearance for a single object. Gordon developed a set of appearance attributes that applied a soft vignette and blue fill to a path symbolizing the Pacific Ocean. To begin building appearance attributes, make sure the Appearance panel is open. Gordon first drew the outline of the water with the Pen tool and then he gave the path a dark blue fill. To create the effect of water lightening as it approaches the shore, he applied an Inner Glow effect. To do this he opened the Appearance panel and clicked on the Fill attribute. Then he clicked the Add New Effect icon at the bottom of the Appearance panel and chose Stylize > Inner Glow from the pop-up menu. In the Inner Glow dialog, he set the Mode to Normal, Opacity to 100%, Blur to 0.25 inches (for the width of the vignette edge), and enabled the Edge option. To finish the glow, he clicked the dialog's color swatch and chose white for the glow color.

2 Creating a style for your highway paths. In the early days of Illustrator, the way you created a multi-stroked line like this "map symbol" for an interstate highway was by overlapping copies of a path and giving each copy a different stroke width. Now you can use the Appearance panel to craft a multi-stroked line that you apply to a single path. Deselect any objects still selected and reset the Appearance panel by clicking the Clear Appearance icon at the bottom of the panel (this eliminates any attributes from the last selected style or object). To make Gordon's interstate highway, click the Stroke attribute (it will have the None color icon) and give it a light color and a 0.5-pt width. Click the Add New Stroke icon to make a second stroke. Next, select the bottom of the two strokes and choose a dark color and a 3-pt width. Because you'll reuse this set of appearance attributes, open the Graphic Styles panel and Option-click/Alt-click the New Graphic Style icon at the bottom of the panel to bring up the Graphic Style Options dialog where you can name your new style.

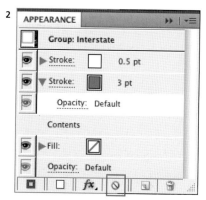

Appearance panel for Gordon's interstate highway symbol, with the Clear Appearance icon indicated

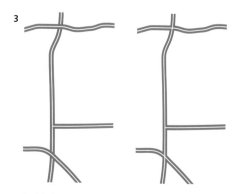

(Left) The interstates with the style applied to the individual paths; (right) the interstate paths were grouped before the style was applied

3 Assigning a style to a group. Draw the paths you want to paint with the new style you created above. Next, select all the paths you just made and Group (⌘-G/Ctrl-G). To get the two levels of strokes to merge when paths on the map cross one another, make sure Group is highlighted in the Appearance panel and apply your new interstate style.

4 Assigning appearance attributes to an entire layer. By targeting a layer, you can create a uniform look for all the objects you draw or place on that layer. Create a layer for the iconic "map symbols" and click the layer's target indicator in the Layers panel. In the Appearance panel, click the *fx* icon and select Stylize > Drop Shadow. Now each "map symbol" you draw or paste on that layer will be painted automatically with the drop shadow. You can modify the drop shadow by clicking the layer's targeting icon and then clicking the Drop Shadow attribute in the Appearance panel and changing values in the pop-up Drop Shadow dialog.

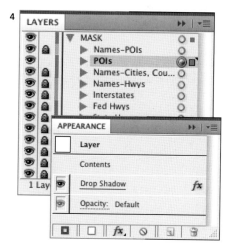

Top, targeting the layer in the Layers panel; bottom, the Appearance panel showing the Drop Shadow attribute (double-click the attribute to edit Drop Shadow values)

Auto-Scaling Art

Apply Effects and Graphic Styles to Resize

Overview: *Draw using picas and points to easily approximate feet and inches; calculate units to work with and amounts to scale by; apply a Transform effect to duplicate, scale, and move artwork in one step, and duplicate the effect to apply different settings; use a Graphic Style to save effect settings.*

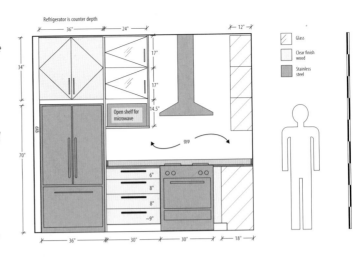

Kitchen West Elevation

WIGHAM

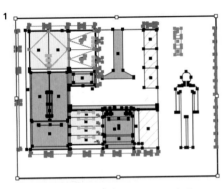

The "master" drawing nearly complete before adding the Transform Effect

---

Getting targeted to move

To target the master layer for an effect, be sure to click directly on the layer's target (circle) and note that the square is large and the Appearance panel shows "Layer" as the selected item. Empty sublayers prevent targeting the master layer, while hidden layers can contain objects that skew the results of the transformation.

As she was designing a kitchen, Laurie Wigham learned she needed to provide others with the same model at different sizes: She worked at 1 pica to the foot, but the builders needed plans at 1/2" to a foot and the city wanted large prints. She chose the Transform Effect to duplicate and scale her art so that changes made to her original plan would automatically be updated in the scaled version.

1 Setting the scale for the architectural drawing. To create and visualize objects in their real-world inches and feet, Wigham set Illustrator's measurement units to picas—there are 12 points per pica, so each point represented one inch and each pica one foot. She drew most of the artwork, including the keys, selected it all, and chose Object > Artboards > Fit to Artwork Bounds. When she needed to submit rough plans to her contractor, she needed to figure out how to get from this small version to the 1/2"= 1' scale. She first changed her ruler to inches and noticed that 1/2" (which would represent 1' in the larger scale) = 3 picas. Therefore if 1 pica = 1', she would need to multiply by 3 (300%) to get 3 picas to equal 1'. She then noted the width of her artboard (2.63 inches), so that plus a bit more for space gave her an approximate distance to use for moving the copy she was going to make.

2 Targeting for the Transform effect. In order for the Transform Effect to duplicate art to other artboards as new objects are added to it, all the art has to be within a master layer, and the master layer itself must be targeted. Once an effect is properly applied to a targeted master layer, any objects added to the layers within will automatically inherit that effect (see the warning Tip at left).

3 Applying the Transform effect. With the layer targeted, Wigham clicked the *fx* icon at the bottom of the Appearance panel and chose Distort & Transform > Transform. Wigham anchored the transformation reference point to the upper left corner (an easy reference point to work from), set the distance for the move and the amount to scale it by—300%, and entered 1 for copies. To check everything was working properly for the transform, she enabled Preview. Once Wigham saw that her artwork duplicated and scaled properly, she clicked OK. To preserve the effect to apply it any time in the future that she needed this same transformation, she created a Graphic Style (Option-click/Alt-click on the New Graphic Style icon in the Graphic Styles panel to name it while adding it). Now she could freely edit, add, and subtract objects in her kitchen's West Elevation. The objects on this artboard weren't selectable or directly editable, but would print. When her plan was finished, she drew an artboard around the scaled artwork and printed it.

To make a version for the city permits, she duplicated the effect in the Appearance panel by dragging it to the Duplicate Selected Item icon. She turned off the visibility for the first instance. She next drew an 11"x17" artboard roughly 20 points to the left from the other side of her master artboard (so the master was now between the two scaled versions). She double-clicked on the Transform effect to open the dialog, and this time played with the settings in the dialog until her drawing filled the page. She saved this as another Graphic Style. With both Transform Effects in the Appearance panel, she toggled their visibility each time she needed one scaled version or another.

2

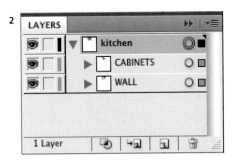

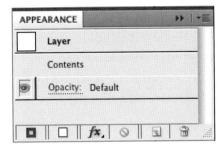

Both the Layers and Appearance panels showing indicators that the master layer, not just objects, is targeted

3

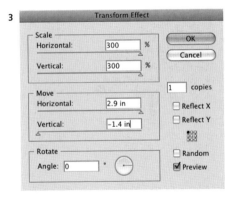

Setting up to duplicate, scale, and move artwork with the Transform Effect—the Vertical setting is for viewing on the monitor only, serving no other practical purpose

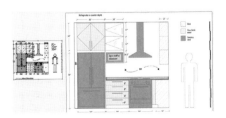

Artboards after creating the 1/2" to 1' scaled model of the elevation

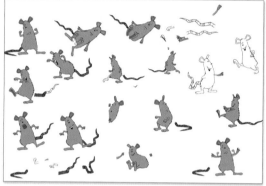

Kevan Atteberry

When Kevan Atteberry starts work on a new book, such as his *Frankie Stein* series of children's books, he first gathers together characters and elements he might use. He works to create them (and parts of them) in various moods and poses; anything, even inanimate objects such as wall sconces and doorknobs, can become a character in Atteberry's world. Before Illustrator featured multiple artboards, Atteberry had to open several files and keep switching his focus from one file to another. Now he creates custom art brushes and swatches that every artboard has immediate access to, builds his characters and the parts he'll later use in a scene, and then begins drawing his final scene. The artboard that is to become a final scene usually begins with a line drawing. As he sets the stage for his characters, he begins dragging them in from the outlying artboards, as he has done here with the mouse. The mouse looks a bit disjointed because it actually resides on separate layers, so that it can be sandwiched later with layers that will make up part of the scene. By keeping the mouse in pieces, Atteberry can build around it, and then size and rotate the mouse parts into place. With multiple artboards, it's easier for him to focus on these complex constructions, rather than having to concentrate on finding his characters in another file. To view one of the finished pieces for this project, see the *Creatively Combining Apps* chapter.

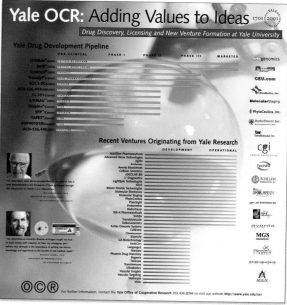

CRISCOLA

Jeanne Criscola

The usefulness of multiple artboards goes beyond storing elements for a single project. When Jeanne Criscola updates a logo or completes an entire project for a regular client, she can store related materials in a client file. Any project or part of a project that might get reused or presented in a different way from the original is a good candidate for storing on its own artboard. One of Criscola's clients, Yale's Office of Cooperative Research, has commissioned artwork at various times. They asked her to produce another project (a mural-sized exhibit illustrated here) into which they wanted her to incorporate some of the memorable projects they had commissioned earlier. Now, instead of tracking down files scattered in many places, Criscola opens her Yale client file (Illustrator can store up to 100 artboards in a single file), and everything is at her fingertips, ready to be pulled together into her new project.

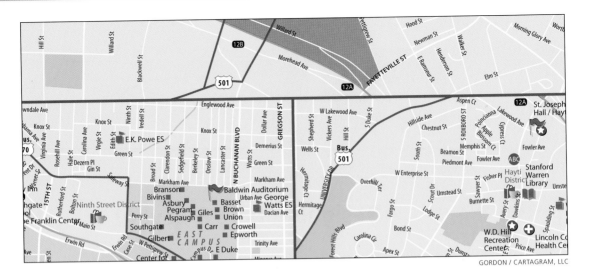

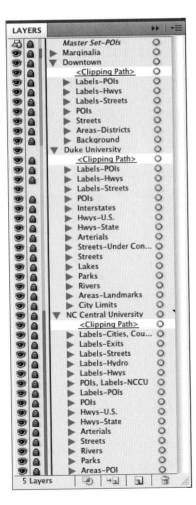

Steven Gordon / Cartagram, LLC

Cartographer Steven Gordon relies on layers to organize geographic features on maps. He places unique kinds of features (like lakes, highways, and street labels) on their own layers. Because this map for the Durham Convention and Visitors Bureau comprises three maps, he created master layers in the Layers panel to organize artwork for each of the three. To more easily find a sublayer within a particular map, Gordon color-coded each map's sublayers to match the layer color of its master layer. He recolored the sublayers of the Downtown map by selecting them in the Layers panel (clicking the first sublayer and then Shift-clicking the last), and then double-clicking one of the selected sublayers to open Layer Options. In the Layer Options dialog, Gordon chose Green from the Color panel menu and clicked OK. With Green now applied to all of the sublayers of the Downtown map, he then used the same method to recolor the sublayers to match the master layers of the two university maps.

2

Designing Type & Layout

Designing Type & Layout

DONAL JOLLEY

Hovering the cursor over the edge of an object reveals the Area Type cursor, then click to enter the desired text; the object can be easily re-shaped, causing the text to reflow

This chapter focuses on tips and tricks related to working with the type tools, as well as design and layout. While Chapter 1 covers the basics of working with multiple artboards, later on in this introduction, and in lessons in this chapter, you'll find some of the more advanced issues of working with multiple artboards.

TYPES OF TYPE

There are three kinds of type objects in Illustrator: *Point type*, *Area type*, and *Path type*. The Type tool lets you click to create a Point type object, click-drag to create a box for an Area type object, or click on a path to create Path type. Click within any existing type object to enter or edit text. To exit type editing mode, press the Esc key, or to be poised to start creating or editing another type object, hold the ⌘/Ctrl key (temporarily turning your cursor into a Selection tool) and click outside the text block, or reselect the Text tool. Some features for manipulating type include the following:

- **Point type never wraps** to a new line. To add another line of text without also adding a new paragraph (so your paragraph style applies to all the lines), press the Shift-Return/Enter key. To add another line that is also a new paragraph (useful when you want to use separate paragraph styles), use just the Return/Enter key.

  To scale Point type, use the Selection tool to select the type and drag on one of the handles of the bounding box. Both the typeface and the bounding box scale together. Use modifier keys as you would with any object to constrain proportions or scale from the center.

- **Area type automatically wraps** to the next line. Use the Return/Enter key to start a new paragraph within an Area type object.

  To scale Area type, use the Selection tool to scale just the bounding box itself; the type will reflow inside the area, but remain the same size. To scale the bounding box *and* the type, choose the Free Transform tool (E) before dragging on the bounding box handles.

Create a custom container for Area type by constructing a closed path with any tool. Choose the Area Type or Vertical Area Type tool and click on the path (not inside the object) to place text within the confines of the path.

Use the Direct Selection tool to distort a container object for Area type by grabbing an anchor point and dragging on it, or reshape the path by adjusting direction lines. The text within your Area type object will reflow to fit the new shape of the confining object.

Use the Area Type Options dialog (Type > Area Type Options) to gain precise control over a number of important aspects of Area type, such as numerical values for the width and height, precise values for rows and columns, offset options, the alignment of the first baseline of text, and how text flows between rows or columns (by choosing one of the Text Flow options).

- **Path type flows text** along the path of an object. Create Path type by clicking on a path with the Type tool; the path become unstroked and unfilled, and is ready to receive text.

A Path type object has three brackets—the beginning bracket, which has an *in port*; a center bracket; and an end bracket, which has an *out port*. Use the ports to thread text between objects (see the Tip "Ports defined" nearby). Use the center bracket to control positioning the type along the path.

To position type on a path, hover your cursor over the path until the cursor turns into an upside down **T**. Dragging the center bracket along the path moves the type toward the beginning or end. Dragging across the path flips the type to the other side of the path. For example, type running outside of a circle will flip to the inside.

To automatically reflow type along a path, use the Direct Selection tool to reshape the path. Set Path type attributes with the Type on a Path Options dialog (Type > Type on a Path > Type on a Path Options). Choose different Type on a Path effects (such as Rainbow or Stair Step),

DONAL JOLLEY

Type on a Path graphic by Donal Jolley

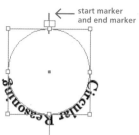

If you try to set Path type on a circle, and the text is set to Align Center, the text will be forced to the bottom of the circle. That's because each Path type object has two handles (the start marker and the end marker) between which the type is centered. When you first draw the circle and apply the Path type to it, those two handles appear together at the top of the circle, due to the fact that the circle is a closed path.

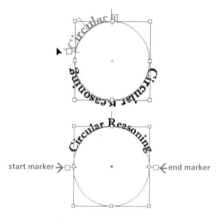

start marker →   ←end marker

To position the text on top of the circle, grab the start marker handle and drag it to the 9 o'clock position, and then drag the end marker handle to the 3 o'clock position. Your text will now be centered between the two handles, on top of the circle.

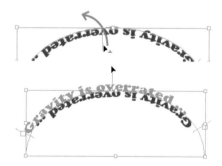

To manually flip type on a path to the other side of the path, select the type and drag the center handle (the thin blue line perpendicular to the type) across the path, as indicated by the red arrow above. Note the tiny T-shaped icon that appears next to the cursor as you position it near the handle; you can also flip type by choosing Type > Type on a Path > Type on a Path Options, enabling the Flip box, and clicking OK.

enable Flip to automatically flip type to the other side of the path, set the alignment of type relative to the path, and use a Spacing control to adjust the type as it moves around a curve. You can also access Type on a Path effects through the Type > Type on a Path submenu.

WORKING WITH THREADED TEXT

If an Area type or Path type object contains more text than it has room to display, you'll see a red plus sign indicating a loaded *out port* (see the Tip "Ports defined" on the next page).

To enlarge an Area type object or a Path type object on an enclosed path, allowing for more text, use the Selection tool to grab the object by a bounding side, and drag to resize it. To lengthen a path for Path type, use the Direct Selection tool to select the last anchor and drag the path longer, or use the Pen tool to start drawing more of the path from the last anchor, then drag the end bracket to the new end of the path. Following are more techniques for dealing with threaded text:

- **To add a new text object to receive overflow text,** use the Selection tool to select the first text object. Next, click on the *out port*; your cursor changes to the "loaded text" cursor. Click on the artboard to create a new text object the same size and shape as the original (this works nicely for custom shapes), or drag to create a rectangular text object of any size. The new text object is *threaded* (linked) to the original, flowing text into the second.

- **To link existing text objects together,** click the *out port* on the first object, and then click on the path of the object that will receive the overflow text. (Keep your eye on the cursor, which will change to indicate valid "drop" locations.) You can also link objects using a menu command: Select both objects and choose Type > Threaded Text > Create, and the objects become linked.

- **To disconnect one object from another,** select the object and double-click its *in port* to break the thread to a preceding object, or double-click its *out port* to break the thread to a subsequent object. Alternatively, you can select the object and click once on either the *in port* or the *out port*. Then click on the other end of the thread to break the link.

- **To release an object from a text thread,** select it, then choose Type > Threaded Text > Release Selection. Or, to remove the threading from an object while leaving the text in place, select it and choose Type > Threaded Text > Remove Threading.

WRAPPING AREA TYPE AROUND OBJECTS

Text wrapping is controlled as an object attribute and is set specifically for each object that will have Area type wrapped around it (known as a *wrap object*). First, in the Layers panel make sure the object you want as a wrap object is above Area type you want to wrap around it (this only works for Area type). Then select the wrap object and choose Object > Text Wrap > Make. To change options for the wrap object, keep it selected and choose Object > Text Wrap > Text Wrap Options. Here, you'll choose the amount of offset; you also have the option to choose Invert Wrap, which reverses the side of the object that text wraps around. To wrap text around multiple objects, add new objects to the text-wrapped group; in the Layers panel, expand the triangle to reveal the layer content, and drag the icon for your new object into the <Group>. To release the text wrap effect, select the wrap object and choose Object > Text Wrap > Release, or move the type above the wrap object in the stacking order.

FORMATTING TEXT

While the Character and Paragraph panels let you format text by changing one attribute at a time, Character Styles and Paragraph Styles panels allow you to apply multiple attributes to text simply by applying the appropriate style.

An open document always has a paragraph style applied to it even before there's any text, so if you select the Type tool, then modify its attributes in the Control panel, Illustrator will think you are modifying the default, [Normal Paragraph Style], on the fly. A plus sign next

The *in port* and *out port* of your text object may appear as:

- A red plus sign in the *out port* means the object contains *overflow text*.
- An arrow in the *in port* means the object is threaded to a preceding text object, and text is flowing into the object.
- An arrow in the *out port* means the object is threaded to a subsequent text object, and text is flowing out of the object.

To join separate Area text boxes or Point type objects, select all the text objects with any Selection tool and copy. Then draw a new Area text box and paste. Text will flow into the box, in the *stacking order* in which it had appeared on the page. (It doesn't matter if you select graphic elements with your text—these elements won't be pasted.) —*Sandee Cohen*

When handling ducks you must always wear protective arm and hand covering. Many unwary duck trainers have lost fingers and even hands and suffered deep puncture wounds from careless handling methods or even brief inattention.

Some of the as the Hookbill, Orpington will and have been burns from the feathers of important that only expert close handling.

more docile breeds such Bali, Muscovy and Buff allow some minor handling even known to cuddle. Acid ducks can be serious so it is handlers attempt such

One particularly nasty Welsh Harlequin. Aptly this uncommon bird has unusual characteristic of itself behind curtains of grass only out and deliver lines in a from Shakespeare's unsuspecting animal

breed is the named, the hiding to jump melodramatic style sonnets whenever an approaches

DONAL JOLLEY

Artist Donal Jolley wrapped Area text around this duck by placing the duck above the text and choosing Object > Text Wrap > Make

When your project calls for several text objects using the same font, consider using a custom paragraph style. Created properly, this prevents Illustrator from applying the default, [Normal Paragraph Style], to all your new text and then adding formatting overrides to apply your specific font attributes. (Using the Control panel, you will merely be creating formatting overrides that must then be cleared in order to apply a different font with different attributes).

- If you'll use the same font attributes in several documents, you can create a New Document Profile that will always include your preferred font attributes as part of the [Normal Paragraph Style]. (See more about profiles in *Your Creative Workspace*.)
- If you only need to change the font for a single document, double-click on [Normal Paragraph Style] and modify the default for just this document, or create a new paragraph style.

—*Cristen Gillespie*

Fonts at small sizes or with fine details won't look as good on the computer screen, or print as clearly at resolutions of 600 dots per inch or less as outlines, as they would if you kept them as fonts.

to the style name in the Paragraph Styles panel indicates you have applied extra formatting, or *overrides*. To avoid unnecessary overrides, see the Tip "Avoiding formatting overrides" at left, and work with styles wherever possible.

- **To create a style based on existing formatting,** format the text as you want it to appear, select it, and click on the New Style button (Option-click/Alt-click to name the style). The selected attributes define the new style.
- **To create a new style based on another,** highlight the style and click the Create New Style icon to duplicate the style. Double-click on the style to open the (Paragraph or Character) Styles Options dialog, rename and modify the style. If you change the original (parent) style, the modifications will ripple down through your new style, as well.
- **To apply a paragraph style to text,** just insert your cursor into the paragraph you want to format and click the name of the style in the Paragraph Styles panel. When you first apply a paragraph style, it won't remove overrides. To remove all overrides, click again on the plus beside the Paragraph style name.
- **To apply a character style,** select all the letterforms you want to change, and then click on the name in the Character Styles panel.

CONVERTING TYPE TO OUTLINES

You can now keep type live and perform many effects that once required you to outline type. Using the Appearance panel you can apply multiple strokes to characters, run type along a curve, use envelopes to distort type, and you can even mask with live, editable type. Following are some cases where you still might need to outline your type:

- **Convert to outlines to graphically transform or distort type.** If Warp Effects and Envelopes don't create the effect you need (see examples in this chapter, and in the *Reshaping Dimensions* chapter for examples of warps and envelopes), then outlining your type will allow you to edit the individual curves and anchor points of letters or words. Your type will no longer be editable as type, but instead will be constructed of standard Illustrator Bézier curves that are editable just like any other object. Type converted to outlines may include compound paths to form the "holes" in the outlined letter forms (such as the see-through centers of an **O**, **B**, or **P**. Choose Object > Compound Path > Release to fill the "holes" with color.

- **Convert to outlines to maintain your letter and word spacing when exporting type** to another application, as many programs don't support the translation of custom kerning and word spacing.
- **Convert to outlines if you can't distribute the font to your client or service bureau,** when you don't have permission to embed the fonts, or your service bureau doesn't have its own license for a font.

USING THE EYEDROPPER WITH TYPE

The Eyedropper tool allows you to copy appearance attributes from one type object to another, including stroke, fill, character, and paragraph attributes. Double-click the Eyedropper tool to check that text attributes are enabled.

For a one-step method, select the type object with appearance attributes you want to change, and then move the Eyedropper tool over the unselected type object that has the attributes you want and click on it.

Alternatively, the Eyedropper tool works in another mode: *sampling* and *applying*. A small **T** means it is in position to sample or apply text attributes. To copy text formatting from one object to another using the Eyedropper tool, position it over an unselected type object. When it angles downward to the left, click the type object to pick up its attributes.

Now position the Eyedropper tool over the unselected text object to which you want to apply the attributes, and hold down the Option/Alt key. In applying mode, it angles downward to the right, and looks full. To apply the attributes that you just sampled, move the cursor to the text you want to change and click. (A simple click will apply the sampled attributes to the whole paragraph; you can also drag the cursor to apply the attributes only to the specific text you dragged over.)

The Every-line Composer

Illustrator offers two composition methods for determining where line breaks occur in lines of text: The Single-line Composer applies hyphenation and justification settings to one line of text at a time (but can look ragged with multiple lines), and the Every-line Composer determines the best combination of line breaks across an entire paragraph of text.

Control tabs and leaders

Use the Tabs panel to control tabs and leaders. As you pan or zoom, you'll notice the Tab ruler doesn't move with the text box. If you lose your alignment, just click the little Magnet button on the Tabs panel, and the panel will snap back into alignment.

*Artist Donal Jolley had to convert type to outlines in order to reshape the **U** and **N** type characters*

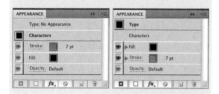
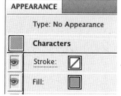

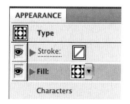

The Appearance panel showing the green fill applied to the type at the Character level

The Appearance panel showing the pattern Quilt 1 (from the Decorative_Ornaments pattern library) filling the type at the type object level

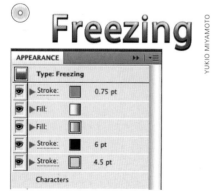

A graphic style created using the Appearance panel with multiple fills and strokes

YUKIO MIYAMOTO

USING THE APPEARANCE PANEL WITH TYPE

When you work with type, you work with the letter characters or with the container that holds the characters—or both. Understanding the difference between characters and their container (the "type object") will help you access and edit the right one when you style type. To help understand the difference, you'll need to watch the Appearance panel as you work.

Type Characters

Type characters entered with the Type tool can have a color or pattern applied to a character's fill and stroke (by default it has a Black Fill and No Stroke). To edit a character's fill and stroke, drag across the text with the Type tool or double-click Characters in the Appearance panel.

With type characters, you can't do the following things (although you can with their containers): move the stroke under the fill or the fill above the stroke; apply a live effect to the fill or stroke; apply a gradient fill; or add multiple fills or strokes.

Type Objects

The Type object contains all the text in a Point, Area, or Path type object. You are working with the type "object" when you select the text with the Selection tool and then move the object around on your page.

With the text object you can add another fill (click on the Add New Fill icon in the Appearance panel). Now there is another listing of Stroke and Fill, in the Appearance panel, but this time they are positioned above the Characters line in the panel. If you reveal the Stroke and Fill for the type by double-clicking the Characters line in the panel, you return to character editing; reselect the type object with the Selection tool to return to editing the type object rather than its characters.

When you add a new Stroke or Fill to the type object, its color and effects interact with the color of the characters. All the strokes and fills applied to type are layered on top of those listed below (including on top of the stroke and fill you see listed when you double-click Characters in the panel). So if you add a new fill to the type object and apply white to it, the type appears white (the white fill of the type object is stacked above the black default fill of the characters).

THE GLYPHS PANEL

Illustrator's Glyphs panel (Window > Type > Glyphs) provides quick access to a wide variety of special characters (like * or ❤), including any ligatures, ornaments, swashes, and fractions included with a given font. Use the list box to narrow your search of a font for the type of letterform you're seeking. With the Type tool, click to place the insertion point, then double-click the character you want in the Glyphs panel to insert it in the text.

WORKING WITH LEGACY TEXT

Any text created prior to Illustrator CS (when Adobe completely re-engineered Illustrator's type engine to become compatible with InDesign), is *legacy text*. It must be updated before it's editable in later versions of Illustrator. Continuing improvements to Illustrator's type engine might result in yet another break between a current and an earlier version. For example, any version prior to CS4 that uses the Type on a Path tool will prompt a legacy text warning when opened in CS4 (or later) before path type can be edited. Adobe will prompt you first to update legacy text from versions before CS, and then to update path type, if necessary. By following the prompts, text in your files will be fully editable in your current version of the software, or you can choose not to edit or work with the text at this time.

ADVANCED FEATURES OF MULTIPLE ARTBOARDS

You can find basic information on artboards in the chapter *Your Creative Workspace*. Following in this section are some of the more advanced features of artboards, which will help you work productively and maintain consistency within a project.

Missing fonts?

If you open a file without the correct fonts loaded, Illustrator warns you. You can still open, edit, and save the file. Illustrator remembers the fonts you were using. However, the text will not flow accurately, and the file won't print correctly until you load or replace the missing fonts. Choose Type > Find Font to then locate and replace each occurrence by clicking Change and then Find, or change every occurrence at once, with Change All.

Glyphs panel showing list of criteria for narrowing what the panel shows to just those characters required

OpenType table on the DVD

We've included a PDF guide by InDesign expert Sandee Cohen on the **WOW! DVD** (look for the file named OpenType.pdf). These pages, which are excerpted from Cohen's *InDesign Visual Quick-Start Guide* from Peachpit Press, give you a handy reference table on how to work with OpenType.

Illustrator's Small Caps option (in the Character panel

SMALL CAPS

SMALL CAPS

SMALL CAPS

menu) converts all selected characters to small caps (top). However, if true-drawn small caps aren't available in a font, Illustrator creates the fake, scaled-down version (middle), which is a typographic taboo. To prevent Illustrator from creating fake small caps, go to File > Document Setup > Type > Options, and change the Small Caps percentage from 70% to 100%. This option is *only* used when Illustrator is faking small caps, so when your small caps are the size of capital letters, you'll instantly recognize it (bottom). This option doesn't persist between documents, so you'll have to choose it each time. (See the **WOW! DVD** for the full creativepro.com article.)

—*Ilene Strizver, The Type Studio*

Using the Transform effect to copy instances of artwork from one artboard to all the others

Illustrator can open and convert Freehand multi-page documents into multiple artboards.

Duplicating Elements to Artboards

Among the more common functions you'll need when you're working in a multiple artboard document is the duplication of elements on multiple pages. Although there isn't currently a built-in "master page" function, there are a number of ways to accomplish this task:

- **To duplicate elements when adding another artboard,** select the Artboard tool, enable "Move/Copy Artwork with Artboard," and hold down the Option/Alt key while dragging an active artboard to a new location.
- **Turn artwork created on one artboard into a symbol,** then drag that symbol from the shared Symbols panel to any other artboard. Now just update the symbol to update all instances of it used on any artboards.
- **To move or copy the artwork a specified distance,** measure the distance between the artwork and where you want it on another artboard. Then use Transform > Move and enter the measurement in the Distance input.
- **To copy "instances" of artwork to another artboard,** use the Transform effect.
- **To copy objects to all other artboards** in the same relative location, use Paste on All Artboards.

Managing Artboards

Many features are available to help you work with artboards according to more specialized needs. If you select the Artboard tool to accomplish these tasks, use the Esc key to return to the tool you were using.

- **Renumbering artboards using the Artboard panel,** either drag artboard names to rearrange them, or highlight one artboard and click the up or down arrow icons Renumbering artboards can be very helpful if you're using them for presentations and storyboarding.
- **Rearrange artboards positions** using either the Artboard panel menu, or Object > Artboards > Rearrange. A dialog lets you determine the order they repeat in both across the monitor and down (their layout), how far apart they are placed, how many columns they're in, and whether or not the artwork is moved with them.

- **Convert any rectangle to an artboard** using Object > Artboard > Convert to Artboard. Or use Object > Path > Split Into Grid to create several rectangles from one before converting them all to artboards.

- **To save artboards as separate files**—from the Illustrator Options section of Save As, choose "Save each artboard to a separate file," and choose all or a range of artboards.

Exporting and Printing Multiple Artboards

All artboards in a file share the same print options, including color mode, bleed settings, and scale, and you can choose to print either to a PDF file or to a printer. In the Print dialog, print artboards as separate pages (the default), or ignore artboards and tile the artwork.

- **Print to PDF** always flattens the file. But you can choose the media, such as screen or slide, ignoring the actual artboard size—this is useful for presentations. Or you can scale the artwork to fit your media, among many other features found in the Print to PDF dialog.

- **Save As PDF** preserves transparency, editing capabilities, and top-level layers, and you can set a level of security.

- **Print only some artboards** using the Range setting. Scale them to fit your print media if desired.

- **Print artboards with landscape orientation, or a mix of landscape and portrait,** with Auto-Rotate when portrait is selected for the media. If your media is landscape-oriented, Auto-Rotate is disabled.

- **Print artwork that is larger than your media** using artboards instead of the Print Tiling tool. The Split Into Grid command (followed by Convert to Artboard) can divide the artwork into media-sized rectangles for you.

- **The boundaries of each artboard are cropped** if your artwork overlaps artboards and you print each artboard as a page.

- **When printing pages in which two or more artboards are overlapping the same artwork,** each artboard will print with whichever portions of the artwork are visible within that artboard.

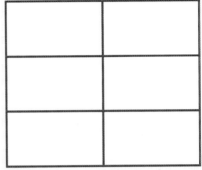

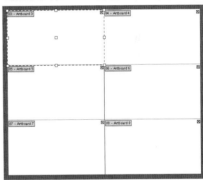

After drawing a rectangle, choosing Split into Grid (original purple stroke is preserved), and Convert to Artboard

Print to PDF dialog, including Auto-Rotate enabled by default when printing landscape artboards to media oriented to portrait

Create an Identity

Working Efficiently with Multiple Elements

Overview: *Create artboards for each type of content; use the Artboards panel to resize the artboards and duplicate some of them; use symbols for logos; optionally, duplicate artboards with artwork for multiple variations.*

1

Setting up multiple artboards

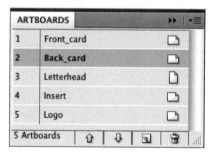

Customize, name, and reorder artboards using the Artboards panel and Artboard Options dialog.

Customizing the layout using the Artboard tool and Smart Guides to help align the artboards

A company's typical identity package may contain several types and sizes of materials, such as letterhead, business cards, web pages, and ad inserts. Instead of needing to keep track of multiple files, Ryan Putnam can rely on multiple artboards and symbols to create the collateral materials in a single file, making additions or updates much simpler and less prone to errors and omissions.

1 Setting up the artboards. Putnam began by setting up four artboards using the default settings in the New dialog plus a standard bleed. Opening the Artboards panel, he double-clicked the first artboard icon, entered the dimensions of the business card, named it "Front_card," and clicked OK. He then customized the sizes and names of the other three artboards: the letterhead, an insert, and the logo design. Since he needed the same size artboard for the front and back of the business card, he used the Artboards panel to duplicate the business card by dragging "Front_card" to the New Artboard icon. He renamed the copy "Back_card," and reordered the artboards (which renumbered them) by dragging "Back_card" to just below "Front_card" in the Artboards panel. Because duplicate artboards automatically get added in a single row to the right of the last artboard drawn, Putnam selected the Artboard tool (Shift-O), to drag the artboards into a custom arrangement. Using Smart Guides (⌘-U/Ctrl-U) he could easily line them up in a well-organized fashion.

2 Making symbols for replication and quick updates.

Putnam began by designing the logo. He then dragged it into the Symbols panel to save it as a symbol, named it, and clicked OK. If he modified the logo, he only had to alter the one symbol to automatically update all instances of it throughout the document. If he needed a variation of the logo, he could break the link to the original symbol to create a new symbol (see the *Expressive Strokes* chapter for more about creating and modifying symbols). Using multiple artboards with symbols adds appreciably to productivity. Artboards in one file share the same libraries, so if there were any changes in the future, Putnam wouldn't have to open separate files for each item in the identity package, and then open the library containing the modified symbol. One file would always contain all the libraries and correctly-sized artboards ready for modifications.

3 Copying and duplicating artwork with artboards.

Putnam created the design for each element of the identity package, placing the logo symbol on the artboard and adding text and artwork as needed. He linked the photo to the insert, making it easy to replace for the next event. Although the letterhead and insert only required a single version, he needed to create a business card that could be duplicated and personalized later for each employee and different events. When he needed to create another business card for a different employee and/or event, he could either duplicate the front and back cards in the Artboards panel as before, or, with the Artboard tool selected and Move/Copy Artwork enabled in the Control panel, he could hold down the Option/Alt key while dragging a selected artboard. With everything in place, Putnam only had to select the text, graphic, or linked image that needed changing and quickly replace it. Because he could add up to 100 artboards in a single file, Putnam was now able to stay organized with just one file.

Sharing artboards and libraries

Any project that shares artwork for different elements—whether they share the same color theme, graphic and type styles, symbols, brushes, etc.—might benefit from using multiple artboards. That way you only need to maintain the libraries belonging to any single document, sharing them among all of the project pieces.

2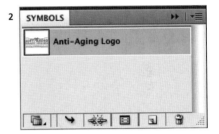

Using symbols for logos to maintain consistency, to make updates a snap, and to modify or place symbols from a shared library onto different artboards as needed

3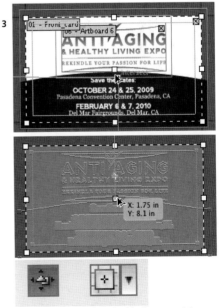

Duplicating the artboard with the artwork by enabling the Move/Copy Artwork with Artboard icon and holding down the Option/Alt key

For Client Review

Creating Presentations from Artboards

Overview: *Use a separate artboard for each variation of a logo; use Recolor Artwork to recolor each version; save the file as a PDF for a client's initial review; create multiple artboards, then place artboards for a new presentation; save the new presentation for the client's final review.*

Need more help?

For more help customizing artboards and using symbols with them, see the "Create an Identity" lesson in this chapter.

When Scott Citron needed to create a new logo for a client, he decided to take advantage of multiple artboards, both to keep each task organized, and to use printing options for his client presentations. With Illustrator's ability to print separate pages for each artboard, and to print only selected artboards, making a PDF presentation becomes quick work using multiple artboards.

1

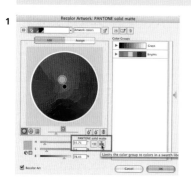

Using the Recolor Artwork dialog to limit to a Pantone Color Book in order to recolor variations for a logo (for more about Recolor Artwork, see the Color Transitions *chapter*)

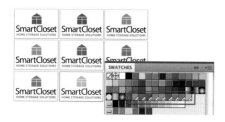

Multiple artboards duplicated with the Artboard tool, then using Recolor Artwork to automatically save Spot colors to the Swatches panel

1 Creating multiple versions on multiple artboards, and preparing a multi-page PDF for review. Citron used a single artboard for the new logo, then he selected the Artboard tool (Shift-O), enabled the Move/Copy Artwork with Artboard icon, and holding down the Option/Alt key he dragged to make several copies (instead you can choose Duplicate Artboards from the Artboards panel menu). Using a workflow designed by Sandee Cohen, he selected one of the logos and clicked on the Recolor Artwork icon in the Control panel. On the Edit tab, he clicked on the Limit to swatches library icon, then he chose Color Books from the list and a Pantone Solid book from the sublist. Citron dragged in the Color Wheel to interactively locate a new Pantone Spot color and clicked OK; the new Spot color was automatically saved to the Swatches panel.

Citron then needed to make a single Acrobat (PDF) document so the client could see and comment on each colored logo separately. To create one multi-page PDF from the artboards, he chose File > Save As > Adobe PDF (also see "Exporting and Printing Multiple Artboards" in the introduction to this chapter).

2 Creating the identity and presentation. Once the client approved a color, Citron copied the chosen logo to a new document, added it to the Symbols panel, and created a new artboard sized for every requested printed piece. Adding the symbol and text, he completed making the collateral materials and saved the file with PDF compatibility enabled. To present the overall effect to the client, Citron wanted to create a pleasing arrangement of the materials. He created a new document at default settings. He didn't worry about the size; he would resize it to fit all the artwork later. He then chose File > Place, with Link enabled, selecting the first artboard in the file he just previously saved.

Because placed artwork can't display a stroke, fill, or drop shadow, Citron used a technique developed by Mordy Golding in order to delineate the boundaries of each visible piece. In the Appearance panel, he first added a new Stroke, and chose Convert to Shape > Rectangle (no added width or height) from the *fx* menu. He then added a new white Fill (temporarily concealing everything), chose Convert to Shape > Rectangle, and with the Fill still targeted, chose *fx* > Stylize > Drop Shadow. He dragged the Fill below "Contents" in the Appearance panel to reveal the artwork. In the Graphic Styles panel, he Option/Alt-clicked the New icon to save this style as "Boundary." For each additional artboard, he chose Place and clicked the "Boundary" style. He arranged the placed artwork and, to prepare the presentation as a PDF, selected the Artboard tool and chose Presets > Fit Artboard to Artwork bounds. Now if he updated the original file containing the collateral materials, he could choose to update his presentation instantly, while the original file was kept "printer-ready."

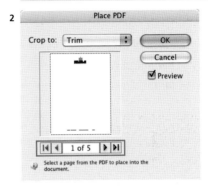

Placing artwork in a file one artboard at a time, cropped to Trim

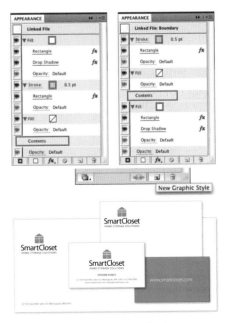

Using a graphic style to create a border as a visual aid—adding a Stroke will define the outline; adding a Fill creates an object that can have a Drop Shadow applied, but first conceals the artwork; after adding the Drop Shadow, the Fill is moved below "Contents," revealing the artwork and defining the boundaries

Book Cover Design

Illustrator as a Stand-Alone Layout Tool

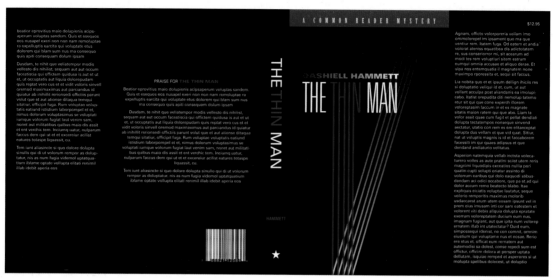

Overview: *Set your document's dimensions and bleeds; make custom guides; make Area type for columns and thread text.*

Even with multiple artboards in Illustrator, you'll still need a page-layout program (such as InDesign or QuarkXPress) for the production of complex multi-page documents. But for simpler projects, such as a book cover design, Scott Citron often finds that after setting up bleeds and custom guides, Illustrator allows him to better work with designs that integrate rich graphic elements.

1 Setting up the page. To create a new document, Scott Citron chose File > New. While in the New Document dialog, he changed the Name of the file and set the Number of Artboards to 1. For the document's dimensions, Citron chose Picas under Units, clicked the Landscape icon under Orientation, and entered the dimensions of his book cover in the Width and Height fields. He also needed a bleed for the book cover, so while still in the New Document dialog, he entered his bleed measurement in the Top Bleed input field and clicked the "Make all settings the same" icon to populate the other Bleed fields with the same measurement. Once he entered all his settings, he clicked OK to exit the New Document dialog.

Changing the name, setting the number of Artboards to 1, changing units to Picas, setting Orientation to landscape, entering dimensions, and entering bleed measurements

2 Customizing your guides. To make it possible to set up guides for the inside jacket flaps, back cover, spine, and front cover, Citron first chose View > Show Rulers. To create the first guide, he first checked to make sure that guides were unlocked (View > Guides), and then click-dragged from the left-side ruler to, roughly, his first position. With the guide still selected, he numerically adjusted the positions of a selected guide by relocating the X (or Y) axis positions in the Transform panel. To create a rectangular guide (rather than a linear one), he could convert a selected rectangle into a guide using ⌘-5/Ctrl-5. With his guides in place, Citron chose View > Guides > Lock Guides. As he worked, if he needed to access lock, hide, and release guide functions, he used the context-sensitive menu.

Choosing View > Show Rulers and dragging a guide into position

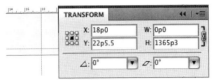

Selecting guide and numerically positioning from the Transform panel

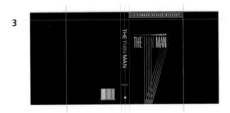

Placing artwork

3 Placing and refining the elements. When the page was set with the correct dimensions, bleeds, and guides, Citron added artwork to the design. Although Citron's book cover contains all vector artwork, you can import a raster image into your document by choosing File > Place.

Citron then created rectangles with the Rectangle tool to define areas for columns of text. With the Area Type tool, he clicked on one of these rectangles, making it possible to type directly into the box or to paste text. He then double-clicked on the Type tool from the Tools panel to open the Area Type Options dialog. Within the dialog, Citron changed the Offset in the Inset Spacing field to inset the text from the edge of the text box. You can also use the Area Type Options dialog to change the Dimensions, Rows, Columns, and Text Flow Options. Citron then repeated these steps for the other rectangles he wanted as text boxes. To make the overset text of one text box flow to another, he used the Selection tool. He clicked on the red box in the overflowing text box and then on the new text box he wanted the text to flow into. As an alternative to using the Area Type tool, you can use the Type tool to create Point type for titles, headlines, and other individual type elements.

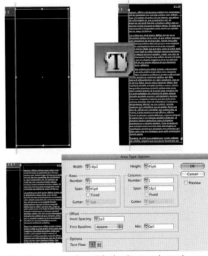

Creating rectangles with the Rectangle tool, using the Area Type tool, and setting Inset Spacing

Flowing overset text to another text box

Curvaceous Type

Fitting Type to Curved Paths

Overview: *Create artwork objects; copy object paths, then cut the paths to workable length; add text to the paths and offset the text; convert type to outlines and edit character paths.*

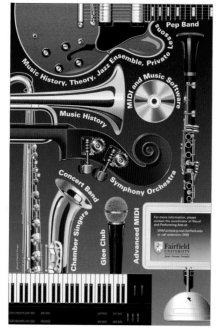

The finished poster for Fairfield University

1

The Outline view of the paths for the guitar

Using the flowing curves of musical instruments coupled with strings of text, designer Gerard Huerta captured the variety of musical studies offered by Fairfield University in this poster promoting its music program to campus and high school students. To give the type characters a more organic fit with the tight curves of some of the instruments, Huerta converted the type to outlines and then edited the shapes of the character paths.

1 Sketching and scanning the shapes, then redrawing them in Illustrator. Huerta started the poster by sketching the shapes of musical instruments by pencil. Then he scanned the drawing and placed the scan in Illustrator as a template layer. By using the Pen tool to draw the shapes, and using gradients and gradient meshes for color, Huerta built the musical instruments and then arranged them to leave space for the text he would create next.

2 Drawing paths for type and creating the type on the paths. You can draw the paths that will parallel your objects with the Pen or Pencil tool for setting type, or, like Huerta, use copies of the objects themselves. First, copy the path you want the type to parallel and paste in front (Edit > Paste in Front) so the copy directly overlays the original. Use the Scissors tool to cut the path so that it's an open-ended path instead of a closed path. Next, with the Type tool, click on the line and type the words you want on that path. Grab the type's I-beam and slide it along the path to position the text—flip it to the other side of the path if the text you typed ended up on the wrong side of the path. Make sure that the Character panel is open and your type is still selected. From the Character panel, enter a negative number in the Baseline Shift field or pick a negative number from the field's pop-up menu. Adjust the offset of the type from its path by increasing or decreasing the Baseline Shift value. Reshape the path by using the Direct Selection tool or by drawing over a section of the path with the Pencil tool.

3 Converting type to outlines, then editing character paths. Violins and guitars have sharply curved bodies that can make some letter characters look too angular and straight when positioned along the curve of the path. To correct this, Huerta changed the shapes of individual letter characters so that their strokes conformed more naturally to the curved shape of the path.

You can change character shapes by first converting the type to outlines. (Make copies of the type first in case you need to edit the type or its paths later.) To do this, select the Type on a Path object (don't select the text itself using the Type tool) and choose Type > Create Outlines. Look for characters with parallel strokes, like **m**, **n**, **h**, and **u**. Using the Direct Selection tool, move points and adjust control handles to reshape characters, or reshape selected paths with the Pencil tool. Huerta relied on the Direct Selection and Pencil tools to add curves to the straight edges of the original character shapes. He also changed the angle of some character strokes so that the characters appeared to bend with the tight curve of their paths.

Spacey characters

Although much improved, the Illustrator type engine may still create some kerning problems with Type on a Path characters. To minimize issues, double-click the Type tool to open Path Options and choose Align to Path: Center (instead of the default Baseline). Also, in the Character panel make sure the Baseline Shift is 0, and manually kern character pairs if necessary.

2

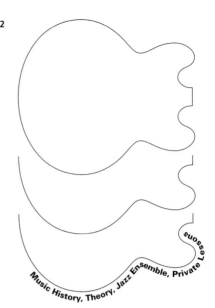

The Outline view of the original outer path for the guitar body (top); path cut from the guitar path (middle); text added to the path and then offset using a negative Baseline Shift

3

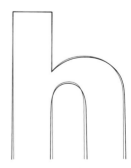

*On the left, the letter **T** character from the Univers font; on the right, the **T** character after Huerta edited the character's outline paths by curving the top stroke of the letter*

*The original letter **h** character shown here as a magenta outline; superimposed on the original letter **h** is the black outline of the **h** that Huerta edited by angling the bottoms of the vertical strokes*

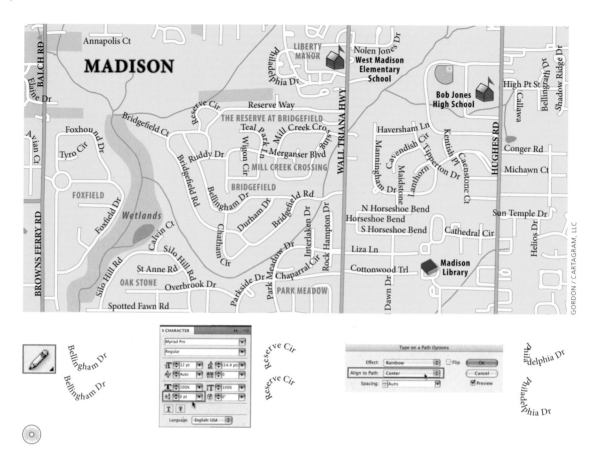

GORDON / CARTAGRAM, LLC

Steven Gordon/Cartagram, LLC

To label curving features like rivers and roads on his maps, cartographer Steve Gordon relies on type on a path. Gordon copies and pastes the river or road paths on a separate layer before applying type to them. He sets the Baseline Shift to 1 pt in the Character panel in order to move the type away from the underlying road or river path. In this map of Madison, Alabama, Gordon encountered paths with sharp turns and tight curves that pinched letters together or spread them apart with unsightly gaps. He smoothed the kinks from some paths by clicking to select a path with type, selecting the Pencil tool, and then dragging it over or near the path. For paths that couldn't be smoothed solely with the Pencil, Gordon reset the path's Baseline Shift to 0 and then dragged the path away from the street path so that its lettering was the same distance away from the street as the labels with the 1-pt Baseline Shift. Some of the type paths required another adjustment: Gordon chose Type > Type on a Path > Type on a Path Options, and in the dialog box changed Align to Path from the default value of Baseline to Center. Gordon employed these techniques, separately or in various combinations, as he worked with hundreds of type objects in the map.

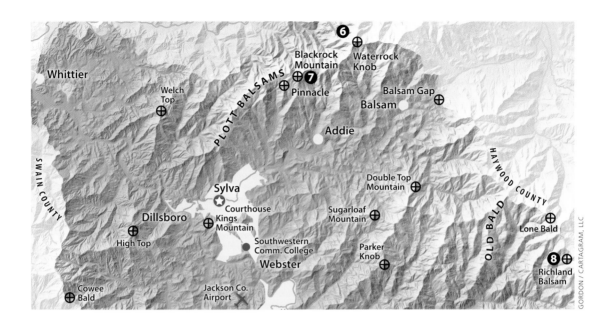

Whittier

Welch
Top

6

Blackrock
Mountain

Waterrock
Knob

PLOTT-BALSAMS

7 Pinnacle

Balsam Gap

Balsam

SWAIN COUNTY

Addie

HAYWOOD COUNTY

Double Top
Mountain

Sylva

Courthouse
Kings
Mountain

Sugarloaf
Mountain

Dillsboro

OLD BALD

Lone Bald

High Top

Southwestern
Comm. College

Webster

Parker
Knob

8

Richland
Balsam

Cowee
Bald

Jackson Co.
Airport

GORDON / CARTAGRAM, LLC

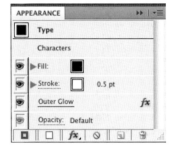

Steven Gordon/Cartagram, LLC

When cartographer Steven Gordon creates a map with a terrain image in the background, he has to ensure that type is not lost in the mountains of the image. For this map of North Carolina's Jackson County, Gordon received directions to create a bold, colorful terrain image by his client, *The Sylva Herald*. He began the map by creating the terrain image in Photoshop, placing it in the Illustrator file, and positioning it on the artboard. After creating the type labels, Gordon opened the Appearance panel, chose Add New Stroke from the panel menu, and dragged the Stroke attribute below Characters in the panel. Next, he set the width of the stroke to 0.5 pt using the Stroke Weight menu and then clicked the Stroke attribute's color icon to pop up the Swatches menu and selected the white swatch. Gordon wanted to soften the contrast between the white stroke and image behind it and decided to add a white glow around the type. To do this he clicked Characters in the Appearance panel and then clicked the Add New Effect icon and chose Stylize > Outer Glow. In the Outer Glow dialog, he clicked the Color Picker, selected white, and changed Opacity to 100% and Blur to 0.04 inches to complete the effect.

Moving Your Type

Setting Type on a Curve and Warping Type

Overview: *Create banners that will go behind curved labels; type label text on a curved path and adjust its alignment on the path; warp text and adjust its tracking; modify the kerning of the space between words.*

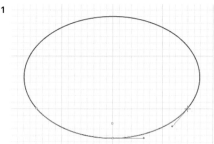

The ellipse with the left and right endpoints of the banner path cut by the Scissors tool

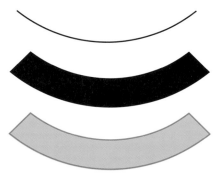

Thickening the banner path's stroke, then outlining the path and giving it stroke and fill colors

Greater Bridgeport Transit hired Jack Tom to design a T-shirt supporting its new campaign to raise public awareness of the local bus system. Tom's design combined the campaign's taglines—"Go Green," "Go GBT.com," and "Go Public"—with artwork illustrating birds, butterflies, and flowery vines.

1 Creating the background art and the two banners.
After drawing the floral, bird, and butterfly figures, Tom created the banners that would serve as backgrounds for the curved "Go Green" and "Go Public" labels. You can make a symmetrical banner by first selecting the Ellipse tool and drawing an ellipse. Then cut the ellipse with the Scissors tool to make the curved path that will form the banner. Using the grid (View > Show Grid) and positioning the ellipse over a horizontal grid line will help you cut the ellipse at the same vertical position on its left and right sides, keeping the curve symmetrical. Next, make a copy of this path; you'll use it later for curving the text of the label. Now give the joined path a thick stroke (Tom used 35 pt) and then outline the path by selecting Object >

Path > Outline Stroke. You can now give the stroke a width and color the stroke and fill.

2 Curving a label. To make the curved labels for "Go Green" and "Go Public," Tom used the path he had copied in the previous step. If you use Paste in Front (⌘-F/Ctrl-F), the path will overlay the banner you created previously. After pasting the path, select the Text tool, click on the path, and type your label text. With the path still selected, click the Align center icon in the Paragraph section of the Control panel. That centers your text horizontally across the banner. Before adjusting the vertical position of the type, realign the position of the type to the path by choosing Type > Type on a Path > Type on a Path Options. From the Type on a Path Options dialog, change Align to Path from the default Baseline to Center. Also, set the baseline shift to 0 in the Character panel. This will minimize any pinching or expanding of space between the letters of the label. Now you can move the path up or down to better center the label against the banner.

3 Arcing and bending a label. Tom wanted the main label, "Go GBT.com," to bend backwards in a gentle arc. To bend type, start by typing your text (you can use an Area- or a Point-type object). With the text object selected, choose Effect > Warp > Arc Lower. In the Warp Options dialog, make sure Horizontal is still active and change Bend by moving the slider or entering a number in the Bend field. A negative number will bend the type backwards (Tom entered –17% for Bend).

When you warp type, the spacing between letters and words may change more than you'd like. Consider resetting the Tracking or the Kerning from the Character panel. Tracking controls the distance between all letters in the selected text, while kerning requires you to adjust the distance between each pair of letters. Also, to tighten the space between words, click on the space between words and narrow the kerned space between words by holding Option/Alt and pressing the left arrow key.

2

The Align Center icon in the Control panel

The Type on a Path Options dialog with the Align to Path changed to Center

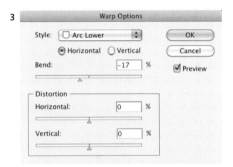

The finished label

3

Above, the Warp Options dialog; below, the type before warping (top) and after warping (below)

Above, the text with a space between words; below, negative kerning inserted between the **O** and **G** characters

TOM

Jack Tom

After creating the color T-shirt design (see previous step-by-step lesson), Tom was asked to develop a design for a new campaign coordinating with the 40th Anniversary of Earth Day. Emphasizing the campaign's goal of planting a tree for every monthly bus pass sold, Tom created a tree using symbols of leaves, flowers, fish, hummingbirds, and dolphins, among other figures. He arranged the symbols around the shape of a bus. For the main label, Tom typed the "Go GBT.com" using uppercase letters. To make the beginning and ending letters larger than the rest of the text, he selected each letter

and entered a larger font size value in the Character panel. Then, with the letter still selected, Tom changed the baseline shift to –5 pt to lower the letter to align its top with the top of the other letters.

TREMBLAY

Jean-Claude Tremblay

When it came time to pair type for his company's name with his newly-designed logo, Jean-Claude Tremblay looked for a typeface that would match the letterforms he had created. He settled on ITC Avant Garde Gothic, Book style, for its echoing roundness, clean simplicity of letterform, and contrast in weight. Since this particular font's **fi** ligature carries a dot that visually closes up and clutters the **f** at display sizes—especially when properly kerned for the entire name—Tremblay chose to create his own ligature for the **fi** combination. First, he spelled out the entire name and converted the type to outlines (⌘-Shift-O/Ctrl-Shift-O). He then used the Group Selection tool (the Direct Selection tool with Option/Alt) to select the dot over each

i, and clicked Delete. Next, after setting the Keyboard Increment to .1 pt (in General Preferences), he Group Selected the two **i** objects that followed an **f**, zoomed in close, and used the left arrow key to nudge both **i** objects until each touched the adjacent **f**'s bar. Still using the Direct Selection tool, he carefully selected each letter following the first **p** and used the arrow keys to move the letters closer together until they looked equally "kerned." He filled the letterforms for each word in the company name with the color that corresponded to their initial. Shown above is the grayscale version as it developed, with the color version in the last example of the type. (Also see his "Interlock Objects" lesson in the *Rethinking Construction* chapter.)

Arcing Type

Transforming Type with Warps & Envelopes

Overview: *Create and color a title using appearances; explore the three Envelope distortions for creating an arc effect; use an Arc Warp effect to arc the type; create a graphic style and apply arc effect to other title elements.*

1

Putnam's 50-point Cabaret font headline

Applying Object > Envelope Distort > Make with Warp and changing the Bend to 20%

Applying Object > Envelope Distort > Make with Mesh, setting the number of Rows and Columns to 1, and editing the anchor points with the Direct Selection tool

Creating an arc-shaped object with the Pen tool over the type, selecting the arc-shaped object and type, and applying Object > Envelope Distort > Make with Top Object

PUTNAM

Adding an arc effect to a headline turns boring type into a dynamic engaging headline that grabs the viewers' attention. With Illustrator you can explore a number of ways to create arcing text; using effects and graphic styles, you can quickly create an arcing effect easily applicable to any other titles or subtitles! (See the *Reshaping Dimensions* chapter for more about warps, blends, and graphic styles.)

1 Creating your headline text. To create headline text, choose a font with distinct, bold characteristics. For his headline text, Ryan Putnam chose 50-point Cabaret font.

Amongst the many ways to create an arcing effect in Illustrator, there are three different Envelope distortions that you can apply to your text: Warp, Mesh, and Make with Top Object.

First, Putnam applied Object > Envelope Distort > Make with Warp. Next, he chose Arc from the Warp options, and changed the Bend to 20%. For a second option, he then applied Object > Envelope Distort > Make with Mesh, set the number of Rows and Columns to 1, and edited the anchor points with the Direct Selection tool. For the final option, he used the Pen tool to draw a separate arc-shaped object over the type, selected the type and arc-shaped object, and applied Object > Envelope Distort > Make with Top Object.

2 Applying an Arc Warp effect to arc the title. Even though using Envelope distortions created the effect Putnam was looking for, and provided significant control for customizing his warp, he ultimately decided that he wanted a quick way to add the same simple arc effect to other titles and subtitles on the cover. Putnam figured out that if he created the arc using Effect > Warp, he could save his effect as a graphic style that he could then apply to additional titles.

There are 15 standard Warp shapes you can choose from when creating a title. For the "Spiritual" title, Putnam applied Effect > Warp > Arc. With Preview enabled, he changed the Bend to 20%, then clicked OK.

3 Saving and applying a graphic style. With the title selected, Putnam clicked the New Graphic Style icon in the Graphic Styles panel. With the graphic style now saved, Putnam could easily apply that style to other titles and subtitles.

To create a variant of this style, he replaced the text with "Muscles:", changed the font to 28 points, the Rotation to 355°, and then clicked the New Graphic Style icon in the Graphic Styles panel.

4 Applying finishing touches. To custom color the individual characters in his headline, Putnam decided to outline the type (Type > Create Outlines). He then applied a custom gradient and adjusted it for each character. (For more about working with gradients, see the *Color Transitions* chapter.)

2

In Effect > Warp > Arc, changing the bend to 20%

3

Selecting the title and clicking the New Graphic Style icon in the Graphic Styles panel

Applying the graphic style

Using Add New Effect from the Appearance panel, apply Distort & Transform, change the Rotation to 355°, and click the New Graphic Style icon in the Graphic Styles panel

4

Applying Type > Create Outlines to the titles

Applying a linear gradient to the titles

Applying a custom gradient

Brush Your Type

Applying Brushes to Letterforms

CRONAN

Overview: *Create, layer, and blur text objects; draw paths and apply brushes; modify paths and brushes; change path transparency.*

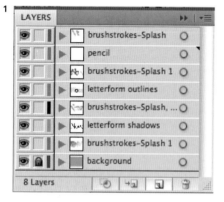

The finished illustration's Layers panel showing the separation of artwork on layers to produce the poster's visual hierarchy

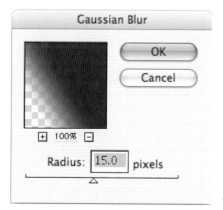

The Effect > Blur > Gaussian Blur dialog with the Radius set to a value appropriate for the smaller working size of the illustration

Designed for a corporate setting where a simple, bold poster could serve as a powerful communication, San Francisco artist Michael Cronan used Illustrator's Pencil and Brush tools to blend artistry with bold type, making the simple words eye-catching and provocative.

1 Converting type to outlines and adding a custom blurred shadow. Cronan began the poster by typing "Now" in the font Didot Regular. Because Illustrator limits the maximum font size to 1296 points, you may need to work at a smaller size and then enlarge the illustration later. (When you enlarge, you may need to convert the type to outlines using Type > Create Outlines if your type will be larger than 1296 points.) To layer artwork you'll create later between the type and a blurred shadow of the type, first duplicate the type layer (drag the type layer and drop it on the Create New Layer icon in the Layers panel). Then, select the type objects on the duplicate layer you just created and from the Effect menu select Blur > Gaussian Blur and choose a blur radius that blurs enough without obliterating the letterforms.

2 Drawing and painting paths with brushes and applying transparency to paths. Painting letterforms couldn't be easier. Using the type you created previously as a visual guide, start by simply drawing lines with the Pen or Pencil tool. Coupling the Pencil tool with a tablet (such as the Wacom tablet) makes drawing even easier and more spontaneous. For a smoother path (with fewer points and more gentle contours) use the Zoom tool to zoom out, *then* draw with the Pencil tool. Cronan mixed paths that followed the shapes of the letterforms with circles and curlicues (letter **o**) and scribbles (letter **w**).

With paths drawn, you're ready to apply brushes. Click the Brush Libraries icon (in the lower left of the Brushes panel) and choose Artistic_Paintbrush. Then click on a path and select the Splash brush from the Artistic_Paintbrush panel. With the path still selected, you can refine the shape of the brushed path by selecting the Pencil tool and drawing over or near the selected path to smooth or reshape it. Use the Zoom tool to zoom in or out before you apply the Smooth or Pencil tools to give your reshaped path a smoother or more angular contour.

Because Illustrator's brushes use a path's stroke color, you can color the path before or after applying a brush. To adjust the thickness of the brushed path, change the path's stroke weight. To change the look of all paths in the illustration painted with a brush, double-click the brush in the Brushes panel and change settings in Art Brush Options. Use the Colorization Method to control how the stroke color is applied to the brush, and adjust the Size > Width field to make the brush stroke wider or thinner.

3 Handwriting with the Pencil tool and setting transparency. Cronan completed the poster illustration by selecting the Pencil tool and drawing paths to mimic handwritten words. Be sure to experiment with the Stroke panel's Cap and Join settings to change the look of the paths. (As an alternative to the Pencil tool, consider using a Calligraphic brush with a small point size from the Brushes panel.) To blend the handwriting-like white-stroked paths with the artwork below, Cronan used the Control panel to reduce the Opacity to 65% for some paths and 31% for others.

On the left, the colored strokes of paths drawn with the Pencil tool; on the right, Splash brush applied to the same paths

Original path on the left; the same path smoothed with the Pencil tool and zoomed out on the right

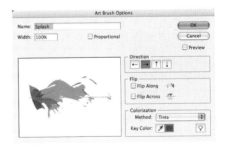

The Art Brush Options dialog showing the Splash brush

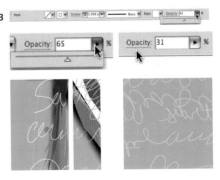

Reducing the opacity of the white-stroked paths in the Control panel

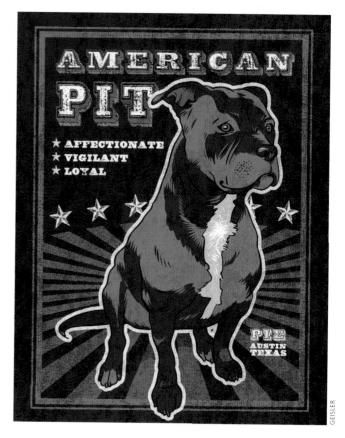

GEISLER

Greg Geisler

When Greg Geisler needed to create a poster for an event showcasing the Pit Bull, he wanted to emphasize the breed's American Heritage. He created a variation on the Stars and Stripes using a sunburst design, adding depth and perspective using Effect > 3D Bevel & Extrude. For the stars he used Western Bullets WF, a dingbat font. Using the star for bullets, Geisler added adjectives describing the Pit Bull in another slab-serif, Gatlin Bold WF. He used Clifford 8 WF to create the main title with a white fill against a black background to enhance the depth he was creating in his poster. He converted the type to Outlines (⌘-Shift-O/Ctrl-Shift-O), and used the Blob Brush to paint over part of the letters, creating a red outline that maintained the 3D appearance of the type. He placed all his Blob Brush strokes in Multiply mode in order to reveal the black texture through the font's transparent areas, as well as the textures he later added to the entire poster. After adding a blue "frame" to complete the Americana style of the poster, he used a photo of a Pit Bull as a template and drew his stylized dog with the Pen tool. Lastly, in order to simulate an old, rough print, he placed two linked texture images. He clicked Opacity in the Appearance panel; he changed the first texture to Overlay blending mode, and then used Luminosity for the second blending mode, reducing the opacity to 18%.

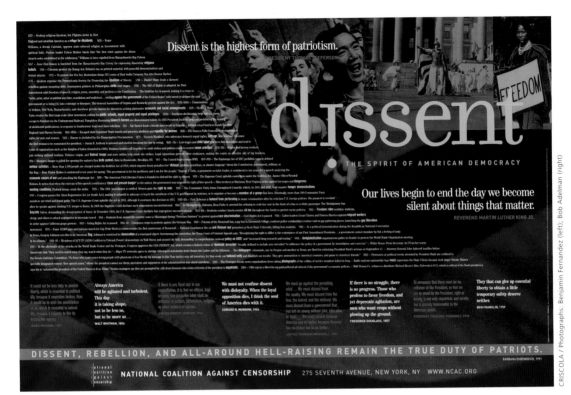

CRISCOLA / Photographs: Benjamin Fernandez (left); Bob Adelman (right)

Jeanne Criscola

When the National Coalition Against Censorship (NCAC) commissioned Jeanne Criscola to create a poster that expressed the need for an engaged public in a democracy, they had in mind the many historic moments when dissent has given rise to momentous decisions, from the founding of our country through every crisis up to today. Criscola wanted to create a poster that would inform the public about the history of free political expression in America, that would be visually appealing, and would immediately convey the thrust of the message, even at a distance. In QuarkXPress she reworked a timeline of historic events and notable quotations and saved it as EPS. She then switched to Illustrator because it provided greater graphical control over individual type elements, and better scaling options for the final poster. Opening the EPS, she next chose type size and color to create both a visual and communicative hierarchy. While her use of red, white, and blue obviously echoed the colors of American patriotism, she alternated the use of sans and serif fonts to echo the structure of free debate. She placed the type dynamically on the diagonal "wave," with "pillars" of paragraphs about dissent running along the bottom as support. Once the layout was approved, Criscola saved universal (EPS and PDF) versions of the poster that the NCAC could easily scale, distribute, and print through their website.

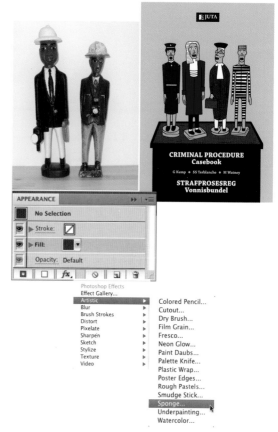

PAPCIAK-ROSE

Ellen Papciak-Rose

When she needs to fully integrate type and illustration elements into her designs, Ellen Papciak-Rose prefers Illustrator to InDesign. She styled the figures for this book cover (Juta Press, Capetown) after wooden Colonial-era African sculptures, similar to sculptures from her own collection (photo center top). Papciak-Rose created a number of variations of the cover, each on its own artboard. Variations included different type treatments (the final version here uses Chaparall Pro with copies of the hand-drawn starburst from the police figure's cap in between the authors' names), and versions with and without textures emulating the texture of the wooden sculptures (untextured illustration,

top right). She began by drawing the statue outlines with the Pen tool. Selecting them all, in the Appearance panel she clicked <u>Stroke</u> (to open the Stroke panel), increased the stroke weight, and chose the more natural-looking round end caps. For the textured version (top left), Papciak-Rose applied different raster effects (such as Texturizer, Artistic, and Sketch) to each fill in her illustration. For example, to create the wood grain for the top of the podium, in the Appearance panel she targeted Fill (the stroke would remain on top without the effect), clicked the *fx* icon, selected a Texturizer effect, chose Canvas, adjusted the attributes, and clicked OK.

3

Rethinking Construction

Rethinking Construction

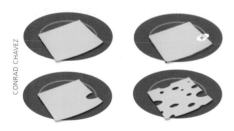

The fastest way to put holes into this slice of cheese is with the Eraser tool; drag the Eraser tool to create holes (automatically turning the "cheese" into a compound path, and revealing the plate underneath

If the Blob Brush tool is set to a fill color different from the unselected path (left), the Blob Brush can't edit the path. When you set the current stroke color to match, dragging the Blob Brush tool over the original path can edit it (right)

Constructing objects is at the heart of artwork in Illustrator, and nowhere has Illustrator been more innovative than in finding new ways to construct new objects from the amalgamation of simple paths and shapes. The early days of painstakingly constructing and joining every path, anchor point by anchor point, is giving way to methods of coloring shapes in ways that create new objects or that more closely simulate drawing with pencil and paper. The chapter works its way from newer methods for combining and editing shapes—using the semi-automatic methods of the Eraser, Blob Brush, the Shape Builder tool, Live Paint, and Live Trace—to older methods such as the Pathfinder panel and working with compound paths and shapes. Here also you'll find drawing assistants—such as drawing inside or behind objects, joining paths, and aligning objects and anchor points—that will help you to combine basic paths and objects.

THE ERASER TOOLS & THE BLOB BRUSH

One of the easiest ways to separate and combine objects is using the Eraser and the Blob Brush tools. With the Eraser tool you can cut an object into many parts, and with the Blob Brush you can combine multiple objects with the same fill attributes (and no stroke).

The Eraser tools

The Eraser tool (or the eraser end of your stylus if you're drawing with a graphics tablet) wipes out anything you drag it over, regardless of whether the paths are selected. The Eraser tool also has the calligraphic attributes of the Paintbrush tool: double-click the Eraser tool in the Tools panel to customize it.

To restrict the effect of the Eraser tool, select the paths you want to edit, and then drag the Eraser tool through them, or enter isolation mode. And, if you want certain paths to be protected from the Eraser tool when nothing

CONRAD CHAVEZ

is selected, lock or hide those paths or their layer. You can constrain the direction of the Eraser tool by Shift-dragging, or by Option-dragging/Alt-dragging a marquee to erase a rectangular area.

The Path Eraser tool (hidden beneath the Pencil in the Tools panel) erases parts of selected paths. To remove a portion of a path, you must drag it along (not perpendicular to) a selected path. Erasing a midsection of a path leaves an open anchor point on either side of the erasure.

The Blob Brush tool

In case you were wondering, the Blob "brush" is in this chapter, and not with the other brushes in the *Expressive Strokes* chapter, because it functions more like the Eraser than a brush. If you paint the same brushstroke using the Blob Brush tool and the Calligraphic Paintbrush, they might at first appear similar; if you switch to Outline mode, however, the difference becomes clear. An Illustrator vector path runs down the middle of a Paintbrush stroke, and the application of the Paintbrush remains live, which means the brushstroke can be restyled or edited like any other path in Illustrator. In contrast, a mark made by the Blob Brush is expanded as soon as you complete a stroke. Where a Paintbrush brushstroke is defined by the single path down its middle, a Blob Brush brushstroke is defined by a path around its outer edge. Following are some rules and tips for painting with the Blob Brush:

- **To paint with the Blob Brush tool,** select it, set a stroke color, and drag a brushstroke. Your stroke is automatically expanded and the fill takes the current stroke color, while the stroke itself is removed. The Blob Brush merges your new brushstrokes into the existing brushstroke depending upon the options you set. As long as you paint with the same color, overlapping brushstrokes will merge. If you change colors, your brushstrokes will stay separated.
- **To customize the Blob Brush tool,** double-click its icon in the Tools panel. If you enable Keep Selected, you can immediately alter the path with the Smooth tool, or make it easy to add to an existing path in a crowded illustration

Here the hub and rim do have the same fill and stroke attributes, but dragging the Blob Brush to draw a connecting spoke (center) still does not connect them, as Outline view reveals (top right). This is because there's a path between the hub and rim in the layer stacking order.

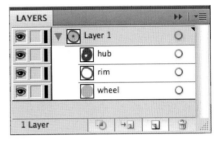

By making the hub and rim adjacent in the Layers panel (top), the Blob brush can connect them, as shown in Outline view (bottom).

Smoothing blobs...

When drawing with the Blob Brush tool, you can temporarily access the Smooth tool by holding Option/Alt as you drag along the outline of a path.

Protection from the Blob Brush

To prevent certain paths from being affected by the Blob Brush tool, you can select the paths and then lock them, hide them, or enter isolation mode. If the paths are on a separate layer, you can lock or hide their layer.

*Using Shape Builder to transform a batch of ovals into a bowl: (upper left) a series of ovals drawn with the Ellipse tool; (upper right) automatically coloring all objects using the Premedia Systems WOW! Artwork Colorizer script (on the **WOW! DVD**); (lower left) after deleting and combining objects using the Shape Builder tool; (lower right) returning to regular editing tools, shown after changing the colors and setting the stroke weight to None*

by enabling the "Merge With Selected" option. When "Merge With Selected" is on, the Blob Brush tool will only affect a path if it's selected and you drag over it, still using the same stroke color. Disabling this option allows the Blob Brush tool to edit paths using the same stroke color regardless of whether or not the paths are selected.

- **To modify a path that was drawn using another tool,** draw the object using any Fill and a Stroke of None. Deselect, and use the Blob Brush with the same Stroke color as the object's Fill, and add your brushstrokes to the object. The Blob Brush won't edit a path with a stroke, and if you edit an open path with the Blob Brush, it will create a closed path. To add to a compound shape, first expand it.

- **To modify and combine multiple objects** that share the same Fill color with no Stroke, make sure they are on the same layer and contiguous in the stacking order.

- **To create calligraphic strokes** with a pressure-sensitive stylus and tablet (such as a Wacom) use the Blob Brush Options dialog to change brush shape and drawing angle.

- **To refine the edges of a Blob Brush brushstroke,** use the Eraser tool. You can't do this with paths stroked with Brushes.

SHAPE BUILDER TOOL

Although it bears some similarities to Live Paint and Pathfinder commands (discussed later in this chapter), the Shape Builder tool presents an entirely new method for constructing objects. When you initially draw, you can allow objects to overlap in the interior of the outline you want, such as by drawing a three-leaf clover from three overlapping circles and an overlapping rectangle for the stem. With the Shape Builder tool, all you need to do is to first select the objects you want to combine into new shapes, then place your cursor over an area. To unite one area with others, simply click-drag across from one highlighted area to another. You can click-drag in a straight line, or Shift-drag a marquee over selected areas to unite multiple areas. Your objects don't need to reside on the same layer to start, but when they are merged with an initial shape, they will be moved to that shape's layer. To delete areas or strokes from your selected artwork using the Shape Builder tool, press the Option/Alt key while clicking on the highlighted area or portion of a stroke.

Depending on how your options are set, you can either select swatch colors as you go (with a Swatch preview cursor), or use the colors already in the highlighted object (double-click the tool to choose which method to use). If you choose "Pick Color From Color Swatches" in the Options dialog, you can enable the Cursor Swatch Preview. Now you can use the left and right arrow keys to switch the current color to the next color in any selected color group in the Swatches panel, or the up and down arrow keys to move to another color group. If you choose "Pick Color From Artwork" then the first object you click on will determine the color that fills the others as you drag. Separate objects can easily become merged into a single object. The rules for filling objects can be complex, so see the Tip "Shape Builder & appearances" at right if an object's appearance isn't what you expected.

One of the most powerful aspects of Shape Builder is that you are actually reconstructing how objects are made and filled, not just how they look on the surface. When working with strokes, those you keep remain live and editable, whereas Live Paint or Pathfinder commands might result in strokes that have become unexpectedly expanded or deleted. You can continue to modify the appearance of your Shape Builder strokes. Your new objects do not become a special kind of group, either, so you can freely switch between regular editing tools and the Shape Builder tool.

WORKING WITH LIVE PAINT

Hidden under the Shape Builder tool are the Live Paint Bucket and Live Paint Selection tools. Whereas the Shape Builder tool helps you to reconstruct and combine objects, Live Paint provides you with a way to recolor objects without modifying the vector paths, ignoring the normal rules about how you define a vector object. Paint lines and

Shape Builder & appearances

Changing the order and direction with which you are applying the Shape builder tool can alter the appearance of the resulting objects. The first object you begin with determines the appearance for the rest of the objects united to it. For instance, if you create the interior of the peace sign first, the background objects take on the "no stroke" appearance, whereas filling those background objects first applies the stroke.

Shape Builder as Paint Bucket

The Shape Builder tool can also be used like an ordinary paint bucket; click (instead of click-drag) to fill shapes without uniting them.

Adding to a Live Paint Group

Add new members to a Live Paint Group by selecting the new paths and the Live Paint Group, then clicking the Merge Live Paint button in the Control panel (or choose Object > Live Paint > Merge). Or even better, enter isolation mode with the Live Paint Group; then anything you paste or create will remain part of the Live Paint Group (see the chapter *Your Creative Workspace* for more on isolation mode).

GUSTAVO DEL VECHIO

Using Live Paint to both construct and color a cityscape: Intersecting open paths created enclosed areas suitable for filling with the Live Paint Bucket tool (bottom)

The Raster View (left) and Vector View (right) buttons in the Control panel for Live Trace

The Ignore White checkbox in the Tracing Options dialog lets you automatically remove a white background from your tracing object

spaces as if you were coloring a drawing by hand. In order to use these tools, you have to first convert your objects into a Live Paint group; all the enclosed spaces, filled or empty, become areas you can potentially fill or clear of color. You can create a "hole" in your Live Paint object by filling with None, or you can fill an "empty" area made from adjacent vector objects with your selected color. All the lines become editable paths that you can keep, color, reshape, or delete, creating new shapes. To convert a selection to a Live Paint Group, choose the Live Paint Bucket tool and click on the object, or choose Object > Live Paint > Make, (⌘-Option-X/Ctrl-Alt-X; like any other grouped object, Live Paint objects all move to the topmost layer that contained the original objects.)

To change the way the Live Paint Bucket behaves, double-click on it and set options, such as whether the Bucket paints fills, strokes, or both, whether you want a Cursor Swatch Preview, or the color and size of the highlight you see when you position the Bucket over an editable area. Choose how Live Paint handles gaps in the Object > Live Paint > Gap Options dialog. To edit paths and reshape areas, use normal editing tools, such as the Pen or Smooth tool. To actually alter or delete segments of paths (created from intersecting paths in Live Paint), use the Live Paint Selection tool.

USING LIVE TRACE

Live Trace renders your raster images into vector graphics that can then be edited, resized, and otherwise manipulated without distortion or loss of quality. It gives you tremendous control over the level of detail that is traced through options that also include the ability to specify a color mode and a palette of colors for the tracing object, fill and stroke settings, the sharpness of corner angles, whether or not to ignore white with black and white, and more. It ships with Tracing presets, and you can create and save your own to suit your projects. Live Trace remains live unless you expand it, so you can adjust the parameters and results of your tracing at any time.

The basics of Live Trace

To trace an image, open or place a raster image, select it, and then trace the object using the default settings by clicking Live Trace in the Control panel, choosing a preset from the drop-down list, or by opening the dialog with the icon on the Control panel. If you open the dialog, you can enable Preview, but Preview can slow you down. As long as your object remains a Live Trace object, you can always open the dialog after first tracing using a preset, and then use Preview in order to finesse the settings. You can also use the Control panel, or the Options dialog to change the way the tracing object, or your original is displayed, change the minimum size of the detail that gets traced, or change the maximum number of colors.

Converting to a Live Paint object or set of paths

From buttons in the Control panel, Live Trace objects can be converted in Live Paint groups (see the section earlier in this introduction for more on Live Paint groups), or expanded into editable object with Fill and/or Strokes. If you click the Expand button, your tracing will no longer be live and editable after you convert it, so don't convert your tracing until you're satisfied with it. If you want to expand exactly what you are looking at according to your Preview options (for example, retaining the original image with the traced image), choose Object > Live Trace > Expand as Viewed. Once it's expanded you can work with the vector paths or convert it to a Live Paint object.

ALIGNING, JOINING, AND AVERAGING
Align and distribute objects

Even though most Align and Distribute controls also appear in the Control panel, Distribute Spacing controls are found only in the Align panel. With an active selection, you can align objects to that selection, or the edges of the artboard, and you can Align to a Key Object (heavy outlines show you which object the others align to). To distribute the space between objects, designate one as the key; in the Align panel, enter an amount in the Distribute

IAN GIBLIN

To create the colored rocket above, Ian Giblin began with the scanned drawing on the left, then used Live Trace to create the tracing in the middle. After he converted the tracing to a Live Paint group, it was easy to color the rocket using the Live Paint Bucket.

Zoom before tracing

You can't change magnification or view from within Live Trace Options; be sure to zoom in to the area you want to see before opening Live Trace Options.

Customize Live Trace colors

To customize colors, create a special swatch library with only the colors you want (or choose a custom library—not Pantone), and then choose its name from the Palette pop-up in the Tracing Options dialog. Be sure the swatch library is open before you open the Tracing Options dialog, or its name won't appear in the Palette pop-up.

Testing a trace

Save a small, representative, cropped version of your image and test your Live Trace settings with that small file. Save your settings, and then apply them to your large file! —*Kevan Atteberry*

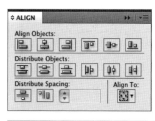

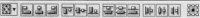

Align controls in the Align panel (top) and on the Control panel (bottom)

Path Simplify command

The Simplify command (Object > Path > Simplify) removes excess anchor points from selected paths. The higher the percentage, the more anchor points will remain, and the closer the new path will be to the original. The endpoints of an open path are never altered. The higher the Angle threshold, the more likely a corner point will remain sharp.

Resizing and stroke weight

Double-click the Scale tool to resize your selection with or without altering line weights:

- To scale a selection while also scaling line weights, enable Scale Strokes & Effects.
- To scale a selection while maintaining your line weights, disable Scale Strokes & Effects.
- To decrease line weights (50%) without scaling objects, first scale the selection (200%) with Scale Strokes & Effects disabled. Then scale (50%) with it enabled. Reverse these steps to increase line weights.

Spacing input box; then click either the Vertical or Horizontal Distribute Space icon.

Easier joins

- It is now easy to join open endpoints without getting an error dialog, and you can even join multiple pairs of endpoints together, at the same time. To join you must first either select one pair of points with the Direct Selection tool, or select one or more open paths with the Selection tool. Next, use ⌘-J/Ctrl-J or Object > Path > Join to join without a dialog, or ⌘-Option-Shift-J/Ctrl-Alt-Shift-J to open the Join dialog, from which you can choose to join with corner, or smooth points, when points are directly on top of each other. If points are not directly on top of each other, you can average them together first (see below for more on averaging), or choosing join will connect them with a line. Be aware that joining multiple open objects joins one object to the next, rather than closing each path to itself. At any time you can convert points from corner to smooth, or smooth to corner, by selecting the anchor points with the Direct Selection tool and clicking the appropriate icon from the Convert section in the Control panel. Below are some rules about joining and averaging:
- **Endpoints that are exactly on top of one another join** with a corner point unless you choose "Smooth" in the Join dialog (⌘-Option-Shift-J/Ctrl-Alt-Shift-J).
- **Joining two or more open endpoints on separate paths that are not exactly on top of each other,** connects the points with a straight segment using corner points. If your paths have different appearances applied, the path topmost in the stacking order determines the appearance of the paths as they are joined to it.
- **Average and join two endpoints that are not on top of each other** using ⌘-Option-Shift-J/Ctrl-Alt-Shift-J.
- **To average (without joining) endpoints,** select any number of points with the Direct Selection or Lasso tool on any number of objects; then use ⌘-Option-J/Ctrl-Alt-J to average the points along horizontal, vertical, or both axes. If you have the path selected, but not specific points,

then all points will be averaged together. If you use the Direct Selection or Lasso tool to select points, then the Align icons in the Control panel or Align panel will average the points, rather than align the objects.

DRAW BEHIND AND DRAW INSIDE

Illustrator has three drawing mode icons near the bottom of your Tools panel: Normal, Behind, and Inside. Once you click the Draw Behind icon, anything that you paste or draw will be the backmost object in your current layer, or, if you have something selected, will be placed directly behind the currently selected object. (Paste in Front and Paste in Back still work as expected, and ignore the drawing mode.) If the Draw Behind mode is active when you add a new layer to your file, it will add it behind the active layer. To create an object with a different appearance from the selected object, create it first, then change the new object's attributes. Or, if you want to be able to set an object's attributes before drawing it, enter isolation mode first. The object you're drawing behind doesn't need to be selected when you're in isolation mode. You can safely deselect it, and then set the attributes for each new object before you draw it.

Draw Inside is only available when one object (or compound path or text object) is selected, and will quickly make a *clipping mask* out of the selected object. When your originally-selected object is automatically converted to this special clipping mask, it loses any attributes beyond the basic stroke and a fill, so art brushes or live effects, for instance, are removed. To set up your object for Draw Inside, first select it, then click on the Drawing Mode icon in the Tools panel and choose Draw Inside. Your selected object will display the dotted corners of a bounding box. Next deselect the object (the dotted box remains); now you can choose your drawing tool or brush and its attributes. Now you only have to draw over the object to have any strokes or fills that extend outside to be clipped to the boundaries of the selected object. Your clipping mask object and whatever you have drawn inside are now a

Using Draw Inside to restrain the Bristle Brush strokes within each object as it's selected

Toggle drawing modes

You can use the keyboard shortcut Shift-D to switch between available modes. Keep an eye on the changing icon to know which drawing mode you have selected.

Compound paths or shapes?

Use compound paths on simple objects for basic combining or hole-cutting. Use compound shapes on complex objects (such as those made with additional effects) and to fully control how your objects interact. Be aware that compound shapes can become too complex to print, or to be combined within some effects, and might have to be released (returning objects to their original state) or expanded (which keeps the appearance, but breaks it apart permanently). Make/release/expand compound shapes from the Pathfinder panel menu, and make/release/expand compound paths from the Object menu.

Using Draw Inside mode to add a gradient-filled rectangle to the text, leaving the text live and the "clipped" object separately editable

Don't forget the drawing mode

IMPORTANT: Drawing modes are persistent! If you forget what mode you're in, you'll get unexpected results. Try to get in the habit of switching to Normal mode (Shift-D) as soon as you no longer need to be in that special drawing mode.

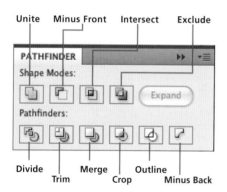

The Pathfinder panel contains two sets of icons: Shape Modes (which combine shapes), and Pathfinders (which divide paths)

Left to right: two ovals (the inner oval has no fill, but appears black because of the black fill of the larger oval behind it); as part of a compound path the inner oval knocks a hole into the outer one where they overlap; the same compound path with inner oval, which was Direct-Selected and moved to the right to show that the hole is only where the objects overlap

group. To edit any part of this new object, use the Direct Selection tool or target it in the Layers panel and edit as a regular vector object. You can even apply effects to the entire group, if you desire. You can also copy and paste artwork in Draw Inside mode, which will clip the artwork inside text, for example. Learn more about working with clipping masks in the *Mastering Complexity* chapter.

COMPOUND SHAPES & COMPOUND PATHS

There are three additional ways to create new objects by combining and subtracting objects with and from each other: compound shapes, compound paths, and by using the commands found in the Pathfinder panel. Compound paths and compound shapes are live and can easily be released to recover the original paths. Compound paths are used primarily to create holes in objects, whereas compound shapes provide more complex ways of combining objects. The Pathfinder panel icons perform operations very much like compound shapes, except that these operations are applied permanently—Undo is the only way to reverse the effects of a pathfinder operation. If you wish to apply a live version of a Pathfinder command to a layer, type object, or a group, instead of using the Pathfinder panel, apply it from either the Effects menu, or the *fx* icon from the Appearance panel.

Compound paths

A compound path consists of one or more paths that have been combined so they behave as a single unit. Compound paths can be used as a single mask, and they can create holes where the original objects overlapped (think of the letter **O**), through which you can see objects.

To create a simple compound path, draw one oval, then draw a smaller oval that will form the center hole of the **O**, and choose Object > Compound Path > Make. Apply the fill color of your choice, and the inner object remains unfilled. To adjust one of the paths within a compound path, use the Direct Selection tool; or select the compound path and enter isolation mode.

Pathfinders

The Pathfinder panel includes the top row of Shape Modes icons and the lower row of Pathfinder commands. The Pathfinder panel's icons alter the selected objects permanently, slicing them up if needed to achieve the icon's effect (see the "Compound shapes" section following about applying the top row as live effects). These permanent alterations to the objects allow you to, for example, apply the Intersect icon to selected objects so that you can pull apart and further edit the resulting pieces. Note that the Trim and Merge commands can be applied only to filled objects.

Compound shapes

A compound shape combines objects with, or subtracts objects from, each other, while leaving the original objects intact. You can make compound shapes from two or more paths or from other compound shapes, text, envelopes, blends, groups, or artwork with vector effects applied. To create compound shapes, hold the Option/Alt key as you click a Shape Mode icon in the Pathfinder panel; if you click without the Option/Alt modifier, original objects are permanently altered (prior to CS4, Shape Modes were live by default). You can also apply the Unite Shape mode by choosing "Make Compound Shape" from the Pathfinder panel menu. Compound shapes take on the attributes of the topmost object in the selection.

As long as you keep compound shapes live, you can continue to apply (or remove) Shape Modes, and add a variety of effects to the compound shape as a unit, such as envelopes, warps, and drop shadows. Compound shapes can also be pasted into Photoshop as editable shape layers, although they won't retain their Illustrator appearance. To retain their appearance and keep them editable, paste them as vector Smart Objects, in which case double-clicking on their thumbnails opens them again in Illustrator. Release the Shape Mode to restore the original objects, or Expand the effect to permanently apply it to the objects, using Pathfinder Options from the panel's menu.

Unite (so that you can see the effects more clearly: the first column shows the original shapes; the second column shows the results of the operation; and the third column shows the resulting objects selected or moved.)

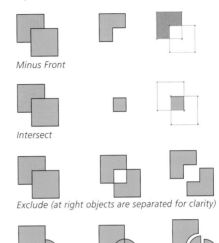

Minus Front

Intersect

Exclude (at right objects are separated for clarity)

Divide (at right objects are separated for clarity)

Trim

Merge (objects only Merge if both objects are the same color; otherwise Merge is the same as Trim)

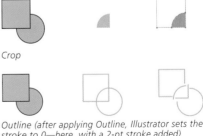

Crop

Outline (after applying Outline, Illustrator sets the stroke to 0—here, with a 2-pt stroke added)

Minus Back

Combining Paths

Basic Path Construction with Pathfinders

Overview: *Create an illustration by joining and intersecting objects using the Pathfinder panel's Unite, Minus Front, and Intersect.*

1

Creating a rounded rectangle by clicking on the Artboard with the Rounded Rectangle tool, setting dimensions, and increasing Corner Radius

Creating a rounded rectangle by clicking on the Artboard with the Rounded Rectangle tool, setting dimensions, and decreasing Corner Radius

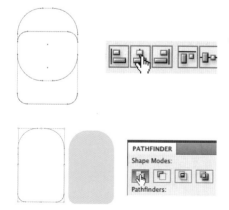

Selecting both rounded rectangles, using Horizontal Align Center, using the Unite Pathfinder command, and changing fill to cyan

To create many eye-catching stock illustrations like the one above, which are used for advertisements, websites, and more, Ryan Putnam frequently uses the Pathfinder panel. Using the Pathfinder's Unite, Minus Front, and Intersect, you too can easily create compelling character illustrations.

1 Constructing the body with the Unite Pathfinder command. Ryan Putnam created the body from two rounded rectangles. To create the first object, he clicked on the artboard with the Rounded Rectangle tool to open the Rounded Rectangle dialog. In the dialog, he set the dimensions of the rectangle to 3 in for Width, 3.5 in for Height and increased the Corner Radius to 1.25. Putnam wanted the bottom corners of the body to be smaller, so he then created a second rectangle with the same dimensions, used .5 for the Corner Radius, and placed the top a third of the way down from the first rectangle.

Putnam selected both rectangles, clicked the Horizontal Align Center icon in the Control panel, used the Unite command from the Pathfinder panel, and chose a Cyan swatch from the Swatches panel.

2 Constructing the mouth with the Minus Front Pathfinder command. With the Ellipse tool, Putnam drew a circle within the body object for the mouth. He then drew an encompassing rectangle halfway up from the center of the circle. He selected both, clicked the Minus Front command from the Pathfinder panel, and chose a brown swatch from the Swatches panel.

3 Constructing the teeth and tongue with Pathfinder commands. To create the tongue, Putnam created two overlapping circles within the mouth shape, selected both, and used the Unite Pathfinder command. To fit the tongue into the mouth, he first copied the mouth shape, and then chose Edit > Paste in Front. Selecting both the mouth copy and the tongue, he applied the Intersect Pathfinder command, and then chose a magenta swatch from the Swatches panel for the fill color.

To create the teeth, Putnam drew four objects with the Rounded Rectangle tool. He rotated one tooth with the Selection tool by moving the cursor along the rectangle until he saw the Rotate icon and then dragged the tooth slightly to the right. He then selected all four teeth and combined them into a single compound path using Object > Compound Path > Make (for more about compound paths, see this chapter's intro). To trim off the portions of the teeth that extend above the mouth, Putnam chose Edit > Paste in Front, selected the copied mouth and teeth, and used the Intersect Pathfinder command.

4 Creating other character features. To finish the piece Putnam added character features as he needed, for instance, a 15-pt stroke for the lips, a circle for the back of the mouth, another pair of circles for eyes, and a rounded rectangle for the stick.

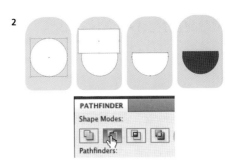

Drawing a circle, drawing a rectangle over the circle, selecting both, using the Minus Front Pathfinder command, and changing fill to brown

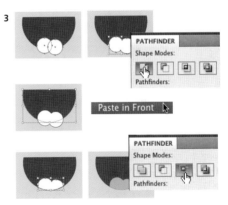

Drawing two ellipses, using the Unite Pathfinder command, Copying the mouth and Pasting in Front, selecting the mouth and tongue, and using the Intersect Pathfinder command

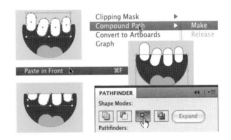

Drawing four rounded rectangles, making a compound shape, Copying the mouth and Pasting in Front, selecting the mouth and teeth, and using the Intersect Pathfinder command

Adding additional features with circles and rounded rectangles

Coloring Line Art

Using Live Paint for Fluid Productivity

Overview: *Draw with the Pen tool to trace the minimum paths needed to define discreet areas; color using Live Paint tools for easy selections.*

DEL VECHIO

1

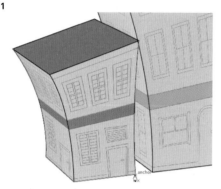

Outlining the 3D model with open paths, using the Pen tool and Smart Guides

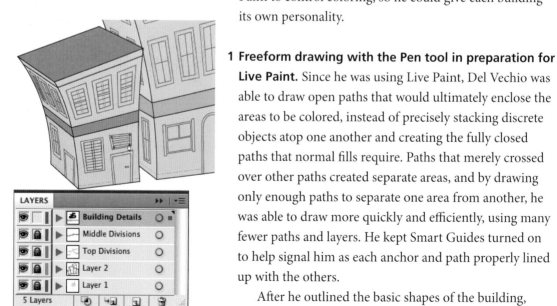

Drawing interior details with the other layers locked and Smart Guides turned off

When Gustavo Del Vechio needed an illustration for his client's urban development proposal, he used Illustrator to draw the initial concept, which he developed more fully in 3D Studio Max. He then rendered the artwork and placed it back into Illustrator as a template. Seeking to create a lively and humanistic interpretation of a crowded city environment, he used the Pen tool for tracing and Live Paint to control coloring, so he could give each building its own personality.

1 Freeform drawing with the Pen tool in preparation for Live Paint. Since he was using Live Paint, Del Vechio was able to draw open paths that would ultimately enclose the areas to be colored, instead of precisely stacking discrete objects atop one another and creating the fully closed paths that normal fills require. Paths that merely crossed over other paths created separate areas, and by drawing only enough paths to separate one area from another, he was able to draw more quickly and efficiently, using many fewer paths and layers. He kept Smart Guides turned on to help signal him as each anchor and path properly lined up with the others.

After he outlined the basic shapes of the building, Del Vechio turned Smart Guides off while he drew the doors and windows more freely on their own layer. Even though the 3D model had curved lines, in order to create the slightly off-kilter look of an illustration, he used only straight segments (except for the arched door and circular window). After tracing the artwork, he selected it all and clicked on it with the Live Paint Bucket tool (hidden under the Shape Builder tool). Once converted to a Live Paint group, the content of all the layers automatically moved into the top layer. Del Vechio next needed to select and delete a few unwanted segments. While the Selection tool selects objects and the Direct Selection tool selects paths, he was able to use the Live Paint Selection tool to select, then delete, individual faces and line segments.

Removing unwanted intersecting edges (highlighted in red) with the Live Paint Selection tool

2 Creating Swatch groups and using Global colors makes it easy to apply, and later edit, color. Del Vechio created a small color group for each building. Using the Live Paint Bucket tool, he colored each building, cycling through colors in a group using the left and right arrow keys, and moving between color groups using the up and down keys. He also assigned all the colors he created as Global swatches. If he later wanted to replace a color, he only had to replace the swatch itself and it would automatically update that color anywhere in the document.

Using Live Paint, small Swatch groups, and the left and right arrow keys to select new colors while filling faces with the Live Paint Bucket tool

To ensure he wouldn't accidentally color a stroke when he only wanted to fill a face on the buildings, Del Vechio double-clicked on the Live Paint Bucket tool and disabled Paint Strokes in the dialog. After he filled the main areas of the buildings, he created a gradient for the lights in the windows. In order to paint some of the strokes (but not all), he again opened the Live Paint dialog to enable Paint Strokes and disable Paint Fills. He then selected all the Strokes and set their weight to None. With the Stroke weight set to .75 pt and choosing various brown colors, he selectively filled some strokes around the windows and doors. Although the strokes were now invisible, Live Paint would highlight them when his cursor passed over them.

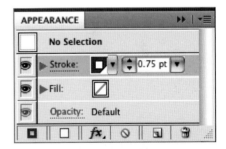

Finally Del Vechio reset the Live Paint Bucket Options to Paint for both Fills and Strokes, then recolored some of the areas and edges to complete his whimsical cityscape.

Painting a few of the edges with Paint Fills disabled, Paint Strokes enabled, and the Stroke set for color and width in the Appearance panel

Blob to Live Paint

From Sketch to Blob Brush and Live Paint

Overview: *Place sketch as a template; trace sketch with the Blob Brush tool; color with the Live Paint Bucket tool.*

1

The original tattoo sketch

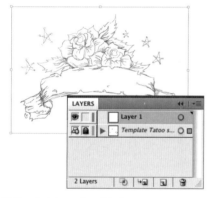

Placing sketch as a template layer

2

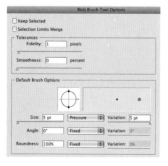

Setting up default Blob Brush tool options

Ryan Putnam has a stock illustration portfolio full of hand-drawn illustrations. Putnam found that using the new Blob Brush tool and his Wacom pen tablet, he could now easily create a hand-drawn look using Illustrator. Moreover, by using Live Paint, he could quickly fill his illustration with color.

1 Creating a sketch and placing it as a template. Putnam first created a tattoo sketch in Photoshop and placed it into Illustrator as a template. Create your own sketch and scan it—or sketch directly into a painting program (such as Painter or Photoshop)—and save it in PSD, JPEG, or TIF format. In a new Illustrator file, choose File > Place, locate your sketch, then enable the Template option and click Place. Illustrator automatically dims the image to make your drawing easier to see. To hide/show the template, click its visibility icon in the Layers panel.

2 Setting Blob Brush tool options and tracing sketch. Putnam wanted to create marks that were very true to his stylus gestures and had minimal smoothness. To create this effect with the Blob Brush tool, he first had to modify the default options. To do this, he double-clicked on the Blob Brush tool in the Tools panel. In the Blob Brush Tool Options, he set the Fidelity to 1, Smoothness to 0, and set Size to 5 pt. From the Size drop-down menu he selected Pressure, changed the Size Variation to 5 pt, and clicked OK. If you don't have a pen tablet, change all the same settings except the Pressure and Size Variation. Using these custom Blob Brush settings, Putnam began to trace the scanned sketch template into the layer above, varying his stylus pressure to re-create the hand-drawn style.

Tracing sketch with the Blob Brush tool

While drawing with the Blob Brush tool, Putnam used the Eraser tool, set up to work with pressure-sensitivity, to modify brush marks and correct mistakes. To do this, Putnam double-clicked the Eraser tool from the Tools panel and changed the Diameter to 5 pt. He then selected Pressure from the Diameter drop-down menu, changed the Diameter Variation to 5 pt, and clicked OK. By setting up the Eraser tool with pressure-sensitive settings, he could move easily between the two tools by simply flipping the stylus around.

Setting up default Eraser tool preferences and erasing with the Eraser tool

3 Filling areas with Live Paint. If Putnam used the regular Brush tool to trace his sketch, he would have had to create additional paths defining fill areas to color the drawing. But Blob Brush objects can easily be converted into Live Paint Groups for quick and simple coloring. To convert the illustration to a Live Paint Group, Putnam selected the illustration with the Selection tool, chose the Live Paint Bucket tool from the Tools panel, and on first click, the object became a Live Paint Group. With the Live Paint Bucket tool, he hovered over the selected illustration to highlight areas to fill. With the left and right arrow keys, Putnam cycled through the swatches from the Swatches panel until he found his desired color (see the *Color Transitions* chapter for more about working with color in Illustrator). Once he found the color, he clicked in the area to fill. He repeated cycling through the swatches and filled in the other enclosed areas of the illustration.

3

Filling areas with the Live Paint Bucket tool

Cycling through swatches with the Live Paint Bucket tool

4

4 Applying finishing touches. Putnam added additional features as needed. For instance, he warped the type and added gradients to the Live Paint fills (see the "Arcing Type" lesson in the chapter *Designing Type & Layout*, and see the *Color Transitions* chapter for details about working with gradients).

Adding a warped type treatment and gradients

JACKSON

Lance Jackson

Sitting on a commuter train, Lance Jackson took advantage of the moment to follow inspiration with a little pencil-and-paper sketching for an animation he was working on, but ideas on paper take extra steps to get into the computer. He'd already started the project in Illustrator using the Blob Brush tool. With the sketch he drew on the train in mind, Jackson found he had no need to tediously construct paths, or create objects that the Pathfinder commands can use; he could adapt his inspiration to Illustrator as freely as he could with a pencil. But unlike using pencil on paper, Jackson could cleanly erase unwanted marks with the Eraser tool, and his drawings didn't need to be scanned and traced afterwards. When he was pleased with the character development in his Blob Brush sketches, he continued to use the Blob Brush to draw them in their finished form, this time filling in the silhouettes using the brush's unique ability to merge paths whenever the brush strokes cross over the same color. These silhouetted characters would be used next in a Flash animation.

David Turton

For a powerful, yet highly detailed drawing of a tiger's head, David Turton relied upon the natural combination of the Blob Brush tool and the Wacom® Cintiq21UX tablet computer. Because Turton could draw directly on the tablet itself, and his paths would join automatically as they overlapped, he felt he had greater control over this kind of meticulous, but still freehand, pen-and-ink drawing, without having to interrupt the flow to create a new brush or adjust his stroke width. He began a rough sketch with brush settings that most closely emulated natural pen strokes. He kept Fidelity and Smoothness at their lowest settings to be as true to his hand as possible, and used a very fine, 2-pixel point. Gradually Turton refined the tiger's features, filling in more detail, and keeping the brush tip fine and allowing his strokes to merge naturally as he drew over them, thickening the detail in some areas for greater definition. As the file size grew, he began to lock layers he was happy with and to add more detail as the drawing progressed. This prevented strokes from merging and forcing constant re-renders of the drawing. Such extensive detail is very demanding of a computer's resources. When he had completed most of the tiger, he unlocked the layers and merged them all. Lastly, he used the Eraser tool to "draw out" the whiskers by erasing next to their lines, creating an interruption in the strokes in order to enhance the illusion of whiskers overlapping the fur.

Rapid Reshaping
Using Shape Builder to Construct Objects

Overview: *Create overlapping objects, color them with a Premedia Systems script, and use the Shape Builder tool to unite some parts and delete others; recolor, use drawing modes and the Bristle Brush to add a background, shading, and textures; resize artboards with another Premedia script.*

Sharon Steuer created this piece for a user group demo highlighting how some newer features in Illustrator—the Shape Builder tool, Drawing Modes, and the Bristle Brush—make constructing objects quicker and easier.

Artboards for a presentation

To save a project in stages for a presentation: duplicate the current artboard in the Artboards panel by dragging it to the New Artboard dialog. Double-click on its name to fit the duplicate in the window (double-click the icon to rename) and continue working.

1

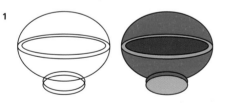

Drawing the oval objects and using the Premedia WOW! Artwork Colorizer script to give each object a different color

Dragging to unite the shapes that make up the bottom of the bowl; then deleting side pieces on foot and top shape (cursors magnified)

1 Constructing the bowl from overlapping objects.

Since the Shape Builder can both unite objects and delete parts of intersecting objects, using it can be much simpler and quicker than either drawing precisely with the Pen tool, or using Pathfinder commands. To follow along with the figures in this lesson, set the fill and stroke to the default (press the D key), then set the fill to None (X toggles focus between fill and stroke; the / key sets the style to None); then, with the Ellipse tool (L), draw a series of ovals that align at the center. (To help you do this quickly and efficiently, make sure that Smart Guides are on (⌘-U/Ctrl-U), use the modifier keys Option/Alt to draw from the center, and use the spacebar key to adjust the position of the oval as you draw.) It's easier to control your use of the Shape Builder tool if each object you'll be working with is a different color. A quick way to do this is to use the Premedia Systems WOW! Colorizer script (install instructions and scripts are on the **WOW! DVD**). With the script installed, select everything and choose File > Scripts > WOW! Artwork Colorizer. In the script dialog, enable "No colors" to let the script select colors and save the used colors as a swatch group (your colors may differ from the ones shown here). For the next step, you'll be using the Shape Builder tool (Shift-M) to hover over the selected shapes, looking at the highlighted areas to see how they will connect. If the areas that you wish to maintain aren't visible (for instance, the purple oval needs to be on top in order to form the foot of the bowl), then adjust the stacking order by cutting and using Paste in Front/Back. With Pick Color From Artwork enabled (double-click on the Shape Builder tool for options), drag from the red bowl through the upper half of the purple oval. To delete the side pieces of the foot and the top of the bowl, hold down Option/Alt while clicking on them.

2 **Completing the composition.** You can select each shape (which is now a separate object) and recolor the bowl, and you can even marquee-select all the objects and set the Stroke to None. To quickly place a background behind all objects, select the Draw Behind drawing mode, either by clicking its icon in the Tools panel, or by pressing Shift-D until you see the icon. Draw rectangles for the background objects. (Steuer drew one rectangle filled with the Plaid 2 Pattern, and another with blue.)

3 **Finishing touches on the bowl.** Select one bowl object (you can only select one at a time), along with the Brush tool, and choose Draw Inside mode (Shift-D), which places dotted corners around the object. Deselect the object and load the Bristle Brush library. Choose a Bristle Brush and paint on the object; Draw Inside constrains your brush strokes within the selected object. When you want to paint another object, you must first exit Draw Inside mode (Shift-D, or double-click with a selection tool). Select the next object and choose Draw Inside again (you can even draw inside a pattern, like the bowl's shadow). When Steuer was done, she wanted to crop the image for the demo she would output to PDF. The easiest way was to resize all the artboards by 72% using the Premedia Systems WOW! Artboard Resizer. This script (also on the **WOW! DVD)** resizes any or all artboards from the center.

Recoloring the bowl with the Grays swatch group; then choosing None for the objects' stroke

3

Draw Normal, Draw Behind, Draw Inside

Using Draw Inside to constrain the Mop Bristle Brush to a single, selected object, denoted by the dotted corners

*Using the **WOW!** Artboard Resizer by Premedia Systems to resize selected artboards smaller*

Easily view drawing modes

You can see (and therefore easily click) each drawing mode if your Tools panel is in double-column view; click the double-arrow in the title bar of the Tools panel to toggle the view between single and double-column. Check your drawing mode if your objects are not going where you intended.

Interlock Objects

Using the Pathfinder Panel & Live Paint

TREMBLAY

Advanced Technique

Overview: *Create a logo from basic geometric objects using Pathfinder commands; create the illusion of interlocking objects and dimension with Live Paint.*

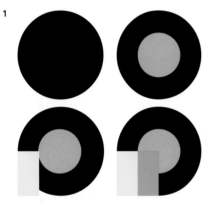

Creating the basic letter form from circles and rectangles

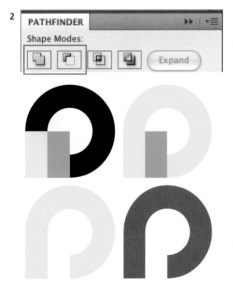

Using Unite and Minus Front in the Pathfinder panel to carve the P form

When Jean-Claude Tremblay decided to design a new logo for his graphics company, Proficiografik, he wanted to emphasize partnership with his clients. Interlocking the shapes in the business name echoed that intention. He not only saw the close relationship in form between an uppercase **P** and a **G,** he recognized that the Pathfinder panel would make it easy to create his new logo using only circles and rectangles. Add in Live Paint's unique ability to recolor overlapping objects, and Tremblay had the basis for his new logo. See his gallery in the *Designing Type & Layout* chapter for the completed result.

1 Starting the P with only circles and rectangles. To easily distinguish the objects at this phase in the project, assign each object its own Fill color and no Stroke. Tremblay used the Ellipse tool and Option-clicked/Alt-clicked to create a perfect circle (70 x 70 pt). With the circle selected, he double-clicked the Scale tool, chose Uniform and 50%, and clicked Copy. Next, Tremblay selected the Rectangle tool and clicked on the artboard to open the dialog. He entered 17.5 x 35 pt (one quarter the width and half the height of the circle), and clicked OK. He then aligned the rectangle to the bottom left of the larger circle using Smart Guides. He duplicated this rectangle by double-clicking on the Selection tool and entering 17.5 pt Horizontal for Position, 0 for Vertical, and clicked Copy.

2 Using Pathfinder commands to punch out the P, and using transform to create the G. Tremblay selected the two circles and, in the Pathfinder panel, he clicked on Minus Front to make a hole in the large circle (creating a compound path). He then selected the compound path and the left rectangle and clicked on the Unite icon in the Pathfinder panel. To separate the stem of the **P** from the bowl, Tremblay selected the compound path and the remaining rectangle and again clicked Minus Front.

Before constructing the **G**, Tremblay created four custom swatches: one gray for the **P**, one red for the **G**, plus a second darker red and darker gray he would later use for the shadows. He filled the **P** with the lighter gray.

To create the **G**, Tremblay selected the **P**, double-clicked on the Reflect tool, enabled Vertical for Axis, and clicked Copy. He filled the new **G** with the lighter red, and rotated it 90 degrees. To move it, he double-clicked the Selection tool, entered half the size of the circle (35 pt) for Horizontal move, and clicked OK. He subtracted 2 pt from the X field in the Control panel to create space between the letters.

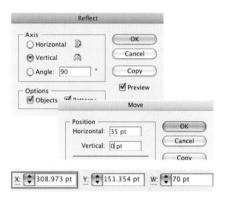

Transforming the P into a G using the Reflect, Rotate, and Move tools; then moving the G by subtracting points in the Control panel's X field

3 Creating an illusion of interlocked letters and shadows.

With the letter forms in place, Tremblay used parts of the original paths of the objects to create the paths for the shadows. With the Direct Selection tool, he selected the lower segment of the **G** where it crossed the **P**. He copied the segment (⌘-C/Ctrl-C) and used Paste in Front (⌘-F/Ctrl-F). So that Tremblay could better see these paths, he temporarily invoked the Swap Fill and Stroke command (Shift-X), then moved the path down and to the right (in the Control panel, he added 2 pt to the X field, and subtracted 2 pt from the Y). He repeated these steps after selecting the lower segment of **P**, where it would later cross over the **G**. Once the paths were in place, he prepared them to be used as part of a Live Paint object by setting them both to no Fill and no Stroke. He selected all four objects and chose the Live Paint Bucket tool. To create the illusion that the bottom of the **P** was crossing over the **G**, he selected the lighter gray swatch and clicked on the lower section of the **P**. Then he filled the shadow on the **P** with the darker gray. To complete the illusion that the letters were dimensional and interlocking (arm-in-arm), he filled the shadow area on the **G** with the darker red.

3

Maintaining the perfect geometric form by creating paths from segments of the objects themselves

Selecting the paths and letter objects, and using the Live Paint Bucket tool to divide the objects into sections for coloring

Using the Live Paint tool to fill the shadow objects with custom colors

Drawing Inside

Building with Multiple Construction Modes

Advanced Technique

Overview: *Create varying types of shading, texture, and detail within objects using Draw Inside mode; alter basic shapes and prepare them for masking using Shape Builder; add soft shading by using Blob Brush in conjunction with Draw Inside mode.*

LEAVENS

1

The intial blocked-in artwork

When in Draw Inside mode, new objects added into the cliff object are clipped

Building and shading complex artwork in Illustrator can be a daunting task. Thankfully, there are clipping masks. Chris Leavens employs a combination of construction methods in his artwork, "The Gardener," including harnessing the artistic and organizational capabilities of both the Draw Inside mode (to quickly create clipping masks) and the Shape Builder tool (to combine objects).

1 Creating masks using Draw Inside, and beginning to add detail. Using the Pen tool, Leavens blocked in the composition by drawing basic, flat, colored forms. He then selected the large cliff object (which spans the width of the artwork's background) and changed the Drawing mode to Draw Inside (Shift-D). Upon entering Draw Inside mode, he deselected by holding Command/Ctrl and clicking outside of the artboard and then added form-defining objects within the cliff object using the Pen tool. He freely plotted new anchor points outside the boundaries of the cliffs, allowing the mask created by Draw Inside mode to keep the edges clean and precise. After finishing the cliffs, Leavens repeated the same steps on the other objects, adding both shading and detail.

2 Preparing objects for Draw Inside mode with Shape Builder. To speed up the drawing process, Leavens used the Pen tool and drew the large, swooping tree in multiple pieces. In order to employ the same shading method he used for the other objects, he selected the various overlapping pieces of the tree. He then chose Shape Builder (Shift-M) and click-dragged over the overlapping objects, quickly combining them into one large object, which he shaded using the method mentioned in step one.

In creating the cactus, Leavens used Shape Builder again, but did so subtractively. To make the cactus look broken and parched, he used the Pen tool to draw jagged forms on top of a pair of the cactus's branches. He then selected the cactus and the new, jagged shapes and switched back to the Shape Builder tool. While holding the Option/Alt key, Leavens click-dragged over the area he wanted to remove, leaving behind a couple of newly-broken branches.

3 **Adding fast shading with Blob Brush and Draw Inside mode.** In order to add soft, feathered shading to the puffy purple foliage on the large tree, Leavens decided to use the Blob Brush. To maintain smooth strokes, he first double-clicked the Blob Brush tool in the Tools panel, and in Options he increased the Fidelity and Smoothness settings. He then predefined a graphic style for the shading by mixing a shade of violet using the Color panel, switching the blend mode to "Multiply" (by clicking Opacity in the Appearance panel), adding a 3-point feather effect (Effect > Stylize > Feather), and saving the style by clicking the New Graphic Style icon in the Graphic Styles panel. To ensure that this style would be properly maintained once he selected and began working with it, he disabled "New Art Has Basic Appearance" from the Appearance panel menu. He selected one of the purple foliage objects, changed to Draw Inside mode (Shift-D), deselected, and chose the Blob Brush tool (Shift-B). Before adding the shading, he clicked on the newly-defined Graphic Style swatch. Finally, Leavens brushed in the shading, using the Blob Brush additively to build up larger masses of darker shading, painting solitary strokes where he wanted lighter shading, and using the Eraser tool to make corrections.

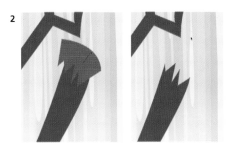

2

Before and after: using the Shape Builder tool to subtractively alter the cactus branch

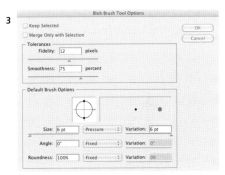

3

Leavens increased the Fidelity and the Smoothness settings in the Blob Brush Tool Options panel

Final, enlarged version of the composition

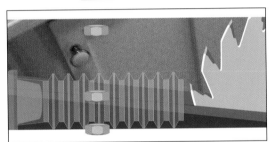

KLEMA

Stephen A. Klema

Stephen Klema found that the Shape Builder tool helped him to save time when creating some of the tool illustrations in his art animation and interactive design piece entitled "100 Days." To construct the drill bit, for instance, Klema began by drawing basic 4-sided objects with the Rectangle tool, and 3-sided objects using the Star tool (reducing it to three sides using the down arrow key). He then added points with the Add Anchor Point tool, and shifted the points using the Direct Selection tool (holding the Shift key to constrain movement). When the basic shapes were in the proper position, he selected them all and then used the Shape Builder tool to start combining some objects by click-dragging from one to the other (e.g., from the bottom orange object to the top triangle), and deleting others and even making holes by holding Option/Alt when clicking (or click-dragging). When the drill bit was properly combined he marquee-Direct-Selected the top anchor points and Shift-dragged the points upwards to elongate the point. Finally, he recolored the newly configured objects. See Klema's "100 Days" project at: www.StephenKlema.com/100days.

4

Expressive Strokes

Expressive Strokes

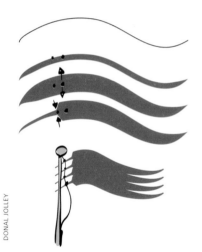

DONAL JOLLEY

Creating discontinuous curves from continuous curves with the Width tool when creating a flag

Almost everything you thought you knew about styling strokes in Illustrator has changed. A path can be manually adjusted with the Width tool to emulate calligraphy, and its form (profile) can be saved in the Stroke panel and applied to another path. Art Brushes can have start and end points protected from alteration, have flexible scale options, and can wrap to fit into tight corners. Tiles for Pattern Brushes offer several scaling options to use with spacing, creating completely different looks when applied to paths. The Bristle Brush emulates traditional brushes, ranging from a round sable to a flat fan, with the texture of multiple "bristles" added at each stroke of the brush. The Symbols we paint with are also discussed here, even though strictly speaking they aren't "strokes."

WIDTH TOOL

The Width tool (Shift-W) varies the width of strokes created with the drawing and geometric shape tools, or Art and Pattern Brushes. The path doesn't have to be selected; hover over it with the Width tool and the path will highlight, along with hollow diamonds indicating existing width points that were either set automatically, such as the end points of a path, or that you have set. As you move your cursor over the path, still hovering, a hollow diamond moves with your cursor, ready to become a width point at whatever location along the path you click on. You can modify paths between two existing width points, and can create either a *continuous*, flowing curve, or a *discontinuous* one with a sharp break between sections of the curve). If the width points are spaced apart, the path gradually gets wider or narrower from one point to the next in a continuous curve. If the width points are placed on top of each other, you create a sharp break between the two widths, causing the curve to abruptly widen or narrow, much like adding an arrowhead to the path. Modify strokes on either side of the path either by adjusting the stroke weight evenly along the path, or placing more weight on one side of the path than the other. Your custom stroke profile is temporarily stored in the Stroke panel, making it possible to apply the same stroke to as many paths in the document as you wish. An asterisk in the Appearance panel beside the Stroke denotes a width profile. You can also save a custom profile as part of a Graphic Style and/or to the Profiles list using the Save icon at the bottom of the Stroke panel list. The Reset icon restores the default width profiles, replacing any custom profiles you've saved, so be careful about choosing to restore the default width profiles. You can modify width points in a variety of ways with the Width tool:

- **To open the Width Point Edit dialog,** double-click on a path or existing width point. Numerically input the stroke weight for each side of the path, and/or choose to have adjoining width points adjusted at the same time.

- **To interactively adjust the width point,** click-drag on a handle to symmetrically adjust the stroke width.

- **To adjust one side of a stroke,** press Option/Alt while dragging on a handle.

- **To adjust the position or width of just some of the points,** Shift-click to first select them, then Shift-drag to move them in tandem or adjust their width.

- **To adjust all the points at once,** select one width point and Shift-drag to adjust all the rest in tandem.

- **To copy selected points,** hold Option/Alt as you drag.

- **To delete a selected width point,** press the Delete key.

- **To deselect a width point,** press the Esc key, hold down Option/Alt and click on an empty space, or use ⌘-Shift-A/Ctrl-Shift-A to deselect all (holding down ⌘ or Ctrl *does not* temporarily switch you to the Selection tool).

THE EXPANDED STROKE PANEL

The Stroke panel controls settings for the many different types of strokes, from how they align to the path of an object to how they join at corners. Dashed lines, end caps, and arrowheads all are part of the Stroke panel, as well as stored width profiles, from a normal even width to a fully

Save those width profiles

The Reset icon in the Strokes panel deletes all custom width profiles and restores the default profiles. To first save your width profiles, apply them to an object, then save that object's Graphic Style in the Graphic Styles panel.

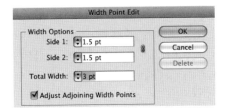

Use the dialog (shown above) to enable Adjust Adjoining Width Points (disabled by default), or select a point and hold the Shift key down while adjusting it in order to bypass opening the dialog

(Top) The starting stroke with width points already added and adjusted; (middle) the width point at the right end adjusted again to make the end wider and Adjust Adjoining Width Points disabled; (bottom) with Adjust Adjoining Width Points enabled when adjusting the same original right-end width point—starting stroke shown for clarity in red on top of both adjusted strokes.

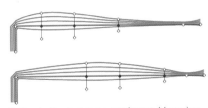

Shift-selecting just some contiguous (shown) or non-contiguous (not shown) width points on a Pattern Brush stroke, releasing Shift, then moving them all at once

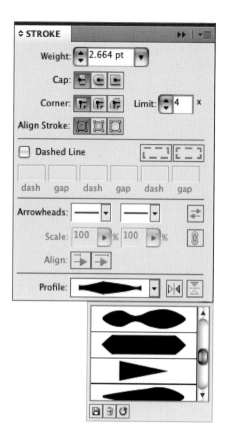

Stroke panel with width profiles list; save or delete one custom width profile at a time; re-setting the defaults removes all custom width profiles

A path shown first in Outline, then in Preview with a Miter join, Round join, and Bevel join

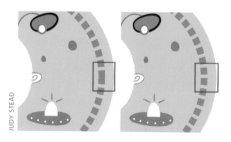

JUDY STEAD

(Left) Choosing to align with mathematically precise spacing; (right) with adjusted spacing for visual appearance, aligning dashes to corners and path ends, which adjusts the space between to fit more uniformly

calligraphic profile. Here you can also customize and save your carefully crafted stroke profiles after creating a variable-width stroke, and preview how your path joins to an arrowhead. Adjust the way dashes follow a path, and scale arrowheads to suit.

Making ends meet

Sometimes stroked lines seem to match up perfectly when viewed in Outline mode but they visibly overlap in Preview mode. You can solve this problem by selecting one of the three end cap styles in the Strokes panel. The default Butt cap causes your path to stop at the end anchor point and is essential for creating exact placement of one path against another. The Round cap is especially good for softening the effect of single line segments. The Projecting cap extends lines and dashes at half the stroke weight beyond the end anchor point. Cap styles also affect the shape of dashed lines.

Corners have joins that serve a similar purpose to end caps. The Join style in the Stroke panel determines the shape of a stroke at its corner points; the inside of the corner is always angled. The default Miter join creates a pointy corner, with the length of the point determined by the width of the stroke, the angle of the corner (narrow angles create longer points), and the Miter limit setting on the Stroke panel. The default Miter join (with a miter limit of 10x) usually looks fine, but can range from 1x (which is always blunt) to 500x. The Round join creates a rounded outside corner with radius of half the stroke width. The Bevel join creates a squared-off outside corner, equivalent to a Miter join with the miter limit set to 1x.

Dashes behave like short lines, and therefore have both end caps and, potentially, corner joins. End caps work with dashes exactly as they do with the ends of paths—each dash is treated as a very short path. However, if a dashed path goes around the corner, it can make that turn in one of two ways: The spacing between the dashes can be precise and constant, so the dash won't necessarily bend around a corner, or even reach to it, or you can click the "Aligns dashes to corners and path ends, adjusting lengths to fit" icon. Dashes won't be precisely spaced, but will look tidy at the corners. The command affects dash spacing for other shapes, from circles to stars, as well.

One more "end" to a path is an arrowhead, and the Stroke panel now offers a choice of both the types of arrowheads and how they are affixed to the ends of the paths. Click on the Arrowheads pop-up list to choose to attach an arrow or feather to the start or end of the path. You can then scale it proportionally or disproportionally, reverse the start and end, or align the arrowhead so that either the tip or the end of the arrow meets the end of the path. To remove an arrowhead (or feather), choose None from the list. You can add custom arrowheads to the list without removing any of the default arrowheads (you'd have to reinstall Illustrator to make them available again if you removed them). Both dash alignment options and arrowheads can be modified again at any time.

BRUSHES

Illustrator's Calligraphic, Art, Scatter, Bristle, and Pattern brushes can mimic traditional art tools, create photorealistic imagery, or provide pattern and texture to your art. You can either create brush strokes with the Brush tool, or you can apply a brush stroke to a previously drawn path.

Calligraphic Brushes create strokes that mimic real-world calligraphy pens, brushes, or felt pens. You can define a degree of variation for the size, roundness, and angle of each "nib." You can also set each of these attributes to respond to a graphics tablet and stylus (like the Wacom) with a variety of different pen characteristics (with a mouse, you can only use Fixed or Random).

Art Brushes consist of one or more pieces of artwork that get fitted to the path you create with them. You can use Art Brushes to imitate traditional painting media, such as drippy ink pens, textured charcoal, spatter brushes, dry brushes, watercolors, and more. Or an Art Brush can represent real-world objects, such as a petal, a leaf, or a ribbon, a flower, decorative flourish, or train. You

Creating custom arrowheads

Illustrator Help provides directions for locating the Arrowheads file on your computer. The file contains instructions for customizing and saving arrowheads without overwriting the original file.

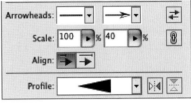

Using the Arrowheads section of the Stroke panel to align the arrowhead so the tail of the arrowhead joins the end of the path with the head extending beyond (left and as shown in the dialog), or to align the arrowhead so the tip of the arrowhead joins the end of the path (right)

Where's the Blob Brush?

Find information on the Blob Brush in the *Rethinking Construction* chapter; even though it's first applied like a brush, it's really more of a modern, fluid method for constructing objects.

Graphics tablets & brushes

Bristle Brushes, which mimic painter's brushes, respond to every hand gesture when using a tablet and pen, such as the Wacom. The Wacom 6D Art or Art Pens also easily retain the appearance of the individual bristles, while allowing full rotation to create unique strokes that imitate real brushes. A mouse is much more limited.

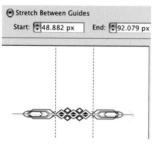

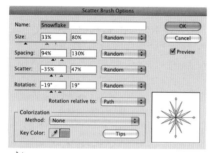

Using the Width tool to alter an Art brush stroke modified by Stretch Between Guides option

The Scatter Brush dialog varies how the artwork is scattered along a path

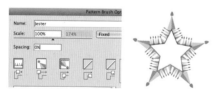

Altering Pattern Scale and Spacing to create a very different look to the brush

can modify Art Brushes and their strokes using a number of different paramters, including variables affected by pressure (if you're using a Wacom tablet and pen). Art Brush marks can be made to scale proportionately to fit the length of your path, or stretched to fit. You can also scale your brush non-proportionally by restricting the area of the Art Brush that can stretch, using two guides to create a segmented brush (choose Stretch Between Guides for the Scale option). Either or both ends of the brush are then protected from being stretched, and the middle portion is stretched to fill in the remaining length. This allows you to stretch the stem of a rose, for instance, without stretching the blossom itself. You can further modify an Art Brush with colorization methods, such as choosing to vary a key color by tint or hue. Modify the way the Art Brush follows a path by flipping its direction, and use the Overlap option to determine whether or not to allow it to overlap itself when turning a corner. You can also use the Width tool to modify an Art Brush.

Use Scatter Brushes to scatter copies of artwork along the path you create with them: flowers in a field, bees in the air, stars in the sky. The size of the objects, their spacing, how far they scatter from the path, and their rotation can be set to a Fixed or Random amount or, with a graphics tablet, can vary according to characteristics such as pressure or tilt. You can also align the rotation of the scattered objects to the direction of the path, or to the edges of the page. Change the method of colorization as you would with a Calligraphic or Pattern Brush.

Use Pattern Brushes to paint patterns along a path. To use a Pattern Brush, first define the tiles that will make up your pattern. For example, a train has an engine, rail cars, links, and a caboose. Each of these constitutes a tile where you have the start of the path, the middle (the side tile), the tiles that turn either an inside or outside corner, and the end of the path. The tiles must be made as individual art and stored in the Swatches panel before you can make your Pattern Brush. Afterwards, however, you can delete them from Swatches. In the Pattern Brush Options dialog, select a tile, then click on the swatch name below the tiles that you want assigned to that tile. You can customize settings for how the tiles fit to, or flip along, the path, and to alter their color. You can also vary the appearance of the Pattern Brush, how it fills sharp angles (by altering the Scale in both Fixed parameters and those affected by tablet features), and the spacing between tiles.

Bristle Brushes emulate traditional paint brushes, showing both the texture of the bristles and the tip shape, which can be round, flat, fan-shaped, etc. To create a Bristle Brush, select it as the New brush type and, in the Bristle Brush Options dialog, choose a tip shape. From there, modify the brush's bristle length, density, and thickness; whether or not the bristles are stiff or soft; and how opaquely it applies the paint. Bristle Brushes use paint opacity for their effect, but even a 100% Opacity isn't completely opaque. Change Opacity on the fly with the numbers on the keyboard. Because calculating transparency for printing often takes a long time, a dialog warns that if you have more than 30 Bristle Brush strokes, you may want to select some or all of the Bristle Brush strokes and choose Object > Rasterize to set raster settings for them before you attempt to print.

Working with brushes

The following describes functional features that apply to most or all brushes:

- **To create Art, Scatter, and Pattern Brushes,** create the artwork for them from fairly basic artwork, including compound shapes, blends, groups, and some live effects such as Distort & Transform or Warp. You *can't* create brushes from art that uses gradients, mesh objects, raster art, and advanced live effects such as Drop Shadow or 3D.
- **To modify the art that makes up a brush,** drag it out of the Brushes panel, edit the object, then drag it back into the Brushes panel. Use the Option/Alt key as you drag to replace the original art with the new art.
- **To set application-level preferences for all brushes,** double-click the Paintbrush tool. (The new preferences

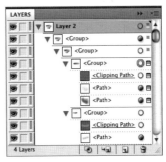

Using a Bristle Brush (the Footprint brush showing) to draw inside a selected path, and the Layers panel showing the Clipping Paths created by Draw Inside

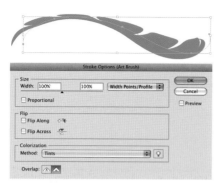

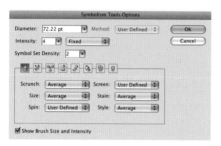

Modifying based on Width Points using Options of Selected Object for an Art Brush that has already been modified with the Width tool

Symbolism Tools Options dialog

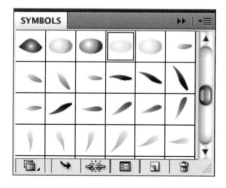

Storing symbols in the Symbols panel, with access to other symbol libraries, editing commands, and the Symbol Options dialog

Quick access to Symbol features on the Control panel with a symbol in the artwork selected; the Reset button not grayed out indicates the symbol has been transformed and the Replace pop-up gives immediate access to the loaded Symbols library

will apply to work you do with the brushes going forward, but won't change existing work.)

- **To modify the properties of a single brush stroke,** select it, then choose Options of Selected Object in the Brush panel's menu. If you've used the Width tool to modify the stroke, your options include using the width points to calculate the profile for your next strokes.

- **To choose how to apply modifications** to existing brush strokes, in the brush's Options dialog choose Leave Strokes to create a duplicate brush, or Apply to Strokes to modify every use of the brush in the document.

- **When Keep Selected and Edit Selected Paths are both enabled,** the last drawn path stays selected; drawing a new path close to the selected path will redraw that path. Disabling either of these options will allow you to draw multiple brush strokes near each other, instead of redrawing the last drawn path.

SYMBOLS

Working with symbols in Illustrator saves file size (since objects converted to symbols aren't duplicated in the file), provides consistency whenever the same artwork needs to be used more than once, and makes it easy to update objects in your artwork simply by editing the symbol to change it wherever it has been used. Symbols can be made from almost any art you create in Illustrator. The only exceptions are a few kinds of complex groups, such as groups of graphs, and placed art (which must be *embedded*, not linked). Symbols are edited and stored using the Symbols and Control panels, and are manipulated in your artwork with the Symbolism tools:

- **To store selected artwork as a symbol,** drag it into the Symbols panel (or click on the New Symbol icon in the panel). Use the Libraries Menu icon to save the current symbols to a new library, or to load other libraries.

- **To add a single instance of a symbol to your document,** drag it into your document or, with it selected, click on the Place Symbol Instance icon. Drag a symbol instance into your document as often as you like, but you can only use the Place Symbol Instance icon once. It's most useful for modifying the symbol (see below).

- **To modify a symbol without modifying the original symbol** in the Symbols panel, click either the Break Link button in the Control panel or the "Break Link to Symbol" icon in the Symbols panel.

- **To modify a symbol and all instances of it** already in the document, place or drag it into your document, then click on the Edit Symbol button in the Control panel. Your symbol will be placed in isolation mode. After you modify it and exit isolation mode, all instances of the symbol, including the symbol in the Symbols panel, are updated.

- **To modify a symbol in the Symbols panel when you have already broken the link,** Option/Alt-drag the modified symbol on top of the symbol in the Symbols panel. This will replace the original symbol with the modified artwork and update all instances of the original symbol.

- **To restore a symbol to its original size and orientation** after transforming it, click the Reset button in the Control panel.

- **To quickly find all instances of a symbol** in your artwork, target the symbol either in the Symbols panel or in your artwork and choose Select All Instances from the Symbol panel's menu.

- **To replace one symbol with another without opening the Symbols panel,** select the symbol in the artwork and click on the Replace list arrow in the Control panel. A miniature Symbols panel opens, which allows you to swap out symbols.

- **To add a sublayer to a symbol's artwork,** in isolation mode click on the topmost layer with the symbol's name, and then click on the New Sublayer icon. You can't add sublayers to a <Group> or <path>.

- **To add a new layer above a group or path sublayer at the same hierarchy level,** target the layer, then Option-click/Alt-click on the New Layer icon. If the layer remains a normal layer (not a group or a path),

Some Control panel options for modifying symbols, including providing a Flash instance name and a Reset button for restoring a symbol to its original size

Symbols for Flash

When creating symbols for use in Flash, take advantage of Illustrator's built-in features for making them ready for use:

- Enable 9-slice scaling, often used for buttons and other interface elements when creating a Flash-based website, from within Illustrator. Doing so reduces distortion when scaling objects, especially noticeable with elements such as buttons that have custom corners.

- Assign a Registration point to the symbol in Illustrator. The Registration point affects any transformations applied inside Illustrator, and Flash also uses the Registration point as the origin point (0,0) for Motion Presets and other commands used to animate or modify the symbol.

- Give a symbol a unique Instance name in the Control Panel so Flash can identify it when using Action Script commands. This is important when creating interface elements, such as buttons, that are otherwise identical.

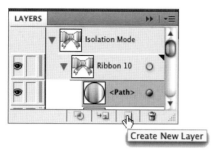

Adding a new layer at the same level as a path sublayer by Option-clicking/Alt-clicking on the Create New Layer icon

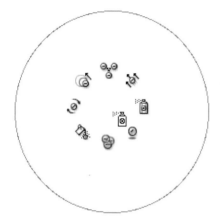

Control-Option-click/Ctrl-Alt-click on an empty spot in the document to reveal this heads-up display of all the Symbolism tools; drag to the desired tool and release the mouse.

Using the Symbolism tools to modify the original set (top) for greater variety (bottom)

you can continue to add new layers at that level merely by clicking on the New Layer icon.

Working with the Symbolism tools

There are eight different Symbolism tools. Use the Symbol Sprayer tool to spray selected symbols onto your document, creating a symbol set. You can't select individual instances inside a set with any of the selection tools. Instead, modify them with any of the other Symbol tools. To display a ring of tools in your document in order to select a new one, press Control-Option/Ctrl-Alt while clicking and holding in an empty spot in your document then drag to a new icon before releasing your mouse. Add symbols to a selected set by selecting a symbol in the Symbols panel—the symbol can be the same as or different from the symbols already present in the instance set—and spray. To add or modify symbols in a set make sure you've selected *both* the set and the corresponding symbol(s) in the Symbols panel that you want to affect. The Symbolism tools will only affect those symbols in a selected set that are also selected in the Symbols panel, thus making it easy to modify just one of the symbols in a mixed set.

To adjust the properties of the Symbolism tools, double-click on one to open Symbolism Tools Options. Vary the diameter (the range over which the tool operates), the rate at which it applies a change, and the density with which it operates on a set. If you're using the default Average mode, your new symbol instances can inherit attributes (size, rotation, transparency, style) from nearby symbols in the same instance set. For example, if nearby symbols are 50% opaque, symbols added to the set will also be 50% opaque. You can also change the default Average mode to User Defined or Random. (See *Illustrator Help* for more information about choosing User Defined.)

To remove symbols from an existing instance set, use the Symbol Sprayer tool with the Option/Alt key, and click on an instance to delete it (or click-drag your cursor over multiple instances—they're deleted when you lift your cursor).

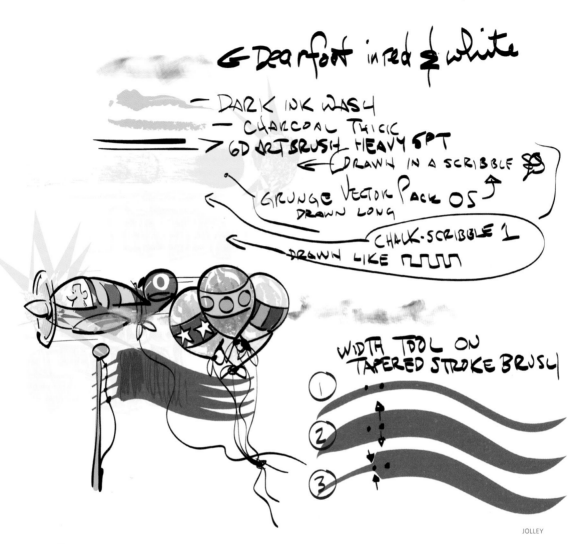

JOLLEY

Don Jolley

This sampler by Don Jolley, using his 6D Art Pen, demonstrates the tremendous variety you get from brushes that ship with Illustrator. When you add a Wacom pressure-sensitive pen and tablet to these out-of-the-box brushes, you can introduce even more variety into your strokes; the standard Grip Pen registers pressure, tilt, and bearing, and the optional, more sensitive 6D Art (Intuos3) or Art (Intuos4) Pens add the

ability to vary each stroke with rotation. The Bristle Brush responds particularly well to the Art Pens, adding a new dimension to painting. You can manually transform your stroke (except those made with the Calligraphic, Scatter, or Bristle Brushes), by modifying its profile with the Width tool, and then saving that profile to apply to other strokes.

Brushes & Washes

Drawing with Naturalistic Pen, Ink, & Wash

Overview: *Start with a placed image as a template; create a custom Calligraphic brush; create variations on the brush to apply to strokes; add a wash layer below the ink layer.*

STEUER

Transparent brushstrokes

By default, brushstrokes are opaque. You can also draw with semi-transparent brushstrokes, which you can use to simulate some types of inks or watercolors; where marks overlap, they become richer or darker. Click <u>Opacity</u> in the Control panel to reduce opacity or choose a blending mode.

(Top) The original photo; (bottom) brush strokes drawn over the dimmed template photo

---

It's easy to create spontaneous painterly and calligraphic marks in Illustrator—and perhaps with more flexibility than in many pixel-based programs. Sharon Steuer drew this sketch of Honfleur, France, using a Wacom tablet, her Art Pen for the Intuos4, and two different Illustrator brushes. She customized a brush for the thin, dark strokes and used a built-in brush for the underlying gray washes.

1 Importing artwork and using template layers. If you want to use a sketch or photo as a reference, set it up as a non-printing template layer. For her template image, Steuer scanned a small photo of Honfleur. To place an image as a template layer so it can be easily resized, choose File > Place, enable the Link checkbox, and click the Place button. If the image imports at too large a size, hold down the Option-Shift/Alt-Shift keys (to resize proportionally from the center) and drag on a corner of the bounding box until the image is the size you want. Then double-click on the layer to open the Layers Options dialog and enable the Template option. Illustrator automatically dims the image to make your drawing easier to see. Toggle between hiding and showing the template layer using ⌘-Shift-W/Ctrl-Shift-W, or toggle the visibility icon in the Layers panel. If you need to unlock the layer, do so in the Layers panel, not the Layer Options dialog.

2 Customizing a Calligraphic brush. In order to sketch freely and with accurate detail, you'll need to adjust the default Paintbrush tool settings. Double-click the Paintbrush tool to open Paintbrush Tool Options. Drag the Fidelity and Smoothness sliders all the way to the left so that Illustrator records your strokes precisely. Disable "Fill new brush strokes," and if you want to be able to quickly draw strokes that overlap, disable Keep Selected.

Customizing the Paintbrush Tool Options

To create a custom Calligraphic brush, click the New Brush icon and select Calligraphic Brush. For this piece, Steuer chose the following settings: Angle=90°/Fixed; Roundness=10%/Fixed; Diameter=4 pt/Pressure/Variation=4 pt. If you have one of the newer Wacom Art Pens, try varying the Diameter with Rotation instead of Pressure, then let the pen barrel rotate between your fingers naturally as you draw. (If you don't have a pressure-sensitive tablet, only Random will have any effect on varying your stroke.) To create a variation of a brush, duplicate it by dragging it to the New Brush icon, then double-click the copy to edit it. By creating and saving a variety of brushes—adding minor variances in Angle, Roundness, and Diameter—you can enhance the hand-drawn appearance of your ink drawing by selecting a brushed path and choosing a new brush for it.

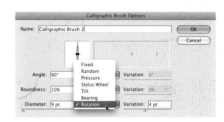

Creating a new Calligraphic brush

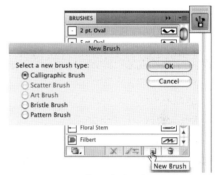

Angle, Roundness, and Diameter can be set to a variety of Pen characteristics, including Rotation if the Pen is one of the newer Art Pens; for mice, Random is the only variation from Fixed.

3 Adding a wash. For this piece, Steuer added depth by introducing gray washes underneath the dark brush strokes. To easily edit the wash strokes without affecting the dark ink strokes, create a new layer, and draw your wash strokes into this layer between the ink and template layers. To avoid altering other layers while you brush in the washes, you may want to lock all the other layers. To toggle between locking all layers except the wash layer, and unlocking all layers at once, including the wash layer, Option-click/Alt-click the wash layer's Lock icon.

For the wash, select a light color. Steuer used the Dry Ink 2 brush from the Artistic_Ink brush library (Swatch Libraries menu). In the Layers panel, click the wash layer to make it the current drawing layer, and paint away.

The final ink drawing after adding a couple of people not in the original photo, and before adding the wash

JACKMORE

Lisa Jackmore

To make interesting brushstrokes, Lisa Jackmore used variations of Calligraphic and Bristle brushes. With a Wacom Intuos4 tablet and Art Pen, Lisa Jackmore created variation in some of her Calligraphic and Bristle brushstrokes, changing the parameters of Pressure, Rotation, and Tilt. When she wanted to customize a brush, she double-clicked the brush, and made changes to the options. For the tree outline, she used a 3-pt Flat Calligraphic brush, set the Diameter to Pressure (with a 2-pt variation), Roundness to Tilt (34°, with a variation of 15°), and set the Angle to Rotation (with a 125° variation). For the long sweeping lines of the tree, she found the combination of using Rotation and a chisel tip of the Art Pen worked the best to vary the brushstroke. As she drew, she slightly rotated and tilted the pen and created variations in her stroke. To create an irregular ink-like appearance in the words, she used a 1-pt Round Calligraphic brush, and set the Angle to 30° (fixed), Roundness to Tilt (60°, with a 29% variation). Jackmore used several other variations of Calligraphic brushes to draw the suitcases and background pattern. To make the pattern, she drew several paths with a customized Calligraphic brush, grouped the brushstrokes, and dragged the pattern tile to the swatches panel. After she drew all of the black brushstrokes, she colored the illustration with a gradient mesh object for the background, and used variations of the Fan, Round Blunt, and Round Point Bristle brushes for other areas, such as the bird, suitcases, and shadows. Finally, Jackmore used the rectangle tool to make a frame, then applied a Charcoal brush to the stroke.

JACKMORE

Lisa Jackmore

For designs as fluid as this floral pattern, Lisa Jackmore finds that initially drawing with the Calligraphic Brush tool is the most natural and intuitive way to begin. However, when she wants to create specific variations to the strokes, she then converts the brushstrokes to Basic stroked paths, so she can use the Width tool (you can't use the Width tool on brushstrokes with a Calligraphic brush). To do this, she clicked on the Basic Brush in the Brushes panel (the basic stroke version is shown directly above). Jackmore then selected the Width tool (Shift-W) and clicked on the stroke itself, dragging the handle outwards to evenly widen the path. To make adjustments to one side, she held the Option/Alt key while dragging the handle. To make even further variations to the strokes,

Jackmore clicked on the stroke, added new width points, and adjusted them. She saved several Width profiles by selecting each modified stroke, clicking on the Add to Profile button in the Variable Width Profile menu in the Control panel, then naming it and clicking OK. To finish the design, she selected each of the remaining paths, applied one of her saved width profiles from the Control panel, and then increased the stroke weight on all of the paths.

Stroke Variance

Creating Dynamic Variable-Width Strokes

Overview: *Place sketch and trace with Pen tool; modify strokes with Width tool; save width profile and apply to other strokes.*

The original sketch

Traced sketch

2 ![icon]

Width tool (Shift-W) adjusting middle of stroke

Ryan Putnam creates many character illustrations for websites, branding projects, and more. Putnam now uses the Width tool to add depth and variance in the strokes of the illustrations. Moreover, he can save the stroke adjustments to new Width profiles to easily apply to other strokes in current and future projects.

1 Placing a sketch template and tracing with Pen tool. Putnam first created a character sketch in Photoshop, chose File > Place in Illustrator, enabled Template, and clicked OK. Putnam then traced basic paths of the sketch with the Pen tool in the layer above.

2 Adjusting strokes with the Width tool. Putnam wanted his strokes to have some variance compared to the uniform strokes created by the Pen tool. He created two distinct stroke widths to use on the majority of the paths in the illustration. For the first stroke adjustment, Putnam created a stroke with a thicker middle and tapered ends. To do this, he used the Width tool to click in the middle of the desired path and drag a width point to the desired width. For the second custom width, Putnam created a stroke with a thicker end and a tapered end. Again, he used the Width tool, but this time clicked on the far right side of the desired path and dragged a width point to the desired width.

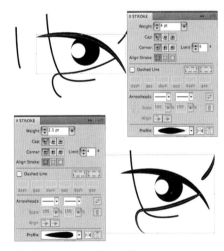

Width tool (Shift-W) adjusting end of stroke

If you like to be precise with your adjustments, you can double-click a width point to open the Width Point Edit dialog, allowing you to numerically adjust the width of the stroke in the Side 1, Side 2, and Total Width fields.

3 Saving stroke profiles and applying to other paths.
Instead of adjusting every path in the illustration to match the two custom widths he created with the Width tool, Putnam saved time and ensured consistency by saving his two custom stroke profiles. To save each profile, he selected the modified stroke and clicked the Add to Profiles icon in the Stroke panel. With both of his strokes saved as custom profiles, Putnam could select a uniform stroke, click the saved Variable Width Profile at the bottom of the Stroke panel, and select the saved profile from the drop-down list. These custom profiles will then be available in other new Illustrator files.

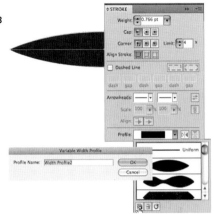

3

Saving new width profile

After Putnam applied the custom profile to all the desired paths, he utilized specific keyboard commands with the Width tool to further adjust individual paths. For example, holding down the Option/Alt key when dragging width points creates non-uniform widths, the Delete key deletes selected width points, and holding the Shift key while dragging adjusts multiple width points. Other Keyboard modifiers with the Width tool include holding down Option/Alt while dragging a width point to copy the width point, holding down Option-Shift/Alt-Shift while dragging to copy and move all the points along a path, Shift-clicking to select multiple width points, and using the Esc key to deselect a width point.

Applying a saved width profile

4 Applying finishing touches. Putnam added additional elements as needed. For instance, he create simple shapes with the Pen tool and filled them with grayscale colors.

4

Adjusting a path with Width tool and keyboard commands

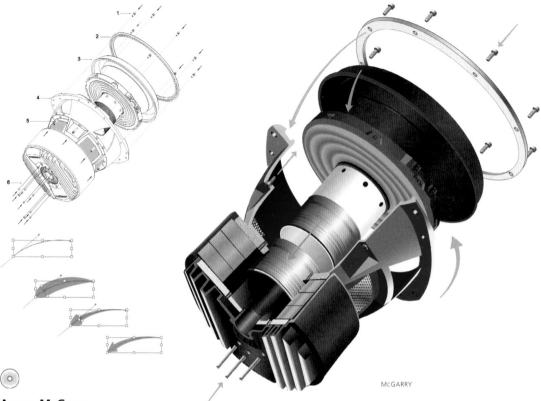

McGARRY

Aaron McGarry

As an illustrator working in the technology industry, McGarry created this exploded view of a subwoofer from a CAD drawing for use as an assembly overview in a re-cone kit. McGarry first placed the drawing as a template layer then created an oval using the Ellipse tool and rotated it to match the angle of the drawing. To preserve this angle and shape throughout the illustration, he used this first object to create all the other ellipses within the illustration by holding Option/Alt to make a copy as he dragged, and resized using the bounding box. McGarry began with the uppermost clamping ring and built each component on a separate layer; this naturally organized each component so that it obstructed the previous components. He used an extensive variety of gradients

from the gradients library (Window > Swatch Library > Gradients) to emphasize the cylindrical structure of the speaker. He made a single screw, dragged it into the Symbols panel, and then used instances of it to create the others. To make his customized arrows, he used the Pen tool to draw a path, stroked it with a color, and then used the Width tool to shape the arrow (see process above left). Ellipse strokes such as the rim of the black cone also employed the Width tool, thinning the stroke as it circled away from view. He used the Pen tool to draw the red surfaces on the main basket and paths forming the cutaway portion of the speaker. He then used the Eyedropper tool to sample various shades of red from a photo of a similar speaker to indicate the red basket shades.

MIYAMOTO

Nobuko Miyamoto / Yukio Miyamoto

Making this intricate beaded necklace at first glance would seem impossibly difficult, but with the use of a Pattern brush, the necklace virtually draws itself. Nobuko Miyamoto designed the necklace and created the bead element (detail above) with a mixture of blended and solid filled objects. Careful attention was paid to the ends of the bead to ensure that when each bead lined up with the next one there would be a seamless connection between them. To make the chained ends, she selected the chain object and dragged a copy (Shift-Option/Shift-Alt) to the other side of the bead. With the chain selected, she chose the Reflect tool and clicked above and below the chain to reflect the chain vertically. Yukio Miyamoto then created the Pattern brush with the bead element. He selected and grouped the bead. Yukio clicked the New Brush icon at the bottom of the Brushes panel, selected New Pattern Brush, and clicked OK. In the Pattern Brush Options dialog, he kept the Colorization method as None, and then under Fit he chose Stretch to Fit. To make the necklace, Nobuko drew a path with the Brush tool and selected the bead Pattern brush in the Brushes panel to apply the brush. Now with the bead as a Pattern brush, the necklace can be easily adjusted to any length or path.

Pattern Brushes

Creating Details with the Pattern Brush

Overview: *Create the parts that will make up a Pattern Brush separately; place the parts in the Swatches panel and give them distinctive names; use the Pattern Brush Options dialog to create the brushes.*

Adjusting Pattern Brush fit

After you've applied a Pattern Brush to a path, you can still scale, flip, and modify its fit along the path. Modify all these settings in the Pattern Brush Options dialog, or, manually reshape and scale the pattern by changing the stroke weight, applying a stroke profile, or using the Width tool.

1

Creating one zipper tooth, using the Blend tool for the highlight, then positioning a duplicate to mimic the teeth

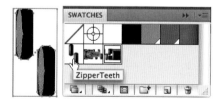

Selecting bounding rectangle and objects, dragging objects for Pattern brushes into the Swatches panel, and naming them

While many Illustrator Brushes mimic traditional art strokes, Greg Maxson often concentrates his efforts on creating Pattern brushes that eliminate the tedious creation of the practical objects he often illustrates. For this product illustration, Maxson saved many hours by creating two zipper brushes, one for just the basic teeth of a zipper, and one that included the zipper pull and stop. Because he would be able to use these brushes over and over again, Maxson knew a little time creating a Pattern brush would save him a lot of time in the future.

1 Creating the parts of the zipper separately.

Maxson first created the zipper teeth. He drew a simple rounded rectangle for the base, and then drew a small, light oval on top of a larger black oval that would become the highlight. Maxson selected both objects and double-clicked on the Blend tool to choose Specified Steps, thus controlling the brush's complexity. He used the keyboard shortcut ⌘-Option-B/Ctrl-Alt-B to blend the highlight, which he placed on the base (you can also blend via the menu by choosing Object > Blend > Make). (See the chapter *Mastering Complexity* for more about working with blends.) Maxson duplicated the zipper "tooth" and positioned the copy as it would be in a real zipper. He then drew a no-stroke, no-fill bounding rectangle behind the teeth to add space around each pair of teeth equal to the space between each tooth, thus keeping the teeth spaced evenly. He selected all the objects and chose Edit > Define Pattern. He gave the swatch a name he would recognize when he built the Pattern brush. Pattern swatches are the "tiles" that make up a Pattern brush.

Maxson then created the pull and stop for the zipper. To create the illusion of the pull and stop overlapping the teeth, he layered them on top of copies of the teeth he had already made. He made sure that the stop and pull were facing in the correct direction relative to the zipper pattern tiles (which run perpendicular to the path), and individually placed them in the Swatches panel.

2 Making and using the Pattern brushes. To make the first Pattern brush for the zipper teeth, Maxson opened the Brushes panel's pop-up menu and selected New Brush. He then chose New Pattern Brush, which opened the Pattern Brush Options dialog. He gave his Pattern brush a descriptive name, chose the first box in the diagram (the Side Tile), and then selected the Pattern swatch that represented the teeth alone. When a thumbnail of the Pattern swatch he had chosen (the teeth) showed in the first box, and the other boxes were left empty, he clicked OK to place the brush in the Brushes panel.

To create the version with the stop and pull, he again selected New Brush from the Brushes panel, and chose the same teeth pattern for the Side Tile. Skipping over the corner tiles, he chose the Zipper Pull swatch as the Start Tile, and the End Tile for the Zipper Stop swatch. He named his new Pattern brush so he would know it was built from all three swatches and clicked OK.

To use his new brushes, Maxson drew a path for each zipper. The long, vertical zipper used the brush with the pull and stop, while the short zipper used the brush with only teeth, since the pull required a unique illustration.

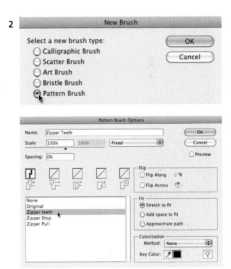

Creating zipper pull and stop, oriented in the outward-facing position Pattern brushes use for their tiles

Creating a new Pattern brush with only a Side Tile repeated along the length of the path to make the zipper with just teeth

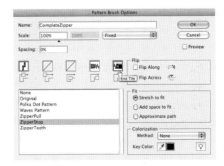

Creating a Pattern brush with Start and End tiles for the zipper with the pull and stop

Symbolism Basics

Creating and Working with Symbols

Overview: *Create a basic background; define symbols; use Symbolism tools to place and customize symbols; add finishing details.*

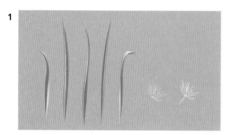

The artwork for the symbols that were used to complete the piece

The Symbols panel containing the library of symbols

The Symbolism tools tear off panel (to tear it off, click and hold a tool, then drag to the right edge

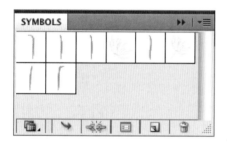

One of several symbol sets of the raw grass after being sprayed with the Symbol Sprayer tool

Lisa Jackmore created this illustration using a variety of effects possible with the Symbolism tools. Jackmore defined a library of symbols and then used the Symbolism tools to place and customize the symbols. Symbols can provide a "brush-like" painting experience, with easier (and more fun!) adjustments and editing.

1 Creating a background and symbols. Because she would be drawing many light-colored objects, Jackmore began by using the Rectangle tool to draw a blue background. Locking the layer with the background, Jackmore created a new layer on top, into which she drew the artwork for each of the symbols she would use to create the illustration. (See the chapter *Your Creative Workspace* for more on layers.) To turn selected artwork into a symbol, either drag it onto the Symbols panel, or press F8; Illustrator automatically takes your artwork on the artboard and swaps it for an instance of the symbol.

2 Applying symbols. Jackmore next selected the grass symbol in the Symbols panel and created the first row of grass with a single stroke of the Symbol Sprayer tool. You can experiment with the Symbol Sprayer by adjusting the Density and Intensity settings (double-click on any Symbolism tool to access the Symbolism Tools Options), and the speed of your spray strokes. Don't worry about getting an exact number or precise placement for each symbol as you spray; you'll fine-tune those and other symbol attributes next by applying Symbolism tools to a selected set.

3 Resizing symbols. To imply depth, Jackmore applied the Symbol Sizer tool to resize blades of grass in a selected set. By default, the Symbol Sizer tool increases the size of symbols within the tool's brush radius; to reduce the size of symbols within the radius, hold down Option/Alt.

To make the diameter of a Symbolism tool visible, double-click on any Symbolism tool and enable the Show Brush Size and Intensity checkbox. To enlarge and reduce the diameter of a Symbolism tool, use the same shortcuts as you do with brushes: the] key enlarges the diameter, and the [key reduces it.

4 Modifying symbol transparency and color. To modify the appearance of a symbol set, use the Symbol Screener, Stainer, and Styler tools. The Screener tool adjusts the transparency of symbols. The Stainer tool shifts the color of the symbol to be more similar to the current fill color, while preserving its luminosity. The Styler tool allows you to apply (in variable amounts) styles from the Graphic Styles panel. (For more details about the Styler and Screener tools, see *Illustrator Help*.) Jackmore used the Symbol Stainer tool, set to Random, to tint the dandelion symbols a lighter shade with just one stroke.

5 Rotating symbols. To make adjustments to the orientation of the dandelion symbol set, Jackmore used the Symbol Spinner tool set to User Defined, which set the spin based on the direction that the mouse was moved. (Search *Illustrator Help* for "Symbolism tool options" for an explanation of the User Defined and Average modes.)

Quick symbol switching

To switch Symbolism tools, hold Control-Option (Mac) or Alt-right-mouse button (Win), and click-drag toward the tool you want until the icon changes. —*Mordy Golding*

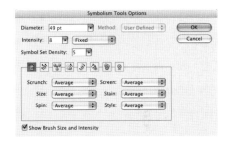

Symbolism Tools Options

3

Jackmore used the Symbol Sizer tool to make some of the blades of grass larger

4

Jackmore used the Symbol Stainer tool to make some of the dandelion symbols a brighter white

5

Jackmore used the Symbol Spinner tool to rotate the dandelion symbols

6

After using the Symbol Shifter tool with a smaller brush size to adjust dandelion symbol positions

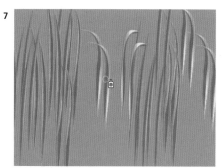

7

Thinning the grass by removing unwanted grass using the Symbol Sprayer tool while holding down the Option/Alt key

8

The background

6 Moving symbols. Jackmore used the Symbol Shifter tool with a smaller brush size to adjust the position of the dandelion symbol set.

The Symbol Shifter tool doesn't easily move symbols across large distances. To maximize symbol movement with the Symbol Shifter tool, first make the brush size as large as you can—at least as large as the symbol you wish to move. Then drag across the symbol, as though you were trying to push the symbol with a broom.

7 Deleting and adding symbols. At this point, Jackmore felt there were too many blades of grass. To remove unwanted grass, Jackmore used the Symbol Sprayer tool with the Option/Alt key held down. She chose a narrow brush size and clicked on the blade to be removed. She worked on the grass symbol set until she was satisfied with the amount of grass. When she needed to add more of that symbol (or even a different symbol) to a selected symbol set, she just applied the Symbol Sprayer tool without any modifier keys.

8 Adding finishing touches. To finish her illustration, Jackmore converted her blue rectangle to a gradient mesh. To create the luminous background, Jackmore applied different colors to individual mesh points. For more about gradient mesh, see the *Color Transitions* chapter.

Making symbols and keeping the art too

To keep your original artwork on the artboard *and* use it to define a new symbol, hold down the Shift key as you drag the artwork onto the Symbols panel.

Symbol stacking order within a layer

You can change the symbol stacking order within a symbol set by adding these modifier keys to the Symbol Shifter tool:

• Shift-click the symbol instance to bring it forward.

• Option-Shift-click/Alt-Shift-click to push the symbol instance backward.

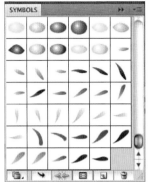

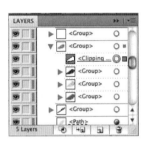

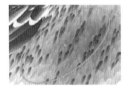

RLSimonson © 2005

SIMONSON

Rick Simonson

When Rick Simonson wanted to create a high level of verisimilitude in his Chipping Sparrow illustration, he turned to Illustrator's symbols as the obvious way to create the hundreds of feathers and seeds he would need. He drew closed paths for single feathers in the different colors and positions necessary to fill the bird's body. He added dimension to the feathers with gradient fills, and he duplicated and rotated some feathers to follow the growth pattern of real feathers. He then Option-clicked/Alt-clicked on the New Symbol icon in the Symbols panel to add the selected object without opening the Symbol Options dialog. Simonson drew the main body of the bird and began filling small areas with layers of feathers, using the Symbol Sprayer with short strokes to manage their placement. To get the look he wanted, he often added feathers one by one instead of in looser symbol sets. He also applied clipping masks to further shape areas of feather symbols. To create the glare and the shading, he used the Transparency panel to reduce opacity and add transparency masks (see the *Mastering Complexity* chapter for more on masks). He used similar methods for adding the seeds.

Painterly Portraits

Painting in Layers with Bristle Brushes

Overview: *Place a sketch as a template; draw with customized Bristle Brushes; continue to paint with custom brushes into separate layers; create frame.*

GEISLER

The myriad Bristle Brushes presented Greg Geisler with an infinite variety of brushes to create his expressive painterly portrait, "Blue Mirror." Commissioned by Adobe Systems, you can find this file, and a PDF ReadMe file explaining more about how he made it, on the **WOW! DVD** and in the Sample Art folder installed with Illustrator.

1 Placing the initial sketch, and customizing Bristle Brush Options. Geisler placed his distorted Photoshop sketch (PSD) as a Template layer. He opened the Bristle Brush Library (Window > Brushes Libraries > Bristle Brush Library) and clicked on the 1-pt Round Bristle Brush, which automatically loaded the brush into the Brushes panel. Geisler next duplicated that brush in the Brushes panel (by dragging its icon to the New Brush icon) and then double-clicked on the brush in the Brushes panel so he could change several settings in Bristle Brush Options. He made changes to Bristle Thickness, adjusted Paint Opacity and increased the Stiffness, and then named it and clicked OK. On a layer above the template, he used this new brush to create the base sketch for the entire illustration. Geisler kept the Brushes panel and the Bristle Brush Library open throughout the drawing session, so he could continue to duplicate and customize brushes as his drawing progressed. For this layer, he created three different variations of the 1-pt Liner brush.

1

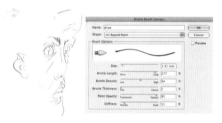

The template; a distorted Photoshop sketch

The initial Bristle Brush sketch made with three variations of a Round Point Bristle Brush; the Bristle Brush Options

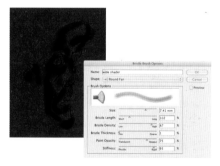

Adding shadows with a wide, fairly opaque Bristle Brush

2 Adding highlights, midtones, and shadows. To make one of the many layers of highlights, such as the strokes in orange, Geisler customized copies of the 3-mm Flat Fan Brush in the Bristle Brushes Library, adjusting Bristle Thickness, Bristle Length, and Paint Opacity. He also drew highlights with a Round Bristle Brush customized with Pointy variations. Geisler continued to draw in separate layers, focusing in particular on midtones, shadows, highlights, or color for each layer, using variations of the Flat Fan and Round Bristle Brushes.

3 Working efficiently and further modifying brush characteristics. Geisler's process is very organic in that he continually defines new brushes, and creates new layers, as he draws. He rarely deletes a stroke, preferring to layer new Bristle Brush strokes upon others, choosing a more opaque brush to cover the underlying strokes. As he's drawing, he presses the [key to decrease the brush size, and the] key, to increase the bristle size. To vary the opacity, he presses the keys from 1, which is completely transparent, through 0, which is completely opaque. To add texture, as in the blue background shown at right, Geisler modifies the settings to increase the brush stiffness toward Rigid, increase the brush density toward Thick, and then decrease the bristle length.

4 Finishing touches. Geisler created an irregular edged black frame that surrounded the portrait, on a layer between the blue texture and the face. He customized a wide Flat Fan brush to 100% Opacity (100% opaque Bristle Brushes lose their character within the stroke, but maintain a ragged edge), and then expanded the brushstrokes (Object > Expand) and clicked Unite in the Pathfinder panel, melding the brushstrokes into one frame object. He then used the Pencil tool to draw a few closed paths, delineating the area between the rectangular frame and the head. Marquee-selecting these paths and the frame, he filled them with black, and again clicked Unite in the Pathfinder panel.

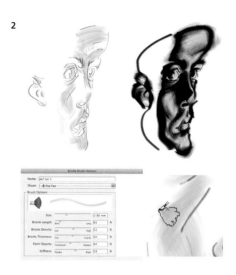

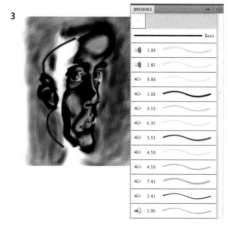

Adding highlights with a Wide Fan Brush, adding shadows; the Bristle Brush icon that appears when using a pressure sensitive pen

Part of the Brushes panel (right), and a later stage of the illustration with blue texture

Black frame made with expanded Bristle Brush strokes and filled paths shown in Preview mode (detail at left), and Outline mode (right)

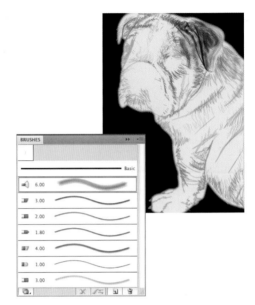

CESAR de OLIVEIRA BALDACCI

Janaína Cesar de Oliveira Baldacci

Based on a photograph taken by Tatiana Bicalho, Baldacci captured the natural undulations of the fur and folds of her pet bulldog with Bristle Brushes. Baldacci first drew a white outline of the dog (against the black background) with the Pen tool and applied a Gaussian Blur effect. Baldacci selected Brush Libraries Menu > Bristle Brush > Bristle Brush Library then selected several brushes to add to the Brushes panel. She chose Bristle Brushes that had varying characteristics in Paint Opacity, Bristle Stiffness, and Bristle Density, such as Round Fan, Flat Blunt, Flat Point, and Round Curve (part of her Brushes panel shown above). Baldacci then selected the Paintbrush tool (B), chose a Bristle Brush and a stroke color, and drew into the first of many layers (the image on the first layer is shown above in Preview and Outline modes). In layers above, she added greater definition and built the fur in stages based on color, such as white, gray, and highlights. On the uppermost layers she added the snout, eye details, and additional layers of fur until the portrait was complete.

Lisa Jackmore

Lisa Jackmore created this pastel-like drawing using Bristle Brushes with a Wacom Intuos4 tablet and a pressure-sensitive pen. After placing a photograph as a Template layer, Jackmore used the Pencil tool to make the line drawing of the flowers and leaves. To add variation to the stroke, she clicked the Variable Width Profile 1 from the Variable Width Profile drop-down menu in the Control panel. Next, she set up her work environment by opening the Brushes panel, the Bristle Brush Library (from the Brush Libraries menu), a TRUMATCH Swatch Library, and the Layers panel. She also set the Wacom tablet's Touch Ring to auto scroll/zoom, so when she needed to magnify an area as she worked, she simply turned the Touch Ring clockwise to zoom in, and counter-clockwise to zoom out. In order to color the inside of the flower using the Draw Inside mode, Jackmore needed to create a simple closed-path outline of each flower, leaf, and stem (without details). She created the outline on a separate layer and then moved that layer below the locked outlines layer (left detail). To draw into each path, she selected it, pressed Shift-D to choose the Draw Inside mode (right detail), then deselected the path (so the Bristle Brush wouldn't be applied to the outline, instead it would be constrained within the path). She selected the Brush tool (B), then chose a Bristle Brush, and a TRUMATCH stroke

JACKMORE

color. When she finished drawing inside a path, Jackmore pressed Shift-D to switch back to Normal drawing mode, then scrolled to the next closed path by dragging the Wacom pen to a new area while holding the bottom Express key on the tablet. She switched between the Brush tool and the Direct Selection tool (pressing the ⌘/Ctrl key), and alternated between Draw Inside and Normal mode. Jackmore used many variations of the Round Point, Fan, and Round Blunt Bristle Brushes. Occasionally she opened Options (by pressing the upper switch on the Intuos4 pen, or by double-clicking the Brush tool) to customize parameters for opacity, Bristle Length, Stiffness, and Bristle thickness. To frame the drawing, she drew two concentric rectangles with the Rectangle tool and applied a Charcoal Art brush to the strokes.

GEISLER

Greg Geisler

Greg Geisler created this graphic self-portrait using a customized Calligraphic Brush. In the Brushes panel, Geisler double-clicked the default 3-pt round Calligraphic Brush, and for the Diameter settings, he changed Fixed to Pressure, and set the Variation to 3 pt. Using a Wacom tablet and pressure-sensitive pen, he drew the facial outline, varying the stroke width as he changed his touch (directly above left). To block out planes of color within the face (such as the chin, beard, and cheek),

he used the Pencil tool to draw color-filled irregular paths on separate layers. Each layer contained one of the many defining areas of color (Layers panel shown above right) for highlights, shadows, or texture. To create the frame, Geisler used the same Bristle Brush, and a technique similar to the one developed in the previous lesson (shown below the artwork). For finishing touches, Geisler drew the bright blue squiggly lines with the Pencil tool.

Cheryl Graham

Cheryl Graham created this vibrant painterly portrait with a custom Art Brush designed to mimic a smudged stroke made with a charcoal stick. To make the "Dreadlock" Art Brush, Graham drew ellipses in different sizes with the Ellipse tool (left detail). She selected the ellipses and applied Pathfinder > Add (middle detail). She then selected the Warp tool and smudged the edges of the ellipse grouping (right detail). She often resized the Warp tool by holding down the Option/Alt key while dragging on the artboard with the tool to change its diameter. Graham selected the artwork and dragged it to the Brushes panel to make an Art Brush and chose Hue Shift to enable quick color changes. She first drew the individual strands of hair with the Dreadlock brush. To make a basic face shape, she drew additional paths with the Pen and Pencil tools. She further defined the face using the Dreadlock and default Calligraphy 1 brushes modified in a variety of ways. Graham could easily, and dramatically, vary the shape and size of the brushes as she painted by merely increasing or decreasing the stroke width. Occasionally she would click *fx* in the Appearance panel and apply an effect to a brushstroke (such as Distort & Transform > Tweak). To create transparency effects, Graham selected brushstrokes or objects, then clicked <u>Opacity</u> in the Appearance panel to reduce opacity

GRAHAM

or change blending modes to Overlay, Multiply, or Screen. She alternated between all of these methods, as well as using the Rotate, Shear, and Scale tools, as she built this dynamic portrait.

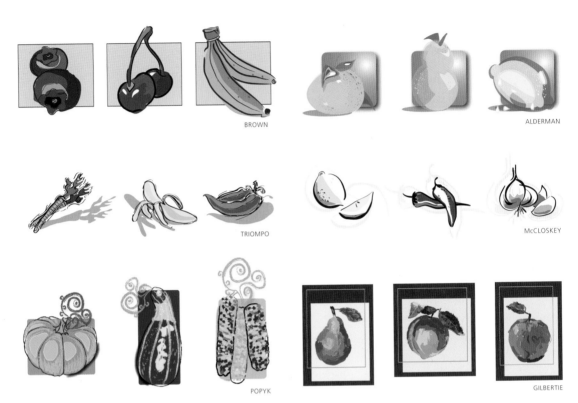

BROWN

ALDERMAN

TRIOMPO

McCLOSKEY

POPYK

GILBERTIE

Stephen Klema's Students:
Dan Brown, Susan E. Alderman,
Matthew Triompo, Laura McCloskey,
Shana Popyk, Nicole Gilbertie

As a class assignment, Professor Stephen Klema challenged his students to create expressive graphic illustrations of organic forms. The students of Tunxis Community College used a variety of default brushes from the Brushes panel. They included both Calligraphy and Art Brushes. Before drawing, the students double-clicked the Paintbrush tool and adjusted the Paintbrush tool preferences. They dragged the Fidelity and Smoothness sliders to the desired positions. The sliders moved farther to the left had more accurate brush strokes, while those moved to the right were smoother. The "Fill New Brush Strokes" and "Keep Selected" options were disabled to allow multiple brush strokes to be drawn near each other without redrawing the last path. Using a pressure-sensitive tablet, the students drew varying widths and angles of brush strokes, many either on top of or close to one another, for a spontaneous, expressive look. Extra points within the brush strokes were deleted using the Smooth tool or the Delete Anchor Point tool.

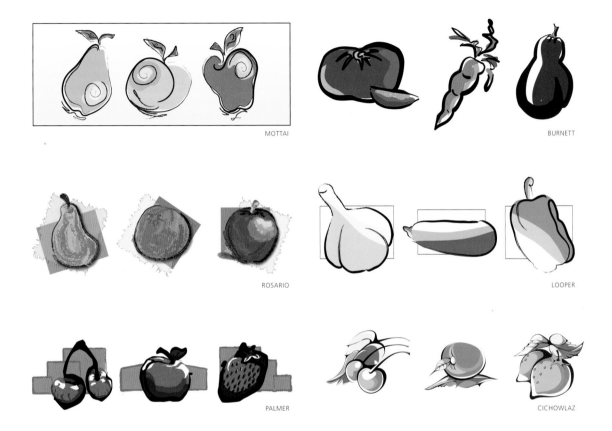

MOTTAI

BURNETT

ROSARIO

LOOPER

PALMER

CICHOWLAZ

Stephen Klema's Students:
Laura Mottai, Cinthia A. Burnett,
Jessica Rosario, Emily Looper,
Theresa Palmer, Kazimiera Cichowlaz

Using the same techniques described on the previous page, additional student creations are shown above. In some of these illustrations, an Art Brush was applied to paths drawn with the Pencil and Pen tools. The Pen or Pencil path was selected with the Selection tool, then a brush was chosen from the Brushes panel. The Pen or Pencil path then changed to that chosen Brush style. Many types of brushes can be found in the Brushes library. To open the Brushes library, click on the Brush Library Menu icon found in the upper right corner of the Brushes panel. Select Open Brush Library > Artistic, then select the brushes you want to add to the Brushes panel. Find more artwork from Professor Klema's students on his website at: www.StephenKlema.com/wow.

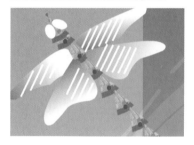

Michael Cronan

Continuing with his series of posters for San Francisco parks, Michael Cronan created Marina Green with his collection of Art Brushes, Scatter Brushes, and Pattern Brushes. He made extensive use of brushes that mimic traditional media. Adobe Illustrator has provided many of these with the program over the years, such as Dry Ink, Charcoal, and Pencil. With Scroll Pen 5 he could draw a variety of elements, from dragon hair to the Golden Gate Bridge and the grassy texture of the Marina Green. He renamed "Scroll Pen 5" to a more descriptive

"Scroll Pen Variable Length" in order to find it easily in his Brushes panel. He created a Scatter Brush for the background stars on the Marina Green strip, and modified a Scatter Brush made from a flying beetle image that he used for one of the kites. A Polynesian design made a Pattern Brush that Cronan used to construct the dragonfly kite's tail, which he drew with the Pencil tool. He also drew vector objects and basic shapes for some of the elements, and colored them with solid or gradient fills.

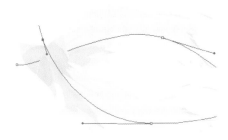

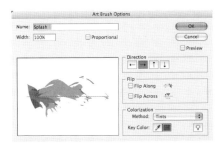

Michael Cronan

To capture the color, ethnic influence, and spirit of San Francisco's popular landmarks, Michael Cronan not only relies on Art Brushes collected over the years, but creates his own. To represent the Japanese Tea Garden, Cronan focused attention on the koi pond, creating the grasses with the Pencil brush and the multi-tones of the shrubbery with the Charcoal brush (both from: Open Brush Library > Artistic > Artistic_ChalkCharcoalPencil). He created a custom Splash brush that included transparency to represent the koi breaking the surface of the pond. Dry Ink and Chalk brushes added to the strong texture in this poster. Cronan also drew individual filled objects that he duplicated repeatedly in order to create pattern texture. By drawing loosely with the Pencil tool and using Pathfinder commands to break objects into abstract patterns, Cronan created informality and freshness in traditional vector drawing that enhanced the Art Brushes' strokes.

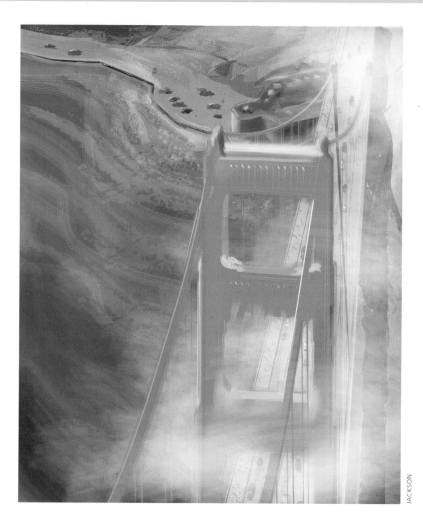

JACKSON

Lance Jackson

To create the cover illustration for the *Adobe Illustrator CS5* **WOW!** *Book*, Lance Jackson generated atmosphere and depth with the Bristle Brush and constructed many of the details using the Blob Brush. He used various tools to block in the main components of his composition. He used the Pen tool to draw the basic cables and roadway for the Golden Gate Bridge, then modified the strokes with the Width tool. Next Jackson began brushing over the water and bridge with various brushes from the Bristle Brush library, especially Deerfoot, Cat's Tongue, Dome,

and Fan. To constrain the brushes to each main element, he often selected a base object and chose the Draw Inside mode. For added texture, he also used brushes from the Artistic and Grunge Brush Vector Pack libraries. Jackson drew a few cars and pedestrians using the Blob Brush, then duplicated and recolored several of them. Jackson toned down his palette, adding fog and more depth, by reducing the opacity of his brushstrokes, layering the strokes, and sometimes even changing the blending mode (by clicking Opacity in the Control panel).

5

Color Transitions

Color Transitions

Color is a big part of what gives your images life. Whether your colors are black and white only, ranges of grays, a limited palette, or a full spectrum of colors, learning how to create transitions between colors, and how to transition one color, or set of colors to another, is essential not only to mastering the power of Adobe Illustrator, but also to unlocking the full potential of your artistic vision. This chapter focuses on the myriad ways of coloring and recoloring your objects in Illustrator, from using the various panels, to creating transitions of colors with gradients and gradient mesh, as well as the group of panels and functions that Adobe calls Live Color.

WORKING WITH THE COLOR AND SWATCHES PANELS

A number of different panels help you work with color, including the Color, Swatches, Color Guide, Appearance, and Control panels. Although you can access the full versions of the Color and Swatches panels, most of the time you'll find it easier to simply access mini versions of the Color and Swatches panels from within the multi-purpose Appearance and Control panels. Click a Fill or Stroke color to reveal an arrow, which in turn accesses a mini version of the Swatches panel, or Shift-click to access the mini Color panel. The Color Guide panel exists only as a full panel.

To save colors from the Color or Color Guide panels (selected contiguously or non-contiguously) to the Swatches panel, drag the color squares to the Swatches panel. To name a single selected color as you create it, click the New Swatch icon at the bottom of the Swatches panel instead. Whenever you copy and paste objects that contain custom swatches or styles from one document to another, Illustrator will automatically add the swatches or styles to the new document's panels.

You can create three kinds of solid fills in Illustrator: process colors, global process colors, and spot colors.

No warning with Trash...

If you click the Trash icon in the Swatches panel, Illustrator does *not* warn you if you're about to delete colors used in the document; Illustrator will simply delete the swatches, converting any global colors and spot colors to non-global process colors. Instead, choose Select All Unused and then click the Trash icon.

Steven Gordon's "Kuler Colors" lesson, later in this chapter, combines Live Trace and Live Color

Accessing the libraries

The Swatch Libraries menu icon (lower left in the Swatch panel) opens Swatch libraries for specific color systems (such as Pantone). Or, choose Other Library to access saved colors from any document. See Illustrator Help for how to save your own libraries, and share them among other Adobe apps.

Where's Kuler?

See the RealWorldAICS5-kuler.pdf on the **WOW! DVD** (adapted from Mordy Golding's *Real World Adobe Illustrator CS5* book) for details on working with Adobe Kuler.

These three kinds of colors each appear differently in the Swatches panel, so they're easy to distinguish visually.

- **Process colors** are mixed from the CMYK colors used for printing with ink. Change the percentage of each ink to change the color, or choose a color from a swatch library, such as Pantone process uncoated.

- **Global process colors** are process colors with an added convenience: If you update the definition for a global process color, Illustrator updates that color throughout the document. Identify a global process color in the Swatches panel by the small triangle in the lower-right corner of the swatch in Thumbnail view, or by the Global Color icon in List view. Create a global process color by enabling the Global option (it's off by default) in either the New Swatch or Swatch Options dialog.

- **Spot colors** are used in print jobs that require a premixed ink or varnish, rather than a percentage of the four process colors. Specifying a spot color allows you to use colors that are outside of the CMYK gamut, or to achieve a more precise color match to the spot color you'll be using than CMYK allows. You can specify a color as a spot color in the New Swatch dialog from the Color Type menu, or you can choose a spot color from a Swatch library, such as the various Pantone libraries (from the Swatch panel's Swatch Libraries Menu icon choose Color Books). All spot colors are global, so they update automatically if you change the definition; and, when the Swatches panel is in Thumbnail view, they have a small triangle in the lower right corner, as well as a small dot or "spot." In List view, they're marked by the Spot Color icon.

Color groups and the Color Guide

The default document profiles that ship with Illustrator include several swatches and a couple of color groups to start using in your document. To create and save your own groups of colors, select multiple colors from the Swatches panel by Shift-clicking contiguous swatches, or by holding ⌘/Ctrl and clicking for non-contiguous selections. Another way to create a color group is to simply

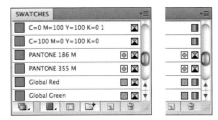

The Swatches panel, shown in list view for color swatches only; the top two swatches are process colors; the middle two are spot colors; and the last two are global colors (at left with the document in CMYK mode; at right the same colors with the document in RGB mode)

The same swatches as in the previous caption, this time shown in large thumbnail view; the left two are process; the middle two are spot (includes a white triangle with a "spot"); the right two are global (includes a simple white triangle)

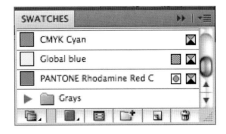

Shown in List view, the Swatches panel includes mini icons that indicate the type of color swatch; from top to bottom the list shows process color (CMYK Cyan), global color (Global blue), spot color (PANTONE), and color group (Grays)

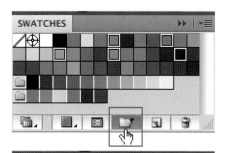

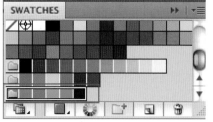

The New Color Group icon makes it possible to organize your Swatches panel by grouping colors that you choose in the Swatches panel or from selected objects; you also specify the name for the group

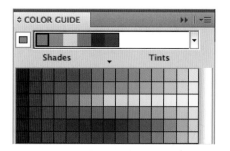

The Color Guide panel after changing the number of steps from the default 4 to 7, via Color Guide Options

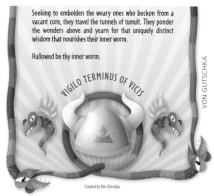

Seeking to embolden the weary ones who beckon from a vacant core, they travel the tunnels of tumult. They ponder the wonders above and yearn for that uniquely distinct wisdom that nourishes their inner worm.

Hallowed be thy inner worm.

VIGILO TERMINUS OF VICIS

VON GLITSCHKA

Created by Von Glitschka

Von Glitschka uses tons of gradients in his pair of fantastical "Loyal Order of the Wormwood" pieces, commissioned by Adobe and included with a PDF ReadMe on the **WOW! DVD**

select objects in your artwork that contain the colors you desire. Click the New Color Group icon to save your colors as a group.

The Color Guide panel helps you mix and match colors according to a color scheme of your choosing. After setting your "base color" (the upper left mini square), you can use the Color Guide panel to apply Harmony Rules (based on scientific color theory) to that color. Or you can select a group from the Swatches panel. You can then preview variations of those colors by choosing to display them (using the Color Guide's panel menu) according to value, temperature, or saturation. Drag a selected swatch (or swatches) to the Swatches panel to save it, or click on the "Save color group to Swatch panel" icon. Clicking on the "New swatch group" icon in the Swatches panel will also save your current harmony.

To access the Harmony Rules menu, click on the pop-up menu to the far right of the base color. Once a new harmony rule is selected, its colors fill the strip beside the base color. Alter how many variations of that color group you see by choosing Color Guide Options from the Color Guide panel's menu. You can change the number of steps in each color's gradient (up to 20) and the amount of variation between steps. Also in the panel's menu you will find the choice to view the colors as shades and tints, warm and cool, or vivid and mute. The Color Guide panel is one that can be resized wider and taller to accommodate the size of the grid. If you want to use your current color group as a base for even more color variations, click the Edit Colors icon at the bottom of the panel to enter the Edit Colors/Recolor Artwork dialog (for more about this icon see the "Live Color" section later in this chapter).

GRADIENTS

Gradients create seamless transitions from one color into another, often creating the appearance of realistic modeling. Illustrator can create either Radial or Linear gradients (with Elliptical gradients formed from Radial). After applying a gradient from the Swatches panel to a selected object or by clicking on the object with the Gradient tool, use the Gradient panel or the Gradient Annotator (View > Show Gradient Annotator) to edit the gradient. When the Gradient tool is active *and* Show Gradient Annotator is enabled, the Gradient Annotator appears as a bar across the gradient on the selected item.

To modify a gradient using the Gradient Annotator, add and/or move the stops along the lower edge of the Annotator. Adjust the blend between the color stops by sliding the diamond shapes along the top of the Annotator. To reposition the start of a gradient, grab and drag the circular endpoint. To resize a gradient, grab and drag the arrow endpoint. To rotate a gradient, move your cursor slightly beyond the arrow end of the Gradient Annotator, then grab and drag the Rotate icon. When you hover your Gradient tool cursor over a radial gradient, its circumference appears as a dashed line and four circles, and you can resize the circumference by dragging one of the circles. With a radial gradient you can also rotate from the circular endpoint, or from anywhere on the dotted circumference. To make a radial gradient elliptical, grab and drag the solid black circle, or enter a value other than 100% into the Aspect Ratio field in the Gradient panel.

When you double-click on a stop on the Gradient Annotator, a special panel with two icons on the left side lets you pick whether this panel behaves like the Swatches or the Color panel. This panel also includes an Opacity field with slider. When you adjust a stop's opacity to be less than 100%, a small rectangle appears hanging from the stop. The Location field and slider numerically relocate the precise position of a selected stop in relation to the beginning of a gradient. Finally, when the panel is another version of the Color panel, its menu allows you to switch between color modes.

The Gradient panel includes some additional features. The Gradient Fill pop-up menu in the top left corner of the panel allows you to choose from or save to a library of gradients. The "Reverse Gradient" toggle allows you to reverse your gradient with a single click. The panel also

Extra big gradient panel

A special feature of the Gradient panel is that you can make it extra tall and wide, and the Gradient slider itself will increase in size, making it much easier to design complex gradients.

Adding color to your gradient

- Double-click the color stop on the Gradient Annotator bar, or slider bar in the Gradient panel, and select a color from the Swatches or Color panels.
- Drag a swatch from the Color or Swatches panel to the Gradient slider until you see a vertical line indicating where the new color stop will be added.
- If the fill is a solid color, you can drag color from the Fill icon at the bottom of the Toolbox.
- Hold down the Option/Alt key to drag a copy of a color stop.
- Option-drag/Alt-drag one stop over another to *swap* colors.
- Click just beneath the Gradient Annotator bar or slider of a gradient where the stops are to add a new stop; a small "+" sign appears next to your cursor when you are in the correct location for adding a new stop.

How long can a gradient be?

Click and drag with the Gradient tool anywhere in your image window; you don't need to stay within the objects themselves.

Aaron McGarry created a custom radial gradient for the flame in his candle illustration

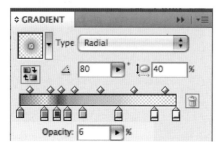

The Gradient panel for the candle flame above; color stops with reduced opacity are indicated by the additional rectangle below the stop, and the opacity of the selected color stop is displayed in the field below the slider.

A detail of the candle flame above showing the gradient annotator on the flame with color stops; the flame has an aspect ratio of 40%, an angle of 80° and various opacity settings for each color stop so that the wick is partially visible through portions of the flame

Missing Gradient Annotator?

If you don't see the Gradient Annotator, then try using the toggle View > Show Gradient Annotator (⌘-Option-G/Ctrl-Alt-G). If you apply one gradient to multiple objects, however, the Annotator won't reliably appear.

has fields for the numerical control of angle and aspect ratio. As with the Gradient Annotator, you can double-click a stop to access the special version of the Swatches or Color panel. Or, simply click on a stop to adjust the opacity or location.

You can create a unified blend by clicking and dragging with the Gradient tool across multiple selected objects. Although you can't apply a gradient to a stroke, you can create the illusion of a gradient within a stroke by first converting the stroke to a filled object (Object > Path > Outline Stroke).

You can save a gradient to the Swatches panel by dragging it from the Gradient panel or clicking the New Swatch icon in the Swatches panel, which gives you a chance to name it. Access additional pre-made gradients from the Swatch Libraries menu icon at the bottom left of the Swatches panel (or by choosing Window > Swatch Libraries > Gradients). Use the Show Swatch Kinds menu icon to show only gradient swatches.

Note: *Aspect ratio and angle information are not saved with gradient swatches. However, if you save your gradient swatch as a graphic style, that information is saved with it.*

GRADIENT MESH

A *gradient mesh object* is an object on which multiple colors can flow in different directions, with smooth transitions between the *mesh points*. You can transform a solid or gradient-filled object into mesh (you can't transform compound paths into mesh). Once transformed, the object will always be a mesh object, so be certain that you work with a copy of the original if it's difficult to re-create.

Transform solid filled objects into gradient mesh objects either by choosing Object > Create Gradient Mesh (so you can specify details on the mesh construction) or by clicking on the object with the Mesh tool, which manually places mesh lines. One way to get a head start in creating a mesh object is to transform a gradient-filled object into a mesh object: select Object > Expand and enable the Gradient Mesh option.

Depending on where you click with the Mesh tool within a mesh object, you'll add points (or lines and points) to the mesh. Reshape the mesh with the Direct Selection tool, using the anchors and their handles as with any ordinary path. Select individual points, groups of points, or patches within the mesh using the Direct Selection tool, the Lasso tool, or the Mesh tool, in order to color or delete them. If the Mesh tool is selected, holding down the Option/Alt key and clicking on a mesh point deletes it. You can sample a color with the Eyedropper and either immediately have it apply to all selected areas of the mesh object, or, with the mesh object completely deselected, use the Option/Alt key to click with the Eyedropper tool on a mesh point or space between points. Adding color to a patch instead of a single point spreads the color to all surrounding points. When adding a new mesh point, the color currently selected in the Swatches panel will be applied to the new point. If you want the new mesh point to remain the color currently applied to the mesh object, hold down the Shift key while adding a new point.

To further modify the shape your gradient mesh takes, you can use any of the Distort tools, such as Warp or Pucker, to reshape it. You don't even have to select points first. Hover over the mesh to highlight it; the size of your distorting tool will determine how many mesh points and patches get distorted at the same time.

You can assign transparency to a gradient mesh object as you can to other vector objects. Simply select either the mesh points or patches you want and use either the Appearance panel (click on <u>Opacity</u>), or the Transparency panel, to reduce the Opacity below 100%. Saving a gradient mesh object with transparency in an AI format earlier than CS5, or to EPS or PDF, results in the transparency becoming converted to an Opacity mask, instead.
Hint: *Instead of applying a mesh to a complex path, try to first create the mesh from a simpler path outline, then mask the mesh with the more complex path. Stack simple objects with gradient mesh applied to them to construct a more complex object.*

Ann Paidrick builds gradient mesh objects in the "Transparent Mesh" lesson later in this chapter

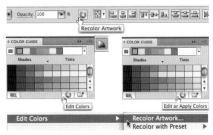

Different ways to enter the Recolor Artwork/Edit Colors dialog: from the Control panel (top); from the Color Guide panel (center), via the menu Edit >Edit Colors >Recolor Artwork

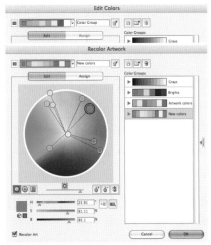

The Edit Colors/Recolor Artwork dialog

LIVE COLOR

Live Color is not just a single panel or feature. Instead, it's an interactive color exploration environment comprised of various interfaces and tools that work together. This chapter and its lessons should help you become more comfortable with Live Color, and add Live Color features and functions to your artistic arsenal.

The heart of Live Color is a dialog that is alternately, and somewhat confusingly, labeled either Edit Colors or Recolor Artwork. The key to how this "heart of Live Color" dialog changes title (and functions you can access from within the dialog) is that the title is different depending on how you enter it.

If you have nothing selected, you can enter a mode called Edit Colors. You can access this mode by clicking the Edit Colors icon at the bottom of the Color Guide panel. Once you're in the Edit Colors dialog, you'll be in Edit mode, which means that you can mix and store col-ors (see the following section for specific instructions on how to do this). You'll see a tab next to the word "Edit" titled "Assign," but it will be grayed out; since you don't have any objects selected, you can't access this tab. You can only assign colors to selected objects.

If, however, you have artwork selected, this dialog will now be titled "Recolor Artwork" and you will have access to the Assign tab of the dialog, as well as Edit mode. As long as your selection contains at least two colors, you'll see the Recolor Artwork icon in the Control panel. Another option is the icon at the bottom of the Color Guide panel mentioned above; note, though, that when artwork is selected this icon will now be called "Edit or Apply Colors." In the Swatches panel, with a color group selected, you can click the Edit or Apply Color Group icon. A final way into this dialog is Edit >Edit Colors > Recolor Artwork.

The Recoloring Artwork (and Editing Color) dialogs

After selecting the object(s) you want to recolor, click the Recolor Artwork button in the Control panel to open the

Recolor Artwork dialog; the colors from your selected art should still be all in order, and the selection edges will automatically be hidden. If you enter the Recolor Artwork dialog via Color Guide's Edit or Apply Colors icon, your image will initially appear with the color group in that panel assigned to your artwork. If that's not what you intended, click the "Get colors from selected art" icon to reload the original colors into your artwork. In fact, any time you want to quickly return to your original colors without canceling the dialog, simply click again on the "Get colors from selected art" icon.

Live Color shows a base color and active colors at the top, with a pop-up menu showing several of Adobe's Harmony Rules, just as the Color Guide panel does. You can drag colors within the Active Colors field to reorder them, and your selected object(s) will be recolored according to their new positions. To change the base color, simply select another color from among the active colors.

The Color Groups section lists any color groups you saved in your Swatches panel before you entered the Recolor Artwork/Edit Colors dialog, as well as any color groups you created during this work session by clicking on the New Color Groups icon. Rename a color group by double-clicking on its name and entering a new one in the pop-up dialog. Clicking on any color group loads those colors into your artwork. Deleting and creating new color groups in the Recolor Artwork dialog will also delete and add color groups in your Swatches panel, so don't click the Trash icon unless you're positive you want to delete that color group from your document entirely. If you create color groups you want to save during a work session, but don't want to apply the changes to your artwork, disable the Recolor Art checkbox and click OK. If you click Cancel instead, all the work you did creating (or deleting) new color groups will be deleted.

The two main tabs are Edit and Assign (remember, Assign is only available with an active selection). The Assign tab displays horizontal color bars, with each long bar representing one of the colors in the artwork currently

Active Colors appear in the upper-left field of the Edit Colors/Recolor Artwork dialog; you can rename and create new Color Groups here; left icon is "Set current color as the base color," right icon is "Get colors from selected art"

The center-right section of the Edit Colors/Recolor Artwork dialog has more powerful mini icons; left icon is "New Color Group," center icon is "Save changes to color group," and right icon is "Delete Color Group"

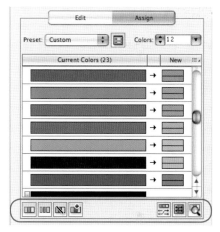

In Assign mode, these icons (circled) allow for merging, separating, excluding, and adding new color rows; you can also randomly change color order, saturation, and brightness, as well as find a particular color in your artwork

Special color sets

If your work requires that you use a very specific set of colors, such as team colors or specific "designer" hues for a season, you'll want to first create and save a Color Group (or groups) in the Swatches panel. Then, when you open Live Color, your Color Groups will be in the storage area, ready to recolor your artwork.

The power of Recolor Artwork

One of the many powerful capabilities of the Live Color toolset is the ability to globally change the colors of almost any kind of colored object in your Illustrator artwork. Colors in envelopes, meshes, symbols, brushes, patterns, raster effects (but not RGB/CMYK raster images), and in multiple fill and stroke objects can all be easily re-colored with the Recolor Artwork dialog! —*Jean-Claude Tremblay*

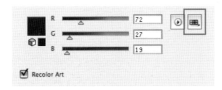

In Edit or Assign mode, clicking the miniature grid-like icon will present a pop-up menu of swatch libraries and the "Limits the color group to colors in a swatch library" icon

The Color Reduction Options icon (under the Assign tab in Recolor Artwork)

The Color Reduction Options icon opens this dialog

selected. To their right is an arrow pointing to a smaller color swatch that's initially the same color as the larger bar. This small swatch is where you can load or mix a replacement color. To protect a color from change, click on the arrow to turn it into a straight bar. You can also drag and drop colors within this area, and access context-sensitive menus.

The Edit tab contains a color wheel with markers representing the colors in the selected artwork. Depending on whether the Lock icon is enabled or disabled, you can move the markers around on the color wheel individually (unlocked) or in unison (locked) to adjust the color in your art. You can also click the display icons to select a segmented wheel or a bar view. In addition to dragging markers on the color wheel, you can use the sliders and controls just below the color wheel to adjust the various aspects of color (hue, saturation, and value). You can work in the standard color modes, or you can choose Global Adjust to affect all colors at once. As you adjust individual colors with the sliders, notice that the color marker you selected moves on the color wheel as you move a slider.

On either the Assign or Edit tabs, you can choose to limit colors to a swatch library such as a Pantone library using the "Limits the color group to colors in a swatch library" icon. On the Assign tab, you have a Preset list and a Color Reduction Options icon for restricting the colors that can be reassigned. When you restrict your colors to a swatch library, the color wheel or bar on the Edit tab displays only the library's colors, while Assign mode will replace all your original colors with those from the library that it thinks are the closest match.

The Presets on the Assign tab also help you limit the number of colors in your palette to 1, 2, or 3. This makes Live Color a huge timesaver when you need to reduce the number of colors used in a full-color project so it can be printed with spot colors, or even need to reduce a 3-color spot color job to 1 or 2. Use the Color Reduction Options to further determine how tints, shades, and neutrals are handled when colors get reassigned.

Ann Paidrick

After hours of intricately creating gradient mesh-based artwork, Ann Paidrick can quickly and easily change colors using Live Color. Because you can't recover colors once you've changed them in Live Color, each time she wants to create a variant of her gold ribbon, she starts by duplicating the original artboard (in the Artboards panel she drags the gold ribbon artboard to the New Artboard icon). Selecting the new ribbon objects, she clicks the Edit Colors icon in the Control panel. Clicking on the Edit mode tab, she enables the Lock icon, then drags the Base Color circle in the color wheel (the largest circle) until she finds a color shift she likes, and clicks OK. Saving this file, she creates the next color variation from another copy of the original.

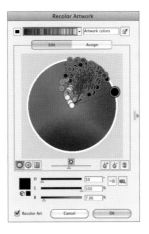

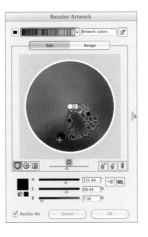

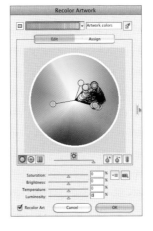

Custom Coloring

Creating Custom Colors & Color Groups

Overview: *Create an illustration; create custom swatches; create a custom color group from custom swatches; save a swatch library.*

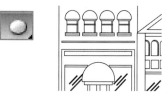

Creating an icon with the Rectangle tool, Ellipse tool, and Pencil tool

Filling icon paths with default swatches from the Swatches panel

Selecting the correct color mode from the Color panel's pop-up menu

PUTNAM

Ryan Putnam designs many illustrations he uses as icons in stock art and client projects. Creating custom swatches is an integral step in creating compelling and consistent icon illustrations. Illustrator comes with some great default color swatches, but they are not suited for most of Putnam's icon illustrations. Moreover, by creating a custom color group, Putnam can easily apply his custom swatches to other related illustrations.

1 Creating an icon illustration. To create the "Destination" icon, Putnam used the Rectangle tool, Ellipse tool, and Pencil tool. Putnam first created the buildings of the icon with varying sizes of rectangles with the Rectangle tool. He then used the Ellipse tool to create windows and awnings for the buildings. Next, he used the Pencil tool to draw the mountains. To distinguish the objects from each other, Putnam filled the building and mountain paths with default swatches from the Swatches panel by selecting each object and clicking the desired swatch.

2 Creating custom swatches. After Putnam roughed out the basic color schemes for his illustration, he then began to customize a more natural set of colors. First, he made sure the Color panel was set to the same color mode as his Document Color Mode. Since Putnam is creating his icon for a website and his Document Color Mode is RGB, from the Color panel pop-up menu he selected RGB. Putnam then selected an object and mixed the desired color with the sliders in the Color panel. Next, he opened the Swatches panel and clicked the New Swatch icon in the bottom of the panel. In the Swatch Options dialog he then named the swatch and clicked OK. Alternatively, you can choose Create New Swatch from the Color panel pop-up menu. Yet another option is to drag the mixed color directly to the Swatches panel, though by doing so, you won't get Swatch Options and the opportunity to name the swatch. Putnam then repeated these steps for every custom color he wanted to create.

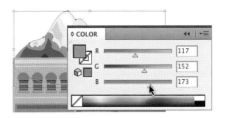
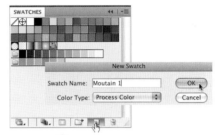

Mixing colors with the color sliders from the Color panel

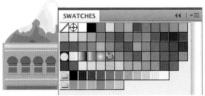

3 Creating a new color group. After creating his custom swatches, Putnam wanted to organize his custom swatches so he could easily apply them to other related illustrations and icons. To do this, he created a custom color group. He selected the desired swatches in the Swatches panel by Shift-clicking to select contiguous swatches, or by holding ⌘/Ctrl and clicking for non-contiguous selections. Then he clicked the New Color Group icon, where he was given the option to name his color group. The new color group was then saved for Putnam and ready for use.

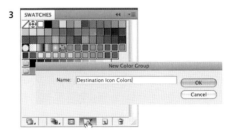

Saving custom swatches in the Swatches panel by clicking the New Swatch icon

To use his custom color group in other documents, Putnam needed to save the color group as a custom swatch library. First, he selected all the swatches he wanted to delete from his custom color group and clicked the Delete Swatch icon in the Swatches panel. Putnam then clicked the Swatch Libraries menu icon at the lower left of the Swatches panel and chose Save Swatches. This saved Putnam's swatch library in the User Defined folder in the Adobe Illustrator CS5 Swatches folder (inside the computer user folder). Now whenever he needs the swatch library in other documents, Putnam clicks the Swatch Libraries menu icon, chooses User Defined, and selects his defined library.

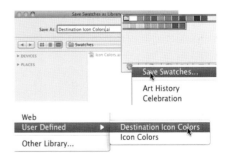

Saving custom swatches as a new color group in the Swatches panel

Opening custom color group in the Swatches panel

Color Guidance

Inspiration from the Color Guide Panel

Advanced Technique

Overview: *Set up the Color Guide panel to generate color groups; create and save color groups based on harmonies in the Color Guide panel; apply, modify, and save color groups from within Live Color.*

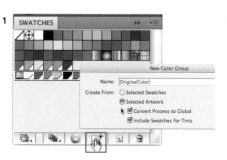

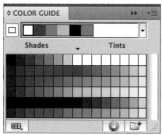

Saving original artwork colors as a color group in the Swatches panel, which automatically places a selected color group with variations into the Color Guide panel

In this "Day at the Circus" poster (created for a children's fundraising event), illustrator Hugh Whyte used a very specific palette of colors. Using Illustrator's Color Guide panel, it's simple to generate and save color groups of new palettes based on existing colors. Live Color allows you to apply your new color groups to an existing design, and then continue to experiment with how colors are applied.

1 Setting up the Color Guide panel to base new color versions on the original. For your first attempt, use the Circus image on the **WOW! DVD**, or one that has a limited number of colors, to avoid having too many swatches in your original artwork to handle easily. Since you'll be working with both your Swatches and Color Guide panels, drag them away from the dock to float free for easy viewing. Select the artwork and, in the Swatches panel, click on the New Color Group icon in order to have the colors that are currently in your artwork saved as a group to work with in the Color Guide panel. When the New Color Group dialog opens, keep the default settings and rename this color group "Original Color." Deselect your artwork. In order to base your color group creations on your original color relationships, click on the small folder icon beside your color group swatches to select the entire group so that it shows up in the Color Guide panel.

2 Creating color groups in the Color Guide panel and saving them to the Swatches panel. Next, you're going to create a variety of color groups in the Color Guide panel. Notice that your original artwork colors run down the middle of the Color Guide's panel of swatches (under the small black triangle). To the right are lighter versions of these colors (tints), and to the left are darker versions (shades). Select the top color in the third row from the right, then Shift-click to select the entire row vertically (⌘-click/Ctrl-click for non-contiguous colors). Click on the Save to Swatches panel icon. Now change the relationship between the colors by clicking on the Color Guide's pop-up menu and choosing Show Warm/Cool. Again select the third vertical row from the right and save this new cooler color group to the Swatches panel. Select the group by clicking on its folder icon, select Color Group Options from the Swatches panel pop-up menu, and rename it something like "Cooler Original" by typing a new name in the dialog. Select this group to place it in the Color Guide panel as the new base group for the Harmony Rules. (For the rest of this lesson, you'll create color groups based on this base group. However, you can click on any swatch, then click on the "Set base color to the current color icon" on the Color Guide panel to change the current color group; changing the base color will affect all of the Harmony Rules that are based on it.)

Click on the Color Guide arrow to the right of your current colors to make another color group, choosing one of the Harmony Rules, such as the Left Complement shown here. Save and rename that group "Left Complement from Cooler." Be aware that if you create new color groups with fewer swatches than your original artwork, you will be reducing the color variation in your artwork. A Harmony Rule contains no more than five swatches, but the panel contains variations based on those five swatches. You can drag any swatch from either the Color Guide panel or Swatches panel into any saved color group in the Swatches panel. You can also drag colors out of a color group in the Swatches panel.

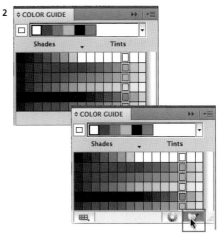

Selecting a tint of all the original colors and saving the new color group to the Swatches panel

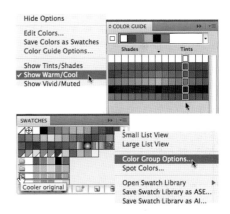

Changing the view of swatches in the Color Guide panel from the menu, selecting, saving, and renaming a new color group

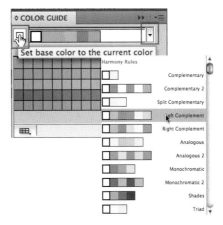

Setting a base color for a Harmony Rule and selecting a new Harmony Rule from the Color Guide list box

Selecting a color group with its folder icon so no color is actually selected or applied, and entering Live Color using the Edit or Apply Color Group icon

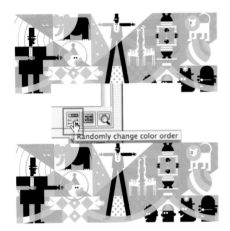

Using "Randomly change color order" icon on the Assign tab

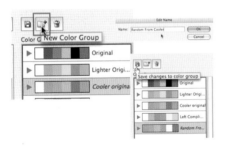

Saving a new color group, or saving changes to an existing color group

Random assignment of saturation and brightness to the pastel color group

3 Applying color groups and creating new ones using Live Color. To protect your original work, choose File > Save As and give your file a new name. (Whenever you create a version you like, repeat saving the file with another file name to protect what you've already created.) Select your artwork and then select the Cooler Original color group by clicking on the folder icon next to it. If you accidentally click on a swatch instead of the color group folder icon, and that color is applied to your artwork, choose Undo. You want to click only on the folder icon so a border shows up around your swatch group, but no color is selected.

Click on the Edit or Apply Color Group icon to enter Live Color. By default, Black and White are protected from being changed by any of the colors in your selected color group. The Cooler Original swatches replace the remaining colors with a random selection of the group's swatches. If you want to try a new version, click on the Assign tab and then on the "Randomly change color order" icon. This command assigns any of the swatches from the Color Group to any of the color bars. You can keep clicking until you see a combination you like, but be sure to do this carefully, because there is no Undo in Live Color, so there's no way to return to a combination you liked. Therefore, every time you find a combination that appeals to you, click on the Save New Color Group icon and save that combination as a new color group. Double-click on the name to rename it. Be careful not to click on the "Save changes to color group" icon (the floppy disk), unless you want to overwrite the color group you had selected and that now has its name in italics. If you don't like the direction your changes are headed, click back on a saved color group you liked for a fresh start at generating different color versions. Whenever you find a version you want to apply, click OK and save it as a new file name. If you want to save your new color groups without changing the art, disable Recolor Art or click on "Get colors from selected art," and then click OK.

Brenda Sutherland

Brenda Sutherland created the original logo for a micro-brewery. With the advent of Live Color, she realized she could easily create color variations to accompany the different micro-brews. Because the original coloring is very complex, she divided the logo into three sections—the text portion, the center of the logo, and the outer circle. The inner circle alone has two gradient fills and multiple strokes, which only Live Color can handle easily. She selected the Text layer and saved the artwork colors to the Swatches panel. She repeated this for both the center and outer circles. Sutherland placed copies of the logo on their own layers. She selected just the outer circle on one layer and opened the Recolor Artwork dialog. There she chose the Edit tab and moved the markers on the smooth color wheel until she found a scheme she liked. She saved the colors as a new color group, then

clicked OK to apply the color scheme and return to the main image. Sutherland repeated this process for the other two areas in the logo, and again to create two more color schemes.

Scripting Colors

Tools for Adding and Editing Colors

Overview: *Use Premedia Systems' WOW! Artwork Colorizer script to automatically fill shapes with color; browse and download color themes with the Kuler panel; assign and edit a color group with the Recolor Artwork dialog.*

1

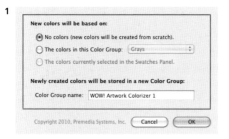

The Premedia Systems' script dialog

City shapes automatically filled with different colors by the Premedia Systems' script

2

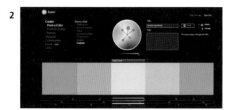

Part of the Kuler webpage showing the color theme Gordon created

Coloring adjacent areas is a common task in making maps—you click each area and fill it with a color. But when there are dozens of areas, special tools can help you perform this task quickly and effectively. For this map of Seattle Southside, Steven Gordon used Premedia Systems' (www.premediasystems.com) WOW! Artwork Colorizer script (included on the **WOW! DVD**) and Illustrator's Kuler and Live Color panels to fill cities with distinctive colors.

1 Creating the map areas and using a script to fill them with different colors. Gordon started the map by importing GIS data using Avenza MAPublisher plug-ins. Once imported, the data produced a layer with 37 cities, each with a black stroke and no fill. You can fill areas with different colors automatically using Premedia Systems' WOW! Artwork Colorizer script (this script and its installation instructions, are on the **WOW! DVD**; install the script before starting or restarting Illustrator). To fill the areas using the script, chose File >Scripts. From the script's dialog, leave the default option of No Colors (new colors will be created from scratch) selected and click OK. This will make the script fill your shapes with colors automatically.

2 Creating a color group using Kuler. Gordon wanted to reduce the 37 unique colors created by the script to a handful of swatches that could be shared among the cities. He decided to tap into the vast collection of color groups (or "themes") from Adobe's online Kuler application. You can access Kuler by opening the Kuler panel (Window > Extensions > Kuler). If you don't find a satisfactory theme navigating the panel, go to http://kuler.adobe.com and create your own, as Gordon did. If you create a theme, give it a unique title, select Public, and click Save.

3 Importing a Kuler theme as a color group and editing its colors. With his color theme, "Seattle Southside," available on the Kuler website, Gordon added it to the Swatches panel using the Kuler panel. To do this, browse themes in the Kuler panel or find one (including one you've created) by typing its name in the Search field. With the theme selected, click the "Add selected theme to swatches" icon. Now your theme is available as a color group in the Swatches panel.

Gordon applied the new color group by selecting all the cities and then double-clicking on the color group's folder icon in the Swatches panel to display the Recolor Artwork dialog. When the dialog displayed, it automatically recolored his selected artwork using the color group he double-clicked. Gordon wanted to fill the cities with the exact colors in his group and avoid using tints. You can limit colors by clicking the arrow on the right of any of the color rows to bring up the New Color pop-up menu and then choosing Exact.

As you work, you may wish to edit your colors. Gordon wanted to lighten the colors in his group so they wouldn't interfere with the legibility of symbols and small type. To change the colors in your artwork, click on the Edit tab in the Recolor Artwork dialog. Lighten or darken colors by moving all of the circular color icons together (with harmony colors linked) or individually (with harmony colors unlinked) toward or away from the center. You can add another color to the group by clicking the Add color tool. When you're done editing the colors, you can save the changes to your group or save them as a new color group. Finally, click OK to exit the Recolor Artwork dialog and return to your artwork.

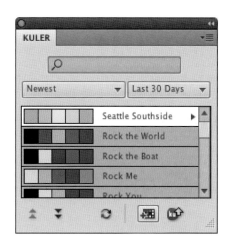

The Kuler panel with the color theme selected

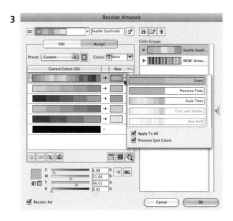

The Assign tab of the Recolor Artwork dialog with the New Color pop-up arrow icon and menu

The Edit tab of the Recolor Artwork dialog with the edited color group saved as a new group and the new group renamed

Kuler Colors

Using Kuler, Live Trace, & Live Color

Overview: *Trace a photograph with Live Trace; recolor artwork using a downloaded Kuler color theme; recolor color with Live Color; create and upload a color group; use a photograph to add detail; use artwork to mask a photograph; create a flare.*

How can you enhance a photograph of a beautiful flower? Steven Gordon sought the answer with Illustrator's Live Trace and Live Color tools—and a trip to Adobe's Kuler website—in making this vibrant advertisement for a botanical garden.

1

The original photograph of the calendula

The Tracing Options dialog

1 Tracing a photograph, expanding the tracing, and moving artwork to new layers. Gordon began by placing a photograph of a calendula flower in Illustrator. Because he wanted to simplify the photograph, Gordon decided to posterize the image by tracing it. To do this, he chose Objects > Live Trace > Tracing Options. In the Tracing Options dialog, he chose the preset "Color 6" from the Preset menu, and then modified the settings by changing Max Colors to 5. Knowing that he would need to select and manipulate some of the traced artwork later, he expanded the trace (Object > Live Trace > Expand) and ungrouped the artwork. Then he added two layers in the Layers panel, one for the green shapes and the other for the orange shapes. He selected and moved all of the green and orange shapes to their respective layers.

2 Browsing Kuler, downloading a color group, and recoloring the traced artwork. After reviewing the traced artwork, Gordon decided to make the traced green leaves and stems more vivid. For inspiration, he opened the Kuler panel (Window > Extensions > Kuler) and browsed the color themes until he found one with a variety of bright greens. Instead of recreating its colors using the Color panel, he downloaded the theme to the Swatches

The traced artwork

panel as a color group by clicking the Kuler panel's "Add selected theme to swatches" icon. Next he selected all of the green artwork and double-clicked on the color group he had just downloaded. In the Assign panel of the Recolor Artwork dialog, Gordon needed to assign three of the color group's five colors to the three greens that had been produced by Live Trace. With Recolor Art enabled he then clicked the "Randomly change color order" icon several times until the green shapes in the illustration looked the way he liked, then clicked OK.

To preserve the traced artwork's colors, Gordon selected all of the green and orange artwork and clicked the Swatch panel's New Color Group icon. After naming the group, he uploaded the group as a Kuler theme that others could access by clicking the Kuler panel's "Upload from Swatch panel to Kuler community" icon.

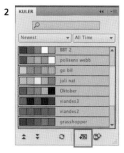

The Kuler panel with the "Download selected theme to swatches" icon highlighted

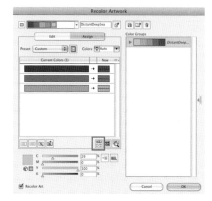

The Recolor Artwork dialog with the "Randomly change color order" icon highlighted

3 Adding detail, brightening the flower center, and creating and uploading a color group. With the traced artwork colored, Gordon wanted to bring some of the original photograph's detail back into the illustration. He created a layer above the traced artwork and placed a copy of the photograph. Selecting the photograph, he opened the Transparency panel and set opacity to 50% and the blending mode to Hard Light.

Because the focal point of the illustration was the flower's center, Gordon wanted to employ the photograph's full color and detail. He created a new layer and placed another copy of the original photograph on it. Then, from the layer with the traced green shapes, he clicked the Lasso tool and selected the green center shapes. He copied and pasted them in place and turned them into a compound path (Object > Compound Path > Make). After moving the compound path to the layer with the photograph, Gordon selected both and chose Object > Clipping Mask > Make. Finally, he brightened the center by drawing a flare with the Flare tool, opened the Transparency panel and changed the flare's blending mode to Soft Light. He finished by adding type to the illustration.

The New Color Group dialog

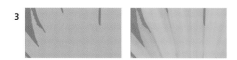

On the left, the flower petals after tracing; on the right, the flower petals overlaid with the photograph set to 50% opacity and Hard Light

At left, the traced flower objects; at right, the photograph masked by the compound path

Unified Gradients

Controlling Fills with the Gradient Annotator

Overview: *Fill objects with gradients; use the Gradient tool with the Gradient Annotator to adjust fill length and angle; unify fills across multiple objects with the Gradient tool and Gradient panel.*

JOLY

1

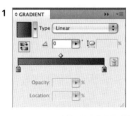

Working with the Gradient panel, Gradient tool, and Gradient Annotator

2

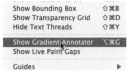

A single click with the Gradient tool on a selected object fills the object with either the default or last-used gradient swatch, and displays the Gradient Annotator, if selected in the View menu (be sure you don't click and drag when applying for the first time—you can click-drag to adjust the gradient later)

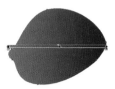

Using the Gradient Annotator to shorten the length of the gradient and to rotate the angle when the Rotate icon appeared

With the advent of the Gradient Annotator in conjunction with the Gradient tool, you can apply and customize gradients in most instances without needing to keep the Gradient panel open. In this illustration, Dave Joly only needed the Gradient panel to switch between Linear and Radial gradients, and to work with creating unified gradients. To control the colors, length, and angle of gradients for individual objects, Joly adjusted each gradient with the Gradient Annotator. He unified gradients across multiple objects using the Gradient tool and Gradient panel.

1 Applying gradients. To apply a gradient to a single object, such as the fish's body, Joly first made sure that the Gradient Annotator toggle was visible (if View >Show Gradient Annotator is available, choose it). Next he selected an object and the Gradient tool, and then clicked once on the object to fill it with either the document's default gradient (for the first object) or with the last gradient used in the document.

2 Editing single objects with the Gradient Annotator. Joly was able to edit a gradient almost exclusively using the Gradient Annotator. With the Annotator, he could modify the gradient length, angle, and colors on the object itself. He only needed to turn to the Gradient panel to choose a different existing gradient swatch, switch the current gradient between linear and radial gradient in Type, or reverse the gradient. Joly began his edits by moving his cursor just beyond the arrow endpoint of the Gradient Annotator. When his cursor turned into the Rotate icon, he dragged to interactively set the angle he wanted the gradient to take. With his cursor directly on top of the arrow end, he click-dragged to lengthen or shorten the gradient, and he dragged on the large circle at the other end to move the whole gradient to another position over the object. To adjust the colors, Joly double-clicked on a color stop along the Annotator, which gave him immediate access to proxies for both the Swatches and the Color panels, and a subset of the Gradient panel, as well. After choosing a suitable color, he dragged the stops on the Annotator to position the color blends more precisely, and on the gradient sliders to adjust their blend.

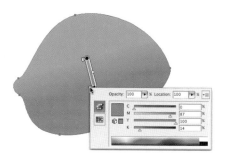

Changing the gradient colors by double-clicking on the Gradient Annotator color stops to pop up both the Color and Swatch panel proxies

3 Unifying gradients across multiple objects. Unifying gradients across multiple objects is a bit trickier with the Gradient Annotator involved. Joly first created the gradient swatch he would need—for the tail fins, for example. Next he selected all the objects and clicked on the swatch in the Swatches panel to apply it. This automatically created a new Gradient Annotator for every object, but Joly wanted to unify the gradients under just *one* Annotator. Still using the Gradient tool with the Gradient Annotator visible, Joly dragged across all the objects. This now appeared to unify the multiple gradients under one Annotator, but it's then only possible to change the length or position of the unifying gradient. Instead, while adjusting one gradient that had been unified across multiple objects, Joly discovered the Gradient Annotator wasn't providing reliable feedback or controls. Therefore, when working with one unified gradient applied to multiple objects, instead of relying on the Gradient Annotator, he would ignore or hide the Annotator (Window > Hide Gradient Annotator). Joly simply used a combination of the Gradient tool (to make length and angle adjustments to the unified gradient) and the Gradient panel itself (for numeric precision, adjustments to color stops, and opacity).

3

After first selecting all objects and applying a gradient tool to them, but before unifying them

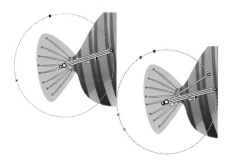

Unified gradients sometimes appear to retain the function of the Gradient Annotator, but if you attempt to edit angles or colors with the Gradient Annotator, you'll discover you aren't actually editing a single gradient

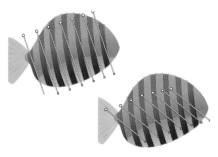

By using only the Gradient panel and/or the Gradient tool to edit unified gradients, you ensure that all changes will be made in unison

Folding Gradients

Simulating Paper Folds with Gradients

Overview: *Create a rectangle and fill with the default gradient; reverse the gradient; add and recolor color stops; reposition stops and midpoints in the Location field; change blending mode and transparency; add shadows underneath the artwork.*

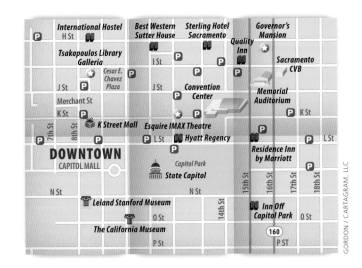

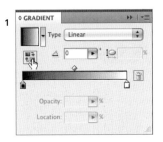

The Gradient panel after selecting the Reverse Gradient icon

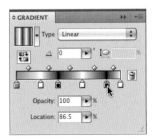

The Gradient panel after adding four new color stops and changing the leftmost color stop to gray

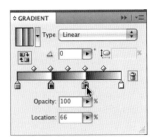

The Gradient with the four color stops positioned using the Location field for each color stop

When Steven Gordon redesigned Cartagram's website, he needed an image that suggested an unfolded paper map. Instead of photographing a printed map, which would have added time and resources, he turned to Illustrator's gradients, transparency, and effects to quickly and easily create the illusion of paper folds and shadows.

1 Making the gradient. Gordon started with a map he had created in Illustrator for the Sacramento Convention and Visitors Bureau. After creating a layer above the map's artwork layers, he drew a rectangle that covered the map and then opened the Gradient panel and clicked on the default black-to-white gradient preview icon in the panel. To make the two vertical folds, he reversed the default gradient by clicking the Reverse Gradient icon. Next, he clicked below the gradient bar four times to create four new color stops that would become the two folds. Selecting the leftmost of the color stops, Gordon filled the stop with gray (50% black). Working to the right, he selected the next color stop and filled it with white, filled the next with black, the next with white, and the next with black. He left the rightmost color stop filled with white.

To create the look of a neatly creased fold, white and black color stops must be positioned on top of each other. Gordon selected the leftmost of the white color stops and entered 33.33% in the Gradient panel's Location field.

Then he entered 33% in the Location field of the black stop to its right. For the next pair of white and black stops, he entered 66% for each stop.

Adjusting the midpoints between each dark color stop and the next white stop to its right controls the fade of the color and how deep the fold appears. Gordon selected each of these midpoints and moved it to the left to shorten the spread of the gray or black color.

To create the horizontal fold, Gordon used Copy and Paste in Front (⌘-F/Ctrl-F) to duplicate the gradient rectangle. Then he entered 90° in the Gradient panel's Angle field, deleted one pair of white and black color stops and repositioned the remaining color stops.

2 **Blending the gradients with transparency.** To simulate the shadows and highlights from folds on a paper map, Gordon modified the transparency of the gradients that overlaid the map artwork. He selected the two rectangles with gradients, opened the Transparency panel and changed the Opacity value (Gordon chose 25%) and then set the Blending Mode to Multiply. (Choosing Multiply instead of the default Normal mode prevents the white in the gradient from lightening the artwork below it.)

3 **Adding shadows underneath the map.** To complete the look of folded paper resting on a surface, Gordon added gently rounded shadows beneath the map. On a layer below the map artwork, he drew a rectangle at the same size as a vertical map fold. Then he duplicated it twice and centered each of the three rectangles below a map fold. He selected the three rectangles, and from the Effects menu chose Stylize > Round Corners. In the Round Corners dialog, he entered 0.08 inches in the Radius field to gently round the corners of each shape. With the three rectangles still selected, Gordon chose Effect > Stylize > Outer Glow. In the Outer Glow dialog, he changed the Opacity to 50% and the Blur to 0.05 inches to make the glows look like soft shadows underneath the paper folds.

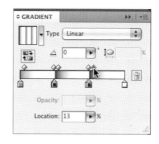

Gradient with the midpoints positioned for the gray color stop and the two black color stops

The Transparency panel with the Blending Mode of Multiply selected and the Opacity value changed to 25%

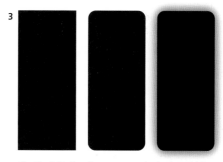

On the left, the drawn rectangle; in the middle, the rectangle with Round Corners applied; on the right, the rectangle with Round Corners and Outer Glow applied

Recycle your gradients

To reuse your gradients, resize the gradient rectangles to fit other art or save the gradients as graphic styles or swatches.

Contouring Mesh

Converting Gradients to Mesh and Editing

Overview: *Draw objects and fill with linear gradients; expand gradient-filled objects into gradient meshes; use various tools to edit mesh points and colors.*

JACKMORE

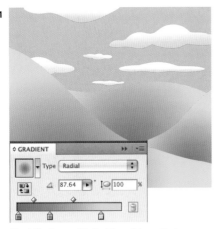

The hills shown filled with radial gradients—although there is some sense of light, it isn't possible to make the radial gradient follow the contours of the hills

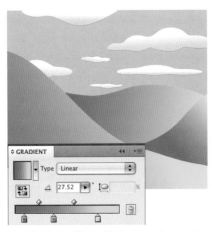

The hills shown filled with linear gradients, which when converted to gradient meshes are easier to edit than radial gradients

For many images, gradients can be useful for showing the gradual change of light to shadow (if you need to learn more about creating and applying gradient fills, first see "Unified Gradients" earlier in this chapter). For these rolling hills, artist Lisa Jackmore expanded linear gradients into gradient mesh objects so she could better control the curves and contours of the color transitions.

1 Drawing objects and then filling them with linear gradients. Begin your illustration by creating closed objects with any of the drawing tools. After drawing each object, fill it with a linear gradient (although in some objects radial gradients might look better before you convert them to mesh objects, linear gradients create mesh objects that are much easier to edit). For each linear gradient, customize the colors, and adjust the angle and length of the gradient transition with the Gradient tool and Gradient Annotator until you can best approximate the desired lighting effect. Jackmore created three hill-shaped objects with the Pen tool, filled them with the same linear gradient, then customized each with the Gradient Annotator.

2 Expanding linear gradients into gradient meshes. To create a more natural lighting of the hills, Jackmore converted the linear gradients into mesh objects so the color transitions could follow the contours of the hills. To accomplish this, select all the gradient-filled objects that you wish to convert and choose Object > Expand. In the Expand dialog, make sure Fill is enabled and specify Expand Gradient to Gradient Mesh. Then click OK. Illustrator converts each linear gradient into a rectangle rotated to the angle matching the linear gradient's angle; each mesh rectangle is masked by the original object (see the *Mastering Complexity* chapter for help with masks).

2

After expanding the gradients into gradient mesh objects

3 Editing meshes. You can use several tools to edit gradient mesh objects (use the Object > Lock/Unlock All toggle to isolate objects as you work). The Mesh tool combines the functionality of the Direct Selection tool with the ability to add mesh lines. With the Mesh tool, click *exactly on* a mesh anchor point to select or move that point or its direction handles. Or, click *anywhere* within a mesh, except on an anchor point, to add a new mesh point and gridline. You can also use the Add Anchor Point tool (click and hold to choose it from the Pen tool pop-up) to add a point without a gridline. To delete a selected anchor point, press the Delete key; if that point is a mesh point, the gridlines will be deleted as well.

3

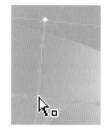

Using the Mesh tool to add a mesh line, then moving the mesh point with the Direct Selection tool

Select points within the mesh using either the Mesh tool or the Lasso tool, using the Direct Selection tool to move multiple selected points. Move individual anchor points and adjust direction handles with the Mesh tool in order to reshape your gradient mesh gridlines. In this way, the color and tonal transitions of the gradient will match the contour of the mesh object. Recolor selected areas of the mesh by selecting points, then choosing a new color, or click on <u>Opacity</u> in the Control panel to reduce the point's opacity, to see through the mesh to objects below.

Using the Add Anchor Point tool, using the Lasso to select a point, moving selected point (or points) with the Direct Selection tool

If you click in the area *between* mesh points with the Eyedropper tool while holding down Option/Alt, you'll add the Fill color to the four nearest mesh points.

By using these tools and editing techniques, Jackmore was able to create hills with color and light variations that suggest the subtlety of natural light upon organic forms.

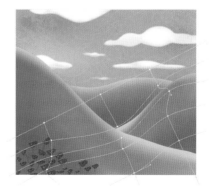

The middle hill, shown after making mesh adjustments

Fashionable Colors

Applying Spot Colors with Live Color

Overview: *Apply colors with Live Paint; duplicate images; use Live Color to create Spot colors; merge colors in Live Color.*

DASHWOOD

1

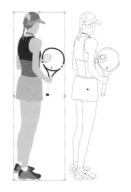

Option-drag/Alt-drag to create duplicates of your artwork on the artboard

Enter the Recolor Artwork dialog by clicking on the Recolor Artwork icon in the Control panel

2

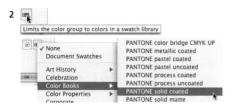

Access color books inside of Recolor Artwork using the flyout menu

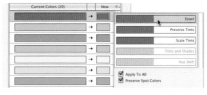

Choose Exact from the New Color pop-up menu to avoid creating tints of Spot Colors

To create these seasonal apparel color changes for an interactive series of instructional materials, Andrew Dashwood used the Recolor Artwork dialog of Live Color to Preview and Assign multiple color variations.

1 Preparing for Live Color. Dashwood began by drawing the tennis player's outline, using the Pen tool to make closed paths. To prepare paths for future recoloring, first block out a basic color scheme by clicking on paths and choosing colors, or use the Live Paint Bucket to convert your figure to a Live Paint object and fill colors with it. Choose the colors first for the parts of the drawing that will not change, in this case, the hair, skin, and tennis racket. Then, choose a random color for each piece of apparel and footwear. You'll find it easier to experiment with color combinations if you begin with a wider variety of colors than you anticipate using in your final image. It's not possible to divide colors inside of the Recolor Artwork dialog, but it is very easy to merge them together.

Create duplicates of your artwork so you'll be able to apply different color changes to each of the versions. Select your artwork, hold Option-Shift/Alt-Shift, and drag it sideways to create a duplicate of your art. Use ⌘/Ctrl-D to create additional duplicates. Select your objects and click the Recolor Artwork icon in the Control panel to open the Recolor Artwork dialog.

2 Working with Live Color and Spot Colors. Once you enter the Recolor Artwork dialog, make sure the Assign tab is active; once it is, you'll be able to change the colors in your image. Since most clients want you to use a specific palette of colors, you can load a color book or custom library of spot, process, or global colors by clicking on the rightmost bottom icon called "Limits the color group to colors in a swatch library." To avoid creating tints of a spot color, choose Exact from the pop-up next to the New Color swatch. Once you return to the artboard, if you select objects containing a Global or Spot swatch, its name will be displayed in the Color panel.

Using Recolor Artwork you can choose to protect colors you don't want to change (such as the skin tone, hair, and tennis racket colors). To protect a color from change, click the arrow to the right of its Current Color icon. The arrow toggles to a straight line, protecting that Current Color from changing to a New Color (click again to toggle protection off). To begin changing the colors, click on the Edit tab. If you chose a custom color book, the color wheel will be divided to display only those colors. Make sure the Link Color Harmony icon is unlocked on the color wheel, so that moving one of the color values on the color won't affect the others. Once you find a tonal range that suits your image well, click on the Link Color Harmony icon to enable the lock option. Once the lock is enabled, you can then drag the linked colors around the wheel to experiment with different color combinations.

3 Reducing colors. To merge two or more Current Colors into a single New Color, click on the Assign tab, select one Current Color, and then drag onto another one. The color bar in the Current Colors will be divided in two, and an arrow to the right of it will show you the changed effect. Alternatively, you can select colors in a row and use the icons at the bottom-left of the section, or access the context-sensitive menu options. Once you've created a color scheme you like, click OK to exit the Recolor Artwork dialog and apply your changes.

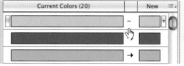

Click on the arrow between a Current Color and New Color to prevent the original color from being modified

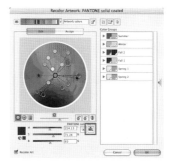

The color wheel when limited to a color book; Link Harmony Color icon highlighted in red

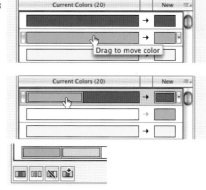

Merging Current Colors by dragging them into one another, or using the icons

Recoloring Black

Using Live Color to Replace Blacks

Overview: *Work with the Recolor Artwork dialog; limit color choices to a Swatch library; choose the right settings to ensure the appropriate colors change; protect specific colors from change.*

1

The original artwork

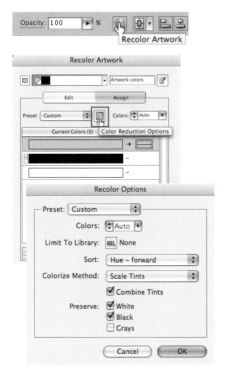

Default settings for Recolor Options and how they affect the assignment of color in Recolor Artwork's main dialog

Live Color provides exciting ways to experiment with color changes, but there are times when you'll get unexpected results if you don't know how to control it. After Laurent Pinabel gave Jean-Claude Tremblay this poster and flyer artwork for printing, a last-minute client request required changing the process black to a Pantone metallic silver spot color. Knowing the ins and outs of the Recolor Artwork dialog made it possible for Tremblay to edit only the black objects without having to select them manually, while protecting the gold and white colors.

1 Opening the Recolor Artwork dialog and changing default settings in the Recolor Options dialog. Tremblay began by selecting the entire graphic. This ensured that he quickly captured all tints and shades of any color, should there be more than one for each. He clicked the Recolor Artwork icon in the Control panel to enter the dialog. With default settings, Black and White are protected colors in Recolor Artwork (meaning new colors will not be assigned to them), so there will not be a color bar for Black in the New column of the dialog. Tremblay clicked the Color Reduction Options icon to open the Recolor Options dialog. This dialog helps set up colors to suit the type of document being worked on before they are edited in the main Recolor Artwork dialog. While Tremblay worked in the Recolor Options dialog, the main Live Color dialog updated to reflect his current settings in the Recolor Options dialog.

If the Recolor Options settings are changed out of sequence, Recolor Artwork will not update properly.

Therefore, Tremblay began adjusting the settings at the top and worked his way down. With only two spot colors used for printing, he first chose Preset: 2 color job. This opens the Limit To Library dialog where he selected Color Book > Pantone metallic coated. In the Live Color dialog, swatch colors were updated, with Black still below the gold. For Recolor Artwork to work properly in a 2-color job when you're only changing one of the protected colors (Black, White, or Grays), you must move that color to the top of the Current Colors column. Tremblay clicked the Color Reduction Options icon and chose Sort: Lightness - dark to light, and disabled Preserve: Black. The Recolor Artwork dialog updated, placing Black at the top.

Tremblay also wanted to make certain that if the artwork had any tints of the Black in it, these would be replaced by a single metallic color. He chose Exact for the Colorize Method and unchecked Combine Tints since he only wanted one color to replace any black found in the artwork. If he had wanted to keep tints of a process color while exchanging it for another process color (a CMYK black to a CMYK purple, for instance), he would have kept the default setting of Scale Tints for the Colorize Method, and kept Combine Tints checked. (For a more complete explanation, search for "colorize method" in *Illustrator Help*.) Tremblay clicked OK to close the Recolor Options dialog. When settings have been changed, some settings in Recolor Options will be remembered, while others will return to their default. It's a good idea to look in the Recolor Options dialog when you first enter Recolor Artwork to see that the settings are appropriate for the current job.

2 Protecting a color from change and assigning a new color. Back on the Assign tab, Tremblay clicked on the arrow connecting the gold color bars to eliminate gold from any further change. He double-clicked on the color bar in the New column to the right of the Black's arrow, and chose 877 C from the Color Picker. Clicking on the color swatch also would bring up the same Color Picker.

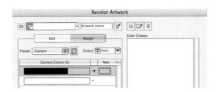

Settings made in random sequence, or not made at all, causing the Recolor Artwork dialog to fail to update properly

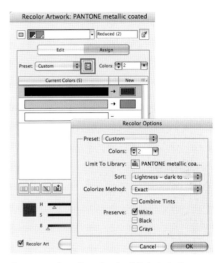

Correct settings for a 2 color job (set via the Color Reduction Options icon) changing a protected color (Black), with Recolor Artwork updating to reflect the new assignment and Swatch Library colors replacing original colors

2

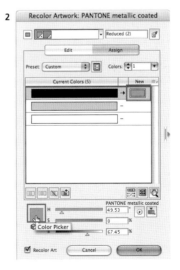

The Recolor Artwork dialog with all Recolor Options settings in place, gold protected from change and a metallic silver being exchanged for Black

Reducing Color

Going Monochromatic with Live Color

Advanced Technique

Overview: *Place color groups in the Swatches panel; reduce colors in a grayscale conversion; make a modified color version using the grayscale values and Global Adjust sliders.*

Why Live Color for grayscale?

With automatic grayscale conversions such as Edit > Edit Colors > Convert to Grayscale, you can't make many decisions about how your image is converted. However, using a grayscale color group and Live Color you can control replacing color with grayscale values to achieve optimal contrast.

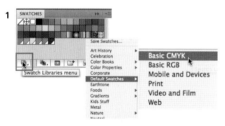

Finding the Grayscale color group in the Default Swatches library

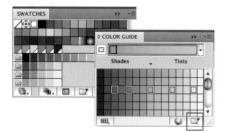

Saving color groups to the Swatches panel; using the Color Guide panel to generate monochromatic palettes

Designers and artists frequently need to reduce the number of colors they used in original artwork in order to feature the same piece in another venue. In this book cover for *Gaborone: The Complete City Guide* by Patricia Farrow, South African illustrator Ellen Papciak-Rose used a full range of bright colors. Using Live Color's remarkable ability to combine and replace colors, you can control the way colors are reduced in number to make subtle or exaggerated changes. Live Color allows you to experiment or to make specific color changes, such as converting color to grayscale, protecting accent colors if desired, and even to create color-tinted versions of your newly converted grayscale image.

1 Placing Color Groups in the Swatches panel for a monochromatic scheme. Before you can convert colors in your image, you need to make sure that your file contains the color groups that you'll be applying to your image. In this case, your file should contain a grayscale color group, and at least one hue-based monochromatic color group. New documents contain a grayscale color group in the Swatches panel. If your image hasn't been saved with the grayscale color group, open the Swatches Libraries icon and select Default CMYK (or RGB) from the menu. For the monochromatic color group, select a swatch or use the Color panel to create a color that will become the base in the Color Guide for your color group. Select a series of tints and shades and click on the "Save color group to Swatch panel" icon. Four or five swatches for the tints and shades (the same number that the Harmony Rules include in a group) are normally enough for a grayscale conversion. Once you've created the color groups you like and saved them to the Swatches panel, select your artwork and click on the Recolor Artwork icon in the Control panel.

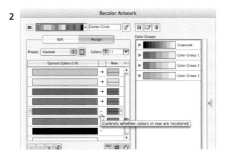

Protecting colors from change in Live Color

2 Reducing colors in Live Color for a monochromatic scheme. When Live Color opens, scroll through the list on the Assign tab until you come to any colors you want to protect from change, such as the red, black, and white of the "Gaborone" image. If any of these colors has an arrow between its color bars, click on it to toggle protection on. To create a satisfactory grayscale conversion, click on the Grayscale color group in the color group storage area, then begin dragging color bars in the Current Colors column from one row to another, combining and changing the value of the gray that has been assigned to each color. Watch the live update in the image as you experiment with combining colors in order to arrive at good contrast. If you now want to "tint" this grayscale, make sure the grays don't exceed the number of swatches in your color group and proceed with Step 3; otherwise, if you want to keep the grayscale conversion, stop here and, with Recolor Art enabled, click OK to apply the change.

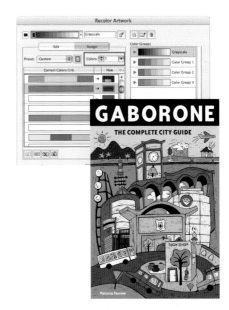

Reducing colors for grayscale by dragging color bars together in combinations that get assigned to the same values and/or hues

3 Using your grayscale conversion to generate "tints." While your grayscale color conversion is still in Live Color, you can now tint your image using the monochromatic color groups you created. Click on a color group to preview the color scheme in the image. If you wish to make adjustments to the selected color scheme, click on the Edit tab, and use the color adjustment sliders (such as Global Adjust, used here) or drag linked color markers. If you find a scheme you want, click the New Color Group icon to add it to your list. Once you like the results, with Recolor Art enabled, click OK to apply the change.

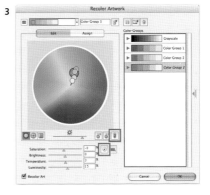

Choosing a monochromatic color scheme to "tint" the grayscale conversion, and modifying the colors on the Edit tab using color adjustment sliders or dragging markers on the color wheel

Transparent Mesh

Molding Transparent Mesh Layers Going

Advanced Technique

Overview: *Draw guides and create gradient mesh objects; contour rectangles; color gradient mesh points with color sampled from reference photo; apply transparency to individual mesh points to create realism.*

1

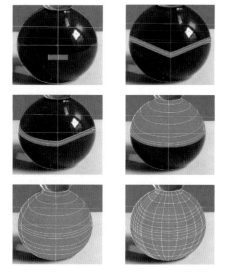

Making guides on top of the photograph in the template layer

Developing the gradient mesh object from a rectangle, adjusting points with the Direct Selection tool, adding rows and columns with the Gradient Mesh tool (left to right, top to bottom)

PAIDRICK

Ann Paidrick transformed simple rectangular objects into complex, contoured gradient mesh objects to create an exact representation of an original photograph. By incorporating actual transparency into her mesh objects, she is able to reuse the finished vase in other settings (see the gallery following this lesson).

1 **Creating guides, drawing basic shapes, then creating gradient mesh objects.** Placing her .jpg as a template into layers above, Paidrick drew a loose grid of paths and then turned them into guides (⌘-5/Ctrl-5) to help position her gradient mesh objects. Paidrick finds that adding a mesh to a rectangle, which she then reshapes, gives her more control over mesh points than if she added mesh to a path drawn with the Pen tool. Therefore, she always begins her gradient mesh objects by drawing one small rectangle with the Rectangle tool. To create the red globe

portion of the vase, she drew a rectangle, filled it with a bright color, chose Object > Create Gradient Mesh, and specified 1 row, 1 column. With the Direct Selection tool (A), she moved points to stretch the rectangle to the edges of the vase base, and eventually the top and bottom. With the Gradient mesh tool (U), she added more rows and columns. She continued to enlarge the mesh object and contour it into the desired shape by pressing U to add mesh points, then A to adjust the points. Paidrick added individual mesh points with the Add Anchor Point tool to further define the shape of the object. She Direct-Selected points and made adjustments to refine the contour of the object and its mesh to closely follow the shading of her reference photo.

2 **Coloring the mesh objects.** To color individual mesh points, Paidrick clicked on a mesh point with the Direct Selection tool (A), then switched to the Eyedropper tool (I) and filled that point with a color sampled from the photograph. She continued to color the mesh points by pressing ⌘/Ctrl to temporarily switch to the Direct Selection tool from the Eyedropper tool, picking up color from the photo, until a pixel in the photograph matched the color she wanted.

3 **Applying transparency to individual mesh points.** For effects such as reflections, she created additional mesh objects on layers above. She then selected individual points in the upper mesh objects and reduced the opacity, creating nearly invisible transitions between different mesh objects on layers above and below. She also reduced the opacity of mesh points when she needed to create smooth color transitions between more- and less-saturated colors (see bottom figure). To reduce the opacity of an individual mesh point, she Direct-Selected a mesh point and clicked on Opacity in the Appearance panel. She continued to choose mesh points and use various transparency settings throughout the illustration until she had matched the color of the reference photo as closely as possible.

2

Coloring mesh points and sampling color from the reference photograph

3

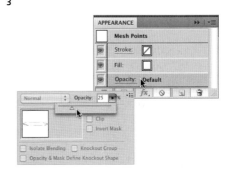

Decreasing the Opacity in the Appearance panel

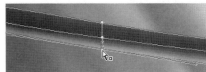

Mesh point before (top) and after (bottom) the opacity is decreased

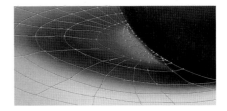

Paidrick applied transparency to mesh points along the edges of the individual rings of color to make smooth transitions between each change of color

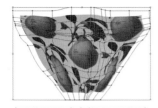

PAIDRICK

Ann Paidrick

Ann Paidrick enhanced her vase illustration from the previous lesson by adding the patterned pear wallpaper to the background. Paidrick locked all the layers of the finished vase and, on a new layer beneath these locked layers, placed a photograph of the wallpaper (saved as .jpg) as the background. With the Pen tool, she drew rough outlines where the distorted pears would be, and then turned these outlines into guides (⌘-5 /Ctrl-5). On a separate layer above the background wallpaper, she placed another photo of the wallpaper, this time one that she had cropped in Photoshop to fit between the top and bottom of the clear glass. In order to use an Illustrator envelope to distort the cropped part of the photo, she had to first embed the photo by selecting the Embed icon in the Control panel. Paidrick then chose Object > Envelope Distort > Make with Mesh (6 rows, 8 columns). She used the Direct Selection tool to adjust the envelope mesh object into the shape of the interior of the glass. To add more rows and columns, Paidrick clicked with the Gradient Mesh tool and added additional mesh points with the Add Anchor Point tool. She continued to adjust the mesh points, referring to her guides until she was satisfied with the distortion results. To make the envelope mesh object fit into the vase shape, on a new layer above, she drew a closed path with the Pen tool, selected the envelope mesh object, then chose Object > Clipping Mask > Make.

PAIDRICK

Ann Paidrick

Gradient mesh objects enabled Ann Paidrick to capture an exact representation of her source photograph (directly above), even the unusual olive reflection in the stainless steel martini glass. Paidrick used the Pen tool to draw rectangular paths of the relative size and shape of each object, filling each object with a base color sampled from the original photograph using the Eyedropper tool. Changing the object into a mesh (Object > Create Gradient Mesh), she specified one row, one column, and a flat appearance. She added more rows and columns with the Mesh tool as needed and adjusted points to form the contour of the mesh objects. To color individual mesh points, Paidrick clicked on a mesh point with the Direct Selection tool,

then switched to the Eyedropper tool (I) and filled that mesh point with a sampled color from the photograph. She continued to color mesh points, pressing the⌘/Ctrl to temporarily switch back to the Direct Selection tool and then releasing to return to the Eyedropper tool. To add further detail to the mesh objects, she added more points with the Add Anchor Point tool, adjusting those points with the Direct Selection tool. To create smooth transitions between one mesh object and another mesh object on a layer below, Paidrick Direct-Selected individual mesh points and reduced the Opacity slider in the Transparency panel (varying from 0–25%). She used the same techniques to create the subtle painterly background texture.

AHUJA

Anil Ahuja/Adobe Systems

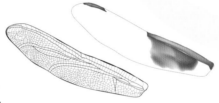

Adobe's Product Specialist Anil Ahuja used a range of tools and techniques to create his dragonfly, and relied upon transparency methods to obtain color accuracy to closely match his reference photo. In his three levels of objects used to create the wings, (shown separately at right) this is readily apparent. After drawing the wing's black-stroked vein structure with Artistic Calligraphic Brushes of various sizes and shapes, he selected the paths and chose Object>Expand (to outline the strokes), then Merge (to create a compound path object). In the Appearance panel he clicked Opacity, and changed the Blending Mode to Darken to reduce the opacity, giving the wing its realistic brown color. With the brown and blue gradient mesh objects (residing on a layer beneath the vein structure), Ahuja used the Direct Selection tool to select individual mesh points to decrease the opacity (ranging from 0–90%). To make the wings appear translucent instead of just transparent, Ahuja used the Pen tool to draw an outline copy of the wings which he put on a layer below the veined structure and the mesh. He filled the outline with a color similar to the background and reduced the opacity to 30%. To complete the illustration, Ahuja created a shadow on a layer between the dragonfly and the gradient mesh background. To make the shadow, he pasted a copy of the wing outline and with the Pen tool added an outline of the body. He then reduced the opacity of the shadow object to 53% and changed the Blending Mode to Darken.

Yukio Miyamoto

Yukio Miyamoto created the numerous complex linear and radial gradients throughout this illustration with ease using the Gradient tool and the Gradient Annotator. Miyamoto drew each path with the Pen tool and filled it either with the default linear or radial gradient from the Swatches panel. He selected the Gradient tool to reveal the Gradient Annotator, which appeared on top of the object. Miyamoto double-clicked on the color stop of the Gradient Annotator to show the options. He clicked on the Swatches icon and chose a custom color from the Swatches panel that he had previously created to color the stop. Miyamoto clicked along the Gradient Annotator to add more color stops. He continued to add color stops and color them until he was satisfied with the results. Miyamoto click-dragged the color stops and moved them into the exact locations to achieve the desired gradient effect. He grabbed the arrow endpoint and stretched the Gradient Annotator to change the length of the gradient. Miyamoto moved the endpoint side to side and adjusted the angle of the gradient. He made additional angular adjustments with the circular endpoint and clicked the center point, then moved it to various positions within the gradient-filled object. The entire illustration is made of gradient-filled objects with two very small exceptions; there is one blended object (the pen tip) and one

Caran d'Ache 1010 I LIMITED EDITION

MIYAMOTO

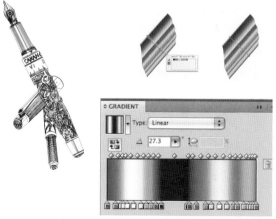

mesh object (grip area, just beneath the tip). The Gradient Annotator enabled Miyamoto to have exceptional control of the gradient fills to achieve exacting realism.

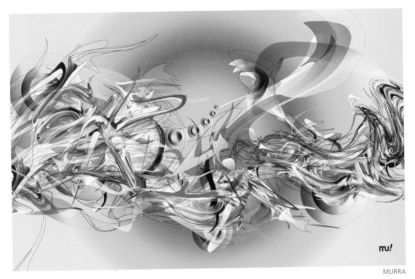

MURRA

Sebastian Murra

When Murra began "In The Scattered Sun," he started with a simple concept ("sun") and several overlapping, gradient-filled rectangles. He used the Hard Light blending mode (by clicking on Opacity in the Appearance panel) on all his objects, so he reduced the opacity of any white or black (which don't blend with other colors) in his gradients. He gave fine black strokes to some nearly transparent rectangles so they would appear as finely-drawn lines in his finished piece. Next he used the Liquify tools—primarily Warp, Twirl, and Bloat—to begin finger-painting his colored objects into an abstraction of swirls and waves. He left these tools at their default settings, but interactively resized them by holding Option/Alt while dragging on a blank spot in the document. Working intuitively, Murra selected some objects and duplicated them, using their bounding boxes to scale or rotate, and reduced the opacity of some objects to increase their ability to blend with others. He copied and pasted objects

both in front and in back to continue filling in his image. To enhance the fluid motion of his objects, he allowed them to extend beyond the artboard and frequently moved or deleted objects until he found a final structure emerge within the "frame" of the artboard. When he wanted to introduce a new color family, he would either select an object and apply a new gradient, or take a group of objects into Live Color and recolor them there. With his abstract sun flares complete, Murra added structure with a background from a radial filled rectangle; then he created his "sun spots" from gradient-filled, stacked circles that he duplicated and distributed across the canvas.

6

Reshaping Dimensions

OCEANMIND@YAHOO.COM
ATTN: ILLUSTRATOR WOW!

Reshaping Dimensions

The three Envelope buttons in the Control panel, from left to right: Edit Envelope, Edit Contents, and Envelope Options

This chapter focuses on the Illustrator tools and functions that allow you to create objects that appear to move beyond two-dimensional space. With warps and envelopes you can easily use familiar vector tools to bend and bow objects (and text) in two dimensional space, and with envelope meshes you can begin to create an illusion of depth as well. Using Illustrator's 3D effects you actually revolve, extrude, rotate, and map objects in three dimensions. Then, the Perspective Grid tool helps you to create art based on linear perspective drawing using one, two, or three vanishing points. All of these demand a bit of a different mindset than flat Illustrator objects and the manipulating of the mesh. In their live states, 3D and the Perspective Grid work quite differently from other Illustrator objects. If you decide to expand the art, they become merely complex vector objects, letting you work upon them using any of Illustrator's editing tools.

WARPS AND ENVELOPES

Warps and envelopes may look similar at first, but there's an important difference between them. Warps are applied as live *effects*—meaning they can be applied to objects, groups, or layers. Warps have two advantages: They are easy to create by choosing from the predefined options in the Warp dialogs, and you can save them within a graphic style to apply them to other objects. Envelopes, on the other hand, are also live, but rather than effects, they're actual *objects* that contain artwork. Envelopes let you edit or customize the envelope shape, and Illustrator will conform the contents of the envelope to the contour.

Warps

Applying a warp is actually quite simple. Target an object, group, or layer and choose Effect > Warp > Arc. (It doesn't matter which warp effect you choose, because you'll be presented with the Warp Options dialog, where you can choose from any of the 15 different warps.) While the warp effects are "canned" in the sense that you can't make adjustments to the effects directly, you can control how a warp appears by changing the Bend value, as well as the Horizontal and Vertical Distortion values.

Once you've applied a warp, you can edit it by opening the Appearance panel and clicking on the warp effect. Like all effects, a warp can be applied to just the fill or just the stroke—and if you edit the artwork, the warp updates as well. Since warps are effects, you can include them in a graphic style, which can then be applied to other artwork.

Envelopes

While warp effects do a nice job of distorting artwork (and allow you to save the effect as a graphic style), Illustrator envelopes provide a higher level of control.

There are three ways to apply envelopes. The simplest way is to create a path you want to use as your envelope. Make sure it's at the top of the stacking order—above the art you want to place inside the envelope. Then, with the artwork and your created path both selected, choose Object > Envelope Distort > Make with Top Object. Illustrator will create a special kind of object: an envelope. This object you created becomes an envelope container, which appears in the Layers panel as <Envelope>. You can edit the path of the envelope with any transformation or editing tools; the artwork inside will update to conform to the shape. To edit the contents of the envelope, click the Edit Contents button in the Control panel or choose Object > Envelope Distort > Edit Contents. If you then look at the Layers panel, you'll notice that the <Envelope> now has a disclosure triangle that reveals the contents of the envelope—the artwork you placed. You can edit the artwork directly or even drag other paths into the <Envelope> in the Layers panel. To again edit the envelope itself, choose Object > Envelope Distort > Edit Envelope.

There are two other types of envelopes, and they're closely related. Both types use meshes to provide even more distortion control. When using the first type, the

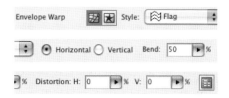

The tools that appear in the Control panel when an envelope warp is selected; you can change the shape of the warp using the pop-up menu

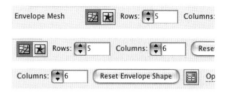

The controls that appear in the Control panel when an envelope mesh is selected; you can easily change the number of rows and columns, as well as restore the object to its original shape using the Reset Envelope Shape button

MICHAEL CRESSY

Michael Cressy turned the building on the left into the one on the right using the drawing tools, then modified with envelopes for each of the windows, the building, and the stacks using Object > Envelope Distort > Make with Mesh.

Isolation mode for envelopes

An easy way to edit an envelope: Double-click it to enter isolation mode. —*Jean-Claude Tremblay*

Envelope distort options

To use envelopes to distort artwork containing pattern fills or linear gradients, choose Object > Envelope Distort > Envelope Options and enable the appropriate options. —*Mordy Golding*

Illustrator's 3D objects are only *truly* three-dimensional while you're working with them in a 3D effect dialog. As soon as you're done tweaking your object and you click OK to close the dialog, the object's three-dimensional qualities are "frozen"—almost as if Illustrator had taken a snapshot of the object—until the next time you edit it in a 3D dialog. On the page, it's technically a 2D rendering of a 3D object that can only be worked with in two-dimensional ways. But because the effect is live, you can work with the object in 3D again any time you want. Just select the object and then double-click the 3D effect listed in the Appearance panel.

Extruding an object using the Effect > 3D > Extrude & Bevel dialog—the two-dimensional object on the left was extruded to create the three-dimensional version on the right

Don't miss Mordy Golding's 3D chapter (3D_RealWorldAICS5.pdf) on the **WOW! DVD**.

To speed up your screen redraw, temporarily hide a 3D effect by clicking on the Eye for that 3D effect in the Appearance panel (click again to make it visible).

envelope warp, you choose the overall envelope form from a pop-up list of options. When you use the *envelope mesh*, instead of starting from presets, you begin by choosing how many rows and columns your mesh will contain.

To create an envelope warp, select an object and choose Make with Warp (Object > Envelope Distort). This will open the Warp dialog. Once you choose a warp and click OK, Illustrator converts that warp to an envelope mesh. The Control panel will display the Envelope Warp controls, including a pop-up menu that lets you choose a different shape for the warp if you want to. You can edit the envelope warp's individual mesh points with the Direct Selection tool to distort not only the outer edges of the envelope shape but also the way art is distorted within the envelope itself. To provide even more control, use the Mesh tool to add more mesh points as desired.

To create an envelope mesh, select your artwork and choose Object > Envelope Distort > Make with Mesh. After you've chosen how many mesh points you want, Illustrator will create the envelope mesh. The Envelope Mesh tools will appear in the Control panel, allowing you to easily change the number of rows and columns, and restore the envelope mesh to its original shape if necessary. You can also use the Direct Selection tool to edit the points and use the Mesh tool to add mesh points. (If you use other tools, however, you'll need to switch back to the Selection tool if you want the Envelope Mesh controls to reappear in the Control panel.)

3D EFFECTS

Illustrator offers you the power to transform any two-dimensional (2D) shape, including type, into a shape that looks three-dimensional (3D). As you're working in Illustrator's 3D effect dialogs, you can change your 3D shape's perspective, rotate it, and add lighting and surface attributes. And because you're working with a live effect, you can edit the source object at any time and observe the resultant change in the 3D shape immediately. You can also rotate a 2D shape in 3D space and change its perspective. Finally, Illustrator lets you map artwork previously saved as a symbol onto any of your 3D object's surfaces. Remember that Illustrator is primarily a 2D program—its 3D capabilities are very limited when compared to the plethora of available 3D programs.

To begin, think of Illustrator's horizontal ruler as the X axis and the vertical ruler as the Y axis. Now imagine a third dimension that extends back into space, perpendicular to the flat surface of your monitor. This is the Z axis. There are two ways to create a 3D shape using 3D effects. The first method is by extruding a 2D object back into space along the Z axis, and the second is by revolving a 2D object around its Y axis, up to 360°.

To apply a 3D effect to a selected object, choose one of the 3D effects from the *fx* icon in the Appearance panel (or via the Effects menu). (To simplify the instructions throughout this chapter, we'll be using the convention "choose Effect > 3D".) Once you apply a 3D effect to an object, it will show up in the Appearance panel. As with other appearance attributes, you can edit the effect, change the position of the effect in the panel's stacking order, and duplicate or delete the effect. You can also save 3D effects as reusable graphic styles so that you can apply the same effect to a batch of objects. Once the style has been applied, you can modify any of the style parameters by clicking the underlined effect name in the Appearance panel or double-clicking the *fx* icon to the right of the effect name. Editing the 2D path will then update the 3D rendering. Following are a few of the key parameters for working in the different kinds of 3D:

- **To extrude a 2D object,** begin by creating a path; the path can be open or closed, and can contain a stroke, a fill, or both (if your shape contains a fill, it's best to begin with a solid color, not gradient or pattern). With your path selected, choose Extrude & Bevel from the Effect > 3D submenu. In the lower portion of the dialog, enter a point size for depth for your object in the Extrude Depth field, or drag the slider. Adding a cap to your object makes the

Customized bevels!

All the 3D Bevel shapes are located inside the file "Bevels.ai" (for Mac: Adobe Illustrator CS5 > Required > Resources > en_US > Bevels.ai, and for Win: Adobe Illustrator CS5 > Support Files > Required > Resources > en_US > Bevels.ai). Each bevel path is saved as a symbol inside this document. To add a custom bevel, draw a new path, drag it to the Symbols panel, name it, and resave the file. — *Jean-Claude Tremblay*

Solid advice on 3D colors

You'll get the best results using solid fill colors for 3D objects. Gradients and pattern fills don't produce reliable results.

3D—Three dialogs

There are three different 3D effects, and some features overlap. If all you need to do is change the perspective of an object, use Rotate. If you want to map a symbol to the object, use either Revolve or Extrude & Bevel (you can still rotate an object from these as well). —*Brenda Sutherland*

Not enough steps...

Click the More Options button to adjust Blend steps; find a setting between the default (25) and the maximum (256) that's smooth enough, but not too slow to draw (and print).

Left to right: Turn cap on for solid, Turn cap off for hollow, Bevel Extent In, Bevel Extent Out

Bevel error messages...

If you apply bevels to some objects (like stars), you might see the error "Bevel self-intersection may have occurred" when you click "Preview"—this may or may not actually mean there's a problem.

For the smoothest 3D

When creating profile objects for 3D, draw as few anchor points as possible. Each anchor point produces an additional surface to render, and might also create potential problems if you're later mapping artwork onto surfaces.

—*Jean-Claude Tremblay*

Revolving an object using the Effect >3D >Revolve dialog—the open path on the left was revolved to create the 3D chess pawn on the right

An example of rotating an object in 3D space

ends appear solid; disabling the cap option makes your object appear hollow (see first two figures at left).

You can choose from ten different bevels to style the edges of your object; bevels can be added to the original using Bevel Extent Out, or carved out of the original using Bevel Extent In (second pair of figures at left).

- **To revolve an object around its Y (vertical) axis,** begin by creating a path. The path can be open or closed and stroked, filled, or both. With your path selected, choose Effect > 3D > Revolve to open 3D Revolve Options. Drag the slider to set the number of degrees or enter a value from 1 to 360 in the Angle text field. An object that is revolved 360° will appear solid. An object revolved less than 360° will appear to have a wedge carved out of it. If you offset the rotation from the object's edge, a 3D shape will appear to be carved out in the center.

- **To Rotate 2D or 3D objects in 3D space,** choose Effects > 3D > Rotate. The 3D Rotate Options dialog contains a cube representing the planes that your shape can be rotated through. Choose a preset angle of rotation from the Position menu, or enter values between −180 and 180 into the X, Y, and Z text fields. To manually rotate your object around one of its three axes, simply click *on the edge* of one of the faces of the white cube and drag. The edges of each plane are highlighted in a corresponding color that tells you through which of the object's three planes you're rotating it. The object's rotation is constrained within the plane of that particular axis. If you wish to rotate your object relative to all three axes at once, click directly on a surface of the cube and drag, or click in the black area behind the cube and drag. Values in all three text fields will change. And if you simply want to rotate your object, click and drag inside the circle, but outside the cube itself.

- **To change the perspective of an object,** enter a number between 0 and 160 in the Perspective field, or drag the slider pop-up. A smaller value simulates the look of a telephoto camera lens, while a larger value simulates a wide-angle camera lens.

Applying surface shading to 3D objects

Illustrator allows you to choose different shading (ranging from dull and unshaded matte surfaces to glossy and highlighted surfaces that look like plastic), as well as customized lighting conditions. The Surface shading option appears as part of both the 3D Extrude & Bevel and the 3D Revolve Options dialogs. Choosing Wireframe as your shading option will result in a transparent object, the contours of which are overlaid with a set of outlines describing the object's geometry. Choosing No Shading results in a flat-looking shape with no discernible surfaces. Choosing the Diffused Shading option results in your object having a soft light cast on its surfaces, while choosing the Plastic Shading option will make your object look as if it's molded out of shiny, reflective plastic. For mapped surfaces, enable "Shade Artwork" in the Map Art dialog.

If you choose either the Diffused Shading or Plastic Shading option, you can further refine the look of your object by adjusting the direction and intensity of the light source illuminating it. By clicking the More Options button, the dialog will enlarge and you'll be able to make changes to the Light Intensity, Ambient Light level, Highlight Intensity, Highlight Size, and number of Blend Steps. You can also choose a custom Shading Color to add a color cast to the shaded surfaces. If you choose to maintain a spot color assigned to your Extruded object during output by enabling the Preserve Spot Colors checkbox, be aware that this removes custom shading and resets your Shading Color to Black. If you choose Preserve Spot Colors, you should enable Overprint Preview (View menu) so you can see your shading and color accurately.

When expanded, the More Options dialog includes the light source sphere (shown at right). The small white dot within this sphere indicates the position of the light source, while the black box around it highlights this light source as currently selected. There is always one light source by default. Click and drag this dot within the sphere to reposition your light. With Preview enabled the lighting will automatically update on your 3D object.

Rotate objects in three dimensions by using the Effect >3D >Rotate dialog (or the upper halves of the Revolve and the Extrude & Bevel dialogs); the symbol on the left, rotated in 3D space to create the figure on the right (any 2D object can be rotated in 3D space, without making the object itself 3D)

3D effect—pass it on

Although in this book we generally recommend working with the New Art Has Basic Appearance setting disabled, you might want to enable it when working with 3D effects. Otherwise, any new paths that you create subsequent to applying 3D effects to an object will also have the same appearance set, unless you first clear the appearance set from the panel or click on the default fill and stroke icon in the Tools panel. On the other hand, if you *want* your next object to have the same 3D effects as the one you just created, leave New Art Has Basic Appearance disabled.

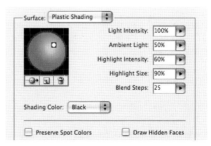

The expanded More Options dialog shows the position of your light source within the sphere; the three icons located below this sphere from left to right are "Move selected light to back of object," "New Light," and "Delete Light"

The above design was mapped onto the ring below it using the Map Art feature. The ring was created using the 3D Revolve effect with an "offset" value added.

Mapping with gradients

Gradients can be saved as symbols, but they are rasterized when mapped. The rasterized resolution of the resulting image is determined from the resolution setting in the "Document Raster Effects Settings." You can adjust this resolution by going to Effects > Document Raster Effects Settings.

Clicking on the "New Light" icon (below the sphere) adds more light sources. This also selects the new light source (indicated by the black "highlight" box around it). Adjust each selected source independently using the lighting controls (to the right of the sphere). The first icon below the sphere, the "Move selected light to back of object" feature, creates back lighting for an object. When your light source is behind an object, the source indicator inverts to a black dot within a white square. When using multiple light sources, this difference helps you see which light sources are behind or in front of an object. Select a light source and click this icon to toggle the light to the front or back of your object, depending on its current position. To delete a light source, first select it, then click the Trash icon beneath the sphere (you can delete all but one default light source).

Mapping art onto an object

To map artwork onto an object (as with the design on the ring to the left) first define the art that you wish to map onto a surface as a symbol; select the artwork you want to map, and drag it to the Symbols panel. You may also want to define a number of symbols. For instance, the design on the ring left is from one symbol. To add engraving inside the ring, you'd create a second symbol and add it in the Map Art dialog.

Map the symbols onto your 3D objects from the Extrude & Bevel or Revolve Options dialogs. In either of these 3D options boxes, you simply click on the Map Art button, then choose one of the available symbols from the menu. You can specify which of your object's surfaces the artwork will map onto by clicking on the left and right arrow keys. The selected surface will appear in the window; then you can either scale the art by dragging the handles on the bounding box or make the art expand to cover the entire surface by clicking the Scale to Fit button. Note that as you click through the different surfaces, the selected surface will be highlighted with a red outline in your document window. Your currently visible surfaces will appear in light gray in the Map Art dialog, and surfaces that are currently hidden will appear dark.

Note: *To see artwork mapped onto the side surfaces of your object, make sure the object has a stroke of None.*

THE PERSPECTIVE GRID

The Perspective Grid allows you to create art on a ground plane representing real world space as viewed by the human eye. Distances between edges converge as you approach the horizon, the terminal point of our vision. This tool is useful for creating scenes such as cityscapes where buildings or roads narrow in view as they recede from our vision, eventually vanishing on the horizon.

With this Perspective Grid toolset you can draw dynamically within the perspective environment itself so that shapes or objects automatically conform to the perspective grid as you create them, or you can attach existing flat vector art to the perspective grid by dragging selected art into the perspective grid using the Perspective Selection tool (see warning tip at right!). You can even position the grid on top of a reference photograph to add vector content. Symbols, text, and objects created with Illustrator's 3D effect are also supported within the perspective environment.

To begin working in perspective you must first define your perspective environment. Click on the Perspective Grid tool in the Tools panel to display the perspective grid on your Artboard, or click View > Perspective Grid > Show Grid. The default is Two Point Perspective consisting of two vanishing points. For one point perspective choose View > Perspective Grid > One Point Perspective > 1P Normal View which has a single vanishing point or Three Point Perspective > 3P Normal View which has three vanishing points (if a perspective grid is customized and saved, it will appear in the respective submenu for 1P, 2P, or 3P Normal View as an additional choice).

When you select the Perspective Grid tool, your grid is displayed with grid plane control points on its extremities (though some disappear when the Perspective Selection

To map or wrap...?

Maps allow you to add designs or texture effects to an object (such as a label on a bottle), but can also cover an entire object (see pawn above mapped with a wood grain image). However, complex objects produce a greater number of surfaces, which can make rendering very slow and perhaps generate errors. If you intend to add lighting and shading options on a mapped surface, enable "Shade Artwork" in the Map Art dialog.

Perspective is permanent!

Unlike other effects, once perspective is applied to an object it cannot be released to return to its original (normal) state, so always work on a copy of the original or, alternatively, use a symbol.

Need to get rid of the grid?

Toggle ⌘-Shift-I/Ctrl-Shift-I (View > Perspective Grid > Hide Grid) to hide the grid.

The Perspective Grid tool (left) opens the perspective grid with grid plane controls visible; the Perspective Selection tool (right) allows you to bring objects, text, or symbols into perspective, move these items in perspective space, or switch active planes

The Plane Switching Widget shown left with the left side highlighted in blue indicates that the left plane (grid) is active; click on a side of the cube with one of the perspective tools (or press 1, 2, or 3 on your keyboard) to activate a different plane (second and third widget); click the area outside the cube within the widget (or press 4) to deactivate perspective mode, which allows you to draw normally (widget at far right).

Grid control points can be manually adjusted on the grid itself or more precisely using the Define Perspective Grid dialog box (View > Perspective Grid > Define Grid). Presets can then be saved for reuse. View > Perspective Grid > Show Rulers displays a ruler on the visible grid.

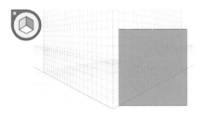

In this example, clicking within the Plane Switching Widget but outside the cube deactivated the perspective grid (note the cyan colored area surrounding the cube), so the rectangle was drawn in normal mode; to later apply perspective to the rectangle, select the Grid Selection tool, click on a Widget side to activate a plane, and drag the rectangle to the desired location.

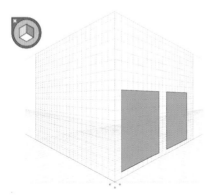

The above image shows a square drawn with the Rectangle tool. Notice the Plane Switching Widget indicates that the right plane is active, hence the illustrated shape in perspective relative to the right vanishing point (the cursor also includes a line and an arrow which also indicates the active plane). The same square copied and moved with the Perspective Selection tool dynamically transforms it as it moves within the perspective plane.

tool is used). These controls allow you to manually adjust parameters such as vanishing points, angles, repositioning of planes, grid height and width, etc. Scrolling the cursor over these controls yields an indicator below the pointer showing the directional choices available for that control.

To save a customized grid choose View > Perspective Grid > Save Grid As Preset. The new grid is saved under the respective perspective type; for example, a customized one-point perspective grid will be saved as an option to 1P Normal View when View > Perspective Grid > Two Point Perspective fly-out menu is displayed. The Define Grid dialog box (View > Perspective Grid > Define Grid) allows you to adjust the grid with greater numerical precision and save as a preset for further uses.

To begin working within your defined environment first select an active plane to work in. The cube in the upper left-hand corner of the work area is the Plane Switching Widget. When you click on a cube side with the Perspective Grid tool (or any drawing or editing tool), the active plane is highlighted with a color. Orange, for example, is the default color for the right plane (see figures at left). The active plane means that anything drawn in perspective will conform to the perspective of that specific plane regardless of where it is drawn on the artboard (only one plane can be active at any time). The Perspective Grid tool cursor also indicates this with the shaded side of a cube below its pointer.

Once you choose an active plane, you can use any drawing or editing tool to draw in perspective mode. Select a tool such as the Rectangle tool and begin drawing on the grid. Use the Perspective Selection tool (hidden under the Perspective Grid tool in the Tools panel) to select and move art within an active plane (the cursor also has a line and an arrow, indicating the active plane). When you move objects within your plane using this tool, your objects appear to recede and advance within the perspective grid (using the normal Selection tool freezes an object's shape to the current viewpoint, so it won't continue to transform as you move it). You can also use the

Perspective Selection tool to (permanently) transform existing (normal) vector objects into perspective. To do so, use the Perspective Selection tool to activate a plane, select objects, and then drag them into the perspective grid. When you use the Perspective Selection tool to select an object that's already attached to the grid, the associated side of the cube automatically becomes highlighted.

Clicking in the circle area outside the cube within the widget (or pressing 4) deactivates all perspective planes so you can draw in normal mode (no perspective applied)—see figures opposite. Once your object is created, use the Perspective Selection tool (or press 1, 2, or 3) to activate a plane by clicking on a Widget side, and then drag the object to position it in perspective. You can also marquee-select multiple objects with the Perspective Selection tool, then drag them (together) into the active plane.

If you wish to move an object perpendicular to its current location, hold down the 5 key (top row of numbers on keyboard only, not 5 on right numeric keypad) as you drag with the Perspective Selection tool; to duplicate an object and move it perpendicular to the original's position, hold Option-5/Alt-5 as you drag.

With the Perspective Grid tool, double-click on any of the grid plane controls (the three circles below where the planes intersect) to open a Vanishing Plane or Floor Plane dialog which allows you to move a plane precisely, with or without the objects associated with that plane.

To work on an object in normal mode after applying perspective, from either the Object menu or the contextual menu, choose Perspective > Release with Perspective (remember, this function does not return an object to a normal state if created initially without perspective but just detaches it from the perspective plane). The object can now be modified normally, however, in order to reattach it to the plane, you must use Object > Perspective > Attach to Active Plane; once an object has been detached from a plane. If the object is not reattached this way, using the Perspective Selection tool will automatically add a new perspective to the object.

Double-click the Perspective Grid tool in the Tools panel to open the Perspective Grid Options dialog for Automatic Plane Positioning options

Warp & Distort

Bending Forms to Create Organic Variations

CRESSY

Overview: *Use Envelope Distort and Distort & Transform live effects to shape objects; use filled rectangles with blend modes to change the time of day.*

When Michael Cressy needed to create scenes for an online video game, he turned to Illustrator's powerful Envelope Distort features and live effects to create a Halloween world where magic changes the shapes of things. By adding a few additional layers to colorize his images for different times of the day, his game scenes took on a consistent look with minimal fuss.

1

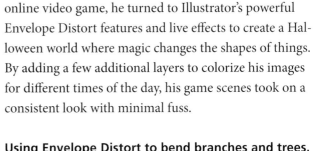

Using Warp Options to bend three rectangles into a curved and pointed arch

1 Using Envelope Distort to bend branches and trees.
To create the blighted trees, Cressy used the Rectangle tool to make three adjacent stripes with different fills (no stroke). He selected them and chose Object > Envelope Distort > Make with Warp. He set the Style to Arch with a Vertical Bend of 25%. He then used a Distortion amount of 99% in the Vertical dimension. These settings created a slightly curved set of stripes so distorted in the vertical dimension that they came to a point. With this horn as his base element, Cressy duplicated and scaled each horn (holding Option/Alt and dragging the bounding box) to be either branches or the main tree trunks. From the context-sensitive menu, he chose Transform > Reflect, and in the dialog chose Vertical to flip half of them. And since Cressy used Envelope Distort, his settings remained live and editable throughout the development of his image.

2

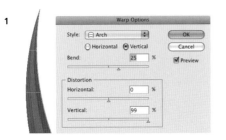

Using Roughen on a duplicate of the envelope layer to add texture to the tree trunks

2 Texturing the tree bark. In order to have some of the tree trunks stand out from the rest, Cressy decided to add texture to them. Since the Roughen effect breaks up smooth outlines with some of the outlines falling inside the original form, Cressy retained the full shape by keeping the basic shape on one layer, then duplicating it to a layer above; this layer he modified by choosing Effect > Distort & Transform > Roughen. After enabling Absolute, Cressy played with the sliders until he found the right amount of the effect to appear like rough bark on his tree trunks—modest settings prevented the Roughen effect here from creating long, sharp needles. Having again chosen a live effect to alter his basic shapes, rather than attempting to draw each of them with the Pen tool, Cressy kept his options open for future editing and was able to work quickly and interactively with the effects.

3 Using Roughen for grass, then warp it to make a broomstick. To construct the grassy hill, Cressy drew a half-oval with the Pen tool, then applied Effect > Distort & Transform > Zig Zag. He next applied Roughen with a low setting, and added another instance of the Roughen effect, this time with a high setting for Details to create the tall, thin strands of grass. To create the bristles of the witch's broomstick he used ⌘-F/Ctrl-F to paste a copy of the grassy hill in front, and applied an Envelope warp using the Shell Upper preset. He then edited the envelope with the Direct Selection tool and Free Transform until he had shaped the broom end.

4 Adding layers to coordinate scenes for different times of the day. Cressy maintained consistency from one scene to the next by adding tinting layers that could be turned on or off, each representing a different time of day. For midday, he added a layer with a light brown rectangle, then clicked <u>Opacity</u> in the Control panel to lower the Opacity to 50% and choose Screen for the Blending Mode. For early evening scenes, he used a white-to-dark brown radial gradient on a layer set to Multiply at reduced Opacity, and for night shots, he used a lavender-colored rectangle set to Multiply at 100% Opacity. He later reused these tinting layers with other scenes he created.

3

Creating the bristles of the broomstick from a duplicate of the grassy hill, then running Envelope Distort >Make with Warp, and choosing Shell Upper for the preset, then further transforming the envelope

4

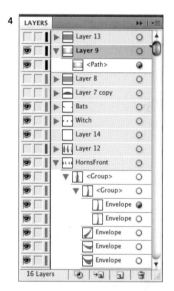

Using rectangles with different colors, blend modes, opacities, and gradients to tint the scenes

3D with a 2D Twist

Using 3D Effects to Achieve 2D Results

Overview: *Start with a sketch; create the 3D objects using the 3D Extrude & Bevel features; rotate and position the objects; use the 3D version as a reference for a 2D version.*

1

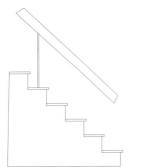

The scanned sketch used for reference and the Illustrator profile of the staircase

2

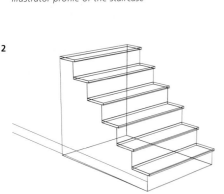

The extruded stairs with surface set to wireframe

Children's book Illustrator Kevan Atteberry creatively uses 3D as a guide to produce a 2D painting of a staircase in this portion of an illustration for his book *Frankie Stein* (see the *Creatively Combining Apps* chapter for a complete illustration that includes these stairs).

1 Creating the 2D line art. Atteberry began by drawing a traditional pencil sketch for the stairs, which he then scanned, and saved. Atteberry next placed his sketch on a template layer in Illustrator so he could create and position his 3D correctly in relation to his sketch. To do this, Atteberry chose File > Place, located his file, enabled the Link and Template checkboxes, and clicked the Place button. Using the Pen and Rectangle tools, he constructed a profile of his stairs. He then grouped the objects making up the stairs (since all of the stair objects would be extruded as a single unit). Next he created the rail and post as separate objects, since he would be extruding each separately (only one post was needed because he later duplicated it to make the rest).

2 Extruding the line art. Atteberry selected his 2D staircase and chose Effect > 3D > Extrude & Bevel. In the Extrude & Bevel Options dialog, he set the Surface field to Wireframe, so that he could still see the sketch through his 3D stairs. He set an estimated depth for the Extrude Depth field (until the stairs were rotated and positioned at the proper angle). After enabling Preview so he could see the 3D image as he worked, he grabbed a side of the 3D cube in the dialog and rotated the stairs until they matched the position of the stairs in the sketch. Atteberry clicked OK to apply the effect and exit the dialog. He then used the Selection tool to move his 3D object into position so that it aligned to the sketch. Once in position, he needed to make adjustments to the dimensions and angle of the stairs; to do this he clicked the underlined 3D Extrude & Bevel effect in the Appearance panel to reopen the dialog, and then he adjusted both the Extrude Depth field and the angle in the Perspective field until the object depth and angle of the stairs matched the sketch.

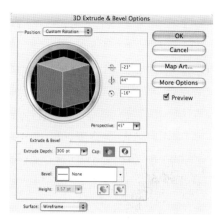

The 3D Extrude & Bevel Options dialog for the staircase

3 **Finishing the 3D.** Once Atteberry positioned the extruded 3D stairs, he repeated the Extrude process for the post and rail. This time, however, it was easier. The dialog remembered the exact X, Y, and Z axes angles from the position of the stairs (it remembers the last applied 3D Extrude & Bevel Options in a working session). The only value he needed to adjust separately for the post and rail was the Extrude Depth. Whereas, while working with the stairs, Atteberry wanted to see through a wireframe to the sketch below for positioning, he wanted the post and rails to appear more solid, so he set the Surface field in the dialog to Plastic Shading for the post and rail. Atteberry returned to the artboard to move and position all the 3D objects in place. To create duplicates of the one rail, he used Option-drag/Alt-drag to move the first post to the second position and then used the Duplicate command (⌘-D/Ctrl-D) to create the others. He made finishing adjustments by clicking on the 3D effect in the Appearance panel for a selected object and adjusted them live.

4 **Returning to 2D.** Atteberry hid the original sketch (in the Layers panel), printed his new 3D art, and used this print as a guide for a traditional ink drawing. Scanning and placing the new drawing back into Illustrator, he revectorized the stairs using Live Trace (see the *Rethinking Construction* chapter for more on Live Trace).

3

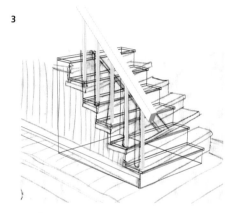

Atteberry's 3D stairs positioned over his scanned hand sketch

Using two windows

When positioning 3D objects in relationship to a template, try working with two windows at once. To create a second window, choose Window > Arrange > New Window. Leaving the first window in Preview mode, set the new window to Outline mode (View > Outline). This way, the outlined objects can be moved in relation to the sketch, and also seen live in the Preview window.

—*Kevan Atteberry*

Dedree Drees

As part of her undersea illustration, "The Dory," artist and instructor Dedree Drees mimicked blades of seagrass by building an intricate blend that she then extruded as a 3D object. Drees started by drawing four overlapping, wavy lines using the Pencil tool and then giving each stroke a unique color. To begin blending, Drees selected all four lines and then double-clicked the Blend tool. In the Blend Options dialog she set Spacing > Specified Steps to 2, and then chose Object > Blend > Make. To make the lines of the blend look like flat seagrass blades, Drees extruded the blend by opening the Appearance panel, and from the *fx* icon choosing 3D > Extrude & Bevel. She experimented with different Extrude Depth values to make sure that the seagrass blades would not appear thick and dense. Drees brought this object into Photoshop where she positioned it among other elements. To finish, she selected individual blades of seagrasses, and created layer masks to make them transparent.

DREES

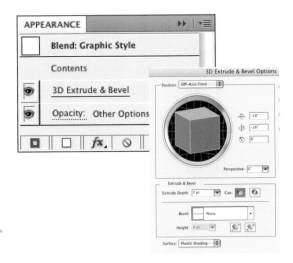

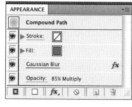

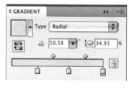

GLITSCHKA

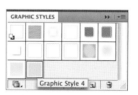

Von R. Glitschka

For "Beautiful," Von R. Glitschka placed his model and Japanese text against one of his intricate patterns (see the *Mastering Complexity* chapter for more on the pattern). He then used Live Effects throughout to create the interaction between his objects and their environment. To lift the Kanji characters from the background, he used Outer Glow in Multiply mode, creating an even shadow around the calligraphy. But to separate his model from the background pattern, he maintained directional lighting. He filled an object that matched her shape with the same blue as the background, and moved it a bit to the right, added a 20 pixel Gaussian Blur, and set the layer to Multiply mode with a slightly reduced opacity. He used the Gaussian Blur effect frequently to create the shadows cast on her skin by her hair and to soften transitions when modeling the skin tones. He used the Inner Glow effect in Multiply mode to add a soft shadow within an object. Because he modeled her in a very detailed fashion, Glitschka streamlined some of his work by creating a few graphic styles to use when creating the fine shading and blending in her skin tones. Gradients—often using transparency—added to the live effects to create a soft, romantically styled illustration.

BOARD2PIECES BY **TED ALSPACH**

Panel 1:
COULD WE FOCUS? I THINK WE'D ALL ENJOY PLAYING MÜ.

OH, I GOT IT NOW. "MÜ" IS THE GERMAN WORD FOR MOUSE DROPPINGS.

RIGHT. LIKE "HANS, CLEAN UP THAT PILE OF MÜ IN THE CORNER."

YUCK.

Panel 2:
WAIT. I BET IT'S ACTUALLY MOOSE DROPPINGS. THESE THINGS ALWAYS GET CONFUSED IN TRANSLATION.

WELL, THAT WOULD EXPLAIN DORIS'S ANIMAL ARTWORK ON THE CARDS.

SO THE NEXT QUESTION IS WHY IS THERE A MOOSE INSIDE? IS IT HANS'S PET?

Panel 3:
STOP. MÜ HAS NOTHING TO DO WITH MICE OR MOOSES.

THE PLURAL OF MOOSE IS MEESE, ISN'T IT?

SURE, AS IN "THERE'S A WHOLE FLOCK OF MEESE ON THE ROAD AHEAD."

SOMEDAY YOU'LL LET ME EXPLAIN THE GAME, RIGHT?

AT LEAST IT HAS A RICH THEME. WOW.

©2007 Ted Alspach 01-11-07

ALSPACH

Ted Alspach

Ted Alspach creates a new version of his comic strip "Board2Pieces" twice a week (plus a large-format bimonthly strip). When creating the whole concept for the strip, he understood he would need to create his characters and their positions and expressions consistently and quickly. To have time to concentrate on the written content instead of repetitive drawing, Alspach chose to use 3D objects for their live, editable effects, and a full Symbols panel of facial expressions to control his characters' appearance frame to frame. Early in the process he determined an extrusion amount for each character, using 3D's ability to rotate the character without the need to redraw the basic figure. Next he created a variety of facial expressions that would allow his characters to respond to each other. Alspach saved even more time by creating some characters that could share facial expressions. He saved all these expressions as symbols in order to be able to use 3D's ability to map symbols as art to a selected surface on the 3D object. (For more on creating symbols, see the *Expressive Strokes* chapter.) Now, instead of laboriously drawing

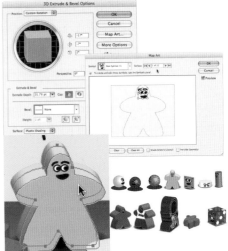

every frame, Alspach can select the desired character and place it where he needs it in the frame. He can then click on the effect name in the Appearance panel to modify the figure's position, and remap its facial expression using a library of symbols, which leaves him a lot more time for writing.

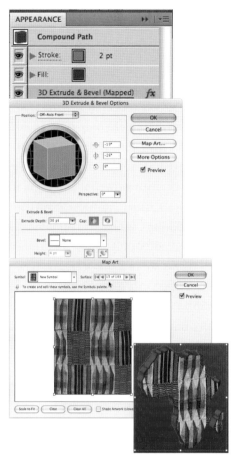

JOGIE

Mohammed Jogie

Mohammed Jogie created this bookcover for the African Peer Review Mechanism, an arm of NEPAD, for an annual progress report on Ghana. He purchased and photographed some of the objects and created the pattern for the map of Africa based on fabrics he bought. The fabric is Kente cloth, entirely hand-woven by Ghanaian weavers, which he obtained from the African art market in Johannesburg. He saved the fabric pattern as a symbol, a step necessary to map art to a 3D object. Jogie next created the flat, 2D object to represent Africa and Madagascar. He used a red Fill and a 2-pt Stroke to give the extruded edge the color and detail he wanted. He selected his "Africa" object and chose Effect > 3D > Extrude & Bevel. He set an amount for the extrusion, set the Cap to produce a solid edge, and rotated the object to the position he wanted, using the Preview to judge the effect. Jogie then chose Map Art and selected the surfaces he wanted to display the fabric. After mapping the fabric pattern, he clicked OK to exit the Map Art dialog, and OK again to exit and apply the 3D Effect. He used other illusions of depth, such as gradients within opacity masks and drop shadows, to complement the 3D structure of the map and used a copy of the 3D map for the reflection.

One Perspective

Simulating a One-Point Perspective View

Overview: *Create a one-point perspective grid; customize the grid by moving its control points; draw tile artwork and move it onto the grid using the Perspective Selection tool; duplicate the artwork to make a row; duplicate the rows to form a floor.*

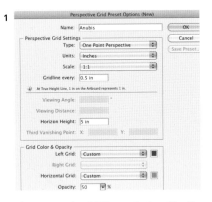

The "Perspective Grid Preset Options (New)" dialog

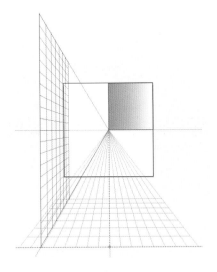

The new one-point grid created by modifying the [1P-Normal View] preset

Elaine Drew is an artist who is equally at home with traditional painting as with the latest digital drawing tools. For this Anubis image, Drew relied on Illustrator's Perspective Grid tool and presets to give the tiled floor and gradient walls the illusion of perspective.

1 Creating the one-point perspective grid. Drew designed the illustration to feature a one-point perspective view. She began by selecting the Rectangle tool and drawing the square that would form the rear wall of the room and serve as a guide for creating the perspective grid in the next step. She filled the square with a gradient.

To start the grid, Drew selected Edit > Perspective Grid Presets, chose the [1P-Normal View] preset, and clicked New. In the "Perspective Grid Preset Options (New)" dialog, she set Units to Inches, and changed Gridlines to every 0.5 inches and Horizontal Height to 5 inches. Drew named the preset and clicked OK.

2 Adjusting the grid to fit the illustration design. To begin customizing the grid to fit her design, Drew chose

View > Perspective Grid > One Point Perspective and selected the preset she had created previously. Selecting the Perspective Grid tool (which made the grid editable), she dragged the left Ground Level control until it met the lower-left corner of the artboard. Then she dragged the Horizontal Level control down and the Vanishing Point control to the right. Finally, to extend the bottom grid plane to the rear wall, she dragged the Extent of Grid control upward so that the grid met the bottom of the wall (to accurately see the full extent of the grid, it may be necessary to zoom in).

3 Creating the floor tiles and moving them onto the grid. With the grid established, Drew was ready to create the two floor tiles. She decided to create the tiles and assemble them into rows outside of the grid before moving them into the grid to form the floor. She turned off the perspective grid by clicking inside the circle of the Plane Switching Widget with the Perspective Grid tool. (The circle's background turns blue.)

Next, Drew created one circular petal and one square tile to fit within the 0.5-inch grid size she specified in the previous step. To soften the look of the artwork, she applied the Effect > SVG Filters > AI_Alpha_1 filter. She duplicated the pair of tiles several times to create a row, then duplicated the row and offset it horizontally by one tile. She continued duplicating and offsetting the rows to complete the floor. To render the tiled floor in the perspective of her grid, she first made sure View > Perspective Grid > Snap to Grid was enabled, and then chose the Perspective Selection tool and clicked the Horizontal Grid plane portion of the Plane Switching Widget. Then she selected all of the tiles with the Perspective Selection tool and dragged them onto the grid.

Drew finished the room by creating the left wall. She drew a rectangle and filled it with a gradient. Then she selected the Perspective Selection tool, clicked on the Left Grid plane portion of the Plane Switching widget, and dragged the rectangle onto the grid.

2

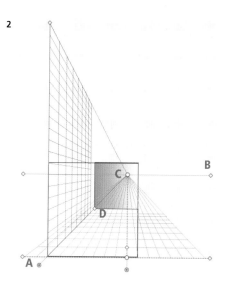

Perspective grid after all adjustments; **A** is the left Ground Level control, **B** is the Horizontal Level control, **C** is the Vanishing Point control, **D** is the Extent of Grid control

3

(Left) Turning off the perspective grid by clicking inside the circle of the Plane Switching Widget with the Perspective Grid or Perspective Selection tool; (right) selecting the Horizontal Grid plane

The original square tile and circular petal tile artwork created in Illustrator before being modified by the AI_Alpha_1 SVG filter

Out of controls?

While only four perspective grid controls were used here, 13 more await you. Find out about them by accessing Help > *Illustrator Help.* Click on Drawing and then Perspective. The About Perspective Grid section shows and describes all 17 grid controls.

Amplified Angles

Creating Details with Two-Point Perspective

Overview: *Set up a two-point perspective grid; use drawing and editing tools to create the basic drawing in perspective; add basic shapes in perspective; add more details to achieve the final result.*

Anil Ahuja, a senior product specialist working for Adobe, created this bus for instructional materials that explain how to work with Illustrator's perspective tools.

1

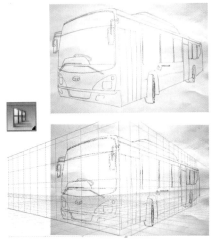

Using the Perspective Grid tool (at left) to set up and position the grid; the ground, right, and left plane controls visible on top of the sketch

1 Setting up a perspective grid. Ahuja sketched the bus from a photo reference, scanned it, and then placed it into Illustrator as a template layer. When you select the Perspective Grid tool, your artboard will, by default, display a two-point perspective grid. Ahuja then adjusted the grid to fit the scanned sketch by aligning the control points on the grid to match the sketch. Using the Perspective Grid tool, he then began by moving the ground level control point (the diamond on either extremity of the ground level), which allowed him to move all the planes together in any direction (this is indicated by the four-way arrow that appears next to the cursor when it is over this control point). Then he moved the left and right planes individually by using the tool to drag the right and left grid plane controls (the small circles beneath each visible grid). He then also adjusted the horizon (the diamond on either extremity of the horizon line) and vanishing points (circles on the horizon line where the planes converge).

2

(Top) Using the Perspective Grid tool to click on a side in the widget to activate a plane (first 3 widgets from left) or outside the cube in the widget to deactivate all planes (far right widget); (bottom) creating the basic bus shapes in perspective using the Rectangle, Rounded Rectangle, and Ellipse tools

2 Drawing in perspective. Clicking a widget side to activate the plane he wished to work in, Ahuja then drew the

basic shapes of the bus in perspective using tools such as
the Rectangle, Rounded Rectangle, and Ellipse tools. After
creating one side window, he held Option/Alt while dragging it to create the others. Duplicating objects this way
automatically transformed them to their new perspective
position as he dragged them.

3 Drawing complex elements. Ahuja created complex elements (such as the wheels) outside of the perspective grid,
then attached them to the perspective grid by dragging
them within the grid using the Perspective Selection tool.
He converted the fills of some grid objects into gradients,
and others into gradient mesh by clicking on them with
the Gradient Mesh tool (meshes must be made by converting objects already in the grid; they can't be created
first and then moved into a grid). He duplicated the outer
rim of the tire to create the inner rim by holding Option/
Alt (this makes the duplicate) and the 5 key (this makes
the drag perpendicular to the original). To create the tire
surface he used the curvature of the tire as a guide, used
the Pen tool to draw a closed path within the space, and
then filled it with a gradient.

Ahuja drew a few doors and windows using the
Rounded Rectangle tool. After creating one door panel
or side window, he duplicated it by holding Option-Shift/
Alt-Shift while he dragged it to the desired location, using
⌘-D/Ctrl-D to transform again if needed. For each door
or window he copied and used Paste in Front, converted
this copy to a gradient mesh, and reduced the opacity of
mesh points by clicking on <u>Opacity</u> in the Control panel.

4 The finishing touches. Ahuja created the most complex
elements (like the logo and text) separately, then attached
them to the perspective grid using the Perspective Selection tool. To create the bus shadow, Ahuja first selected
the ground plane and drew a rectangle on the plane using
the Rectangle tool choosing Effect > Blur > Gaussian Blur.
He created the building side by drawing a series of filled
and stroked rectangles in the perspective grid.

3

(Left) The wheels created outside the perspective
grid; (middle) using the Perspective Grid tool to
move the wheel into perspective and duplicating the outer rim (holding Option-5/Alt-5 while
dragging); (right) after drawing a closed path to
create the tire surface

(Left) Building one door panel by layering versions
(shown alongside one another for clarity); (right)
after creating one of each door panel and window type, duplicating them within the Perspective Grid tool to create the others

4

Creating the bus logo separately before attaching
it to the perspective grid

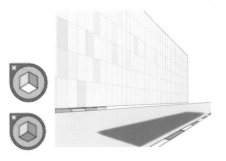

Selecting the right plane to draw the building
side and the ground plane to create the bus
shadow

Modifying a Photo

Inserting Photographs in Perspective

Overview: *Place a photograph and adjust the perspective grid to conform to the perspective of the image; add graphic elements in perspective; modify the photo to create a new product.*

M·GARRY

1

(Top) The original product; (directly above) shown after drawing two pink lines on the left side, extending back until they intersect to form the left vanishing point, and relocating the horizon line to this point using the Perspective Grid tool

Aaron McGarry, an illustrator working for the electronics industry in California, was able to use a photo of an existing product and the perspective grid to conceptualize the next generation of the device.

1 Working with an established perspective. In order to add new elements to this photo, McGarry needed to find a way to fit a two-point grid to this uneven perspective. Using the Perspective Grid tool, he first grabbed the Ground Level control point and moved the entire grid so that the three-plane intersection point rested at the foremost point on the device. McGarry then needed to adjust the grid to the photo perspective. He began by identifying two parallel edges on the left side of the device. To use these edges as a guide, he used the Line tool to draw two lines along these edges, extending the lines into the background until they intersected (see heavy pink lines in image at left). This gave him the left vanishing point. He then used the Perspective Grid tool to grab the Horizon Line control point and move the horizon line up to meet the intersection point of the two guide lines.

Since the right plane of the device is essentially rounded with no straight edges to reference for guide lines, McGarry took the foremost straight edge on the top surface (heavy blue line in image) and extended a line back to intersect the horizon line, which gave him the right vanishing point. Since the horizon line was already in position only one guideline was needed for this side.

2 Creating the side buttons. McGarry began detailed items, like the icons and buttons, outside of the perspective grid. He sampled a light and dark color from the original buttons using the Eyedropper tool, then saved them as swatches. To make it appear that the button was recessed, he created a linear gradient using the sampled swatches, then adjusted the gradient stops so that the lighter color was pushed to a far edge. After rotating the icons 90° clockwise (you can't rotate objects within the perspective grid!), he activated the left plane, marquee-selected the buttons using the Perspective Selection tool, and then positioned them. After resizing the buttons using the bounding box, he completed the bottom ledge on the buttons by drawing a narrow rectangle in perspective mode, then added a gradient; since gradients do not transform when put into the grid, he adjusted the angle in the Gradient panel to match the plane angle. He held Option/Alt as he dragged this ledge to create the other.

3 Creating the LCD screen. Activating the floor plane, McGarry used the Rectangle tool to create a rectangle in perspective and filled it with a Sky gradient (from Swatch Libraries). Outside of the perspective grid, he next created the screen text and icon, rotated them, and then attached them to the perspective plane with the Perspective Selection tool. To create the illusion that the LCD screen was backlit, he layered an offset transparent copy of the LCD above the text. To do this he selected the LCD object, then used perpendicular movement by clicking on the Floor Plane control point to open the Floor Plane dialog. Entering a 2-pt value in the Location field, he selected Copy Selected Objects and clicked OK. With this duplicate now selected, he created a new layer and moved the duplicate to this layer by dragging the selection square (in the Layers panel). Using the bounding box, McGarry then brought the two foremost edges of the top LCD screen out to match the edges of bottom one. Finally, he reduced the opacity of the top LCD using the Transparency panel, giving depth to the glass while also fading the text and icon.

2

(Left) Two buttons that needed to be relocated from the top of the device to the side to make room for the new LCD and LED; (right) after being rotated and color matched to the originals on the image

With the left plane activated, McGarry used the Perspective Selection tool to attach the buttons to the perspective grid

(Left) Before adding the light bottom ledge; (right) after adding the ledge by duplicating the first one (by holding Option/Alt while moving it with the Perspective Selection tool)

3

Selecting the LCD with the Perspective Selection tool and then clicking on the Floor Plane control point opens the Floor Plane dialog; moving a copy of the LCD up 2 points

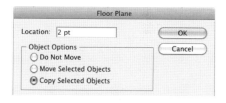

Text and icon are on a separate layer between two LCD layers, with opacity of the top LCD reduced showing the text, icon, and bottom LCD below

Establishing Perspective

Aligning Grids & Planes to an Architectural Sketch

MARIC

Advanced Technique

Overview: *Import a sketch with a visible horizon line; set up and align a perspective grid; construct the rendering using the perspective grid.*

Horizon line shown in red

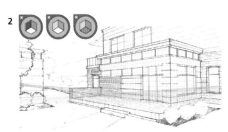

Detail of the original drawing on a template layer with a perspective grid placed accurately over the sketch

Creating architectural renderings in Illustrator got a whole lot easier with the addition of the Perspective Grid tool. For traditional illustrators like Pete Maric, who learned how to create architectural renderings by hand, this tool is similar to setting up vanishing points on a drafting board. Upon constructing the perspective grid, all lines and forms drawn snap to the grid for a faster workflow and provide perspective accuracy. The perspective grid can be repositioned for adjacent walls or turned off to create "out-of-perspective" elements.

1 Creating a reference image. Maric relied on a hand-drawn sketch as reference for the illustration, making certain that there is a strong visible horizon line to later help him establish the vanishing points. In Illustrator, using File > Place, he enabled the Template option to import the sketch into a locked template layer.

2 Constructing the perspective grid. Selecting the Perspective Grid tool in the Tools panel activated the default grid. Maric then began to align the grid to the sketch by moving the grid plane control handles until the grid matched the perspective of the sketch. Starting with the left (blue) plane, he click-dragged the control handle to align with the right front of the building. He aligned the right (orange) plane to the receding front wall and the bottom (green) plane to the porch. He then click-dragged each vanishing point control handle, moving them into position until both were aligned to the visible horizon line in his sketch.

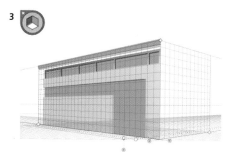

3 Creating the architectural elements in perspective.

Leaving the perspective grid active and sketch template layer visible, Maric was able to easily focus on the current active drawing plane using the Plane Switching Widget. Maric primarily used the Rectangle tool to create the front entrance of the building and main architectural elements. He organized drawn elements (façade, windows, mullions) in the Layers panel in accordance with the way they appear in real life. So, windows would be lower on the layer stack, mullions would be in front of windows, and the façade would be on top of the layer stack. By selecting the right plane in the Plane Switching Widget, he created the receding front wall, windows, and mullions to align with this plane.

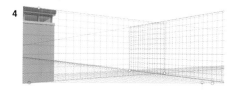

Creating architectural elements in perspective using the Perspective Grid tool and Plane Switching Widget

4 Moving the perspective grid to create additional architectural geometry and adding detail.

Once one portion of the building was complete, he could reposition the perspective grid to create walls in other areas of the illustration. However, before moving the grid to adjacent walls, Maric saved customized grids for each plane of the structure by using View > Perspective Grid > Save Grid as Preset. Then he could realign the perspective grid by clicking and dragging the grid plane control handles so he could use the grid to construct different walls. To create repeating linear details within the walls, Maric needed to draw only one line, he then duplicated it in perspective by holding Option/Alt while dragging it.

Aligning the perspective grid to adjacent walls and creating detail with the Line tool

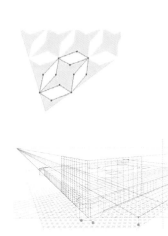

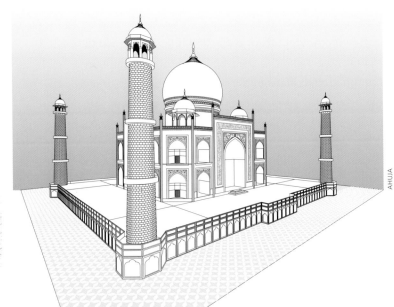

AHUJA

Anil Ahuja/Adobe Systems

Adobe Systems Product Specialist Anil Ahuja used a number of visual references to create this majestic Taj Mahal. To help him in the construction of the building in perspective, he created front- and plan-view sketches. He then referred to photos to set up the basic two-point perspective grid. As with a real structure, he built from the ground up using layers to organize his assembled pieces. The floor is a single design that he created normally (top left) and saved as a symbol. Then he dragged an instance of the symbol into the perspective grid using the Perspective Selection tool. Using a combination of Option-Shift/Alt-Shift, he dragged to create a duplicate, then used Transform Again (⌘-D/Ctrl-D) to repeat the floor pattern. The next object was the plinth (raised base) upon which the mausoleum sits (bottom left). Drawing a rectangle in perspective on the ground plane first, he then used the Automatic Plane Positioning feature when creating the sides. Though he created symmetrical objects such as squares and rectangles in perspective, he created the more intricate designs such as the curved archways of the iwan and pishtaqs normally and then placed them into perspective. The onion dome began as outlines on the plinth. He used the perpendicular movement feature to duplicate and precisely move an outlined ring straight up off the floor plane by using the Floor Plane dialog options (click Floor Plane control point to open). Once he had positioned the rings, he drew straight lines alongside the rings to complete the cylinder and drew a simple circle without perspective behind to create the dome shape. For more info about how he created this, see his ReadMe on the **WOW! DVD**.

7

Mastering Complexity

Mastering Complexity

Use transparency with...

- **Fills and Strokes:** Apply opacity, blend mode, or an effect that uses transparency (e.g., Feather).
- **Gradient Stops and Gradient Mesh points:** Apply opacity to a gradient stop or mesh point.
- **Brush Strokes:** Make brushes transparent, or make brush strokes from transparent artwork by applying an opacity, blend mode, or effect that uses transparency.
- **Text:** Apply transparency to selected text characters and/or the entire text object.
- **Groups:** Select a <Group> and apply an opacity, a blend mode, or an effect that uses transparency (selecting an entire group automatically targets it).
- **Layers:** Target the layer and apply an opacity, a blend mode, or an effect that uses transparency.
- **Charts:** Apply transparency to the entire chart or the elements that make up the chart.

Change your artboard color...

Enable the Simulate Colored Paper option and change the top grid swatch to a color to change your artboard color. Neither the transparency grid nor simulated paper color will print.

The organized whole is more than the sum of its parts. Combining tools and techniques in Illustrator can yield **WOW!** results. In this chapter we'll look at such synergy.

Please keep in mind that this chapter will be quite daunting, if not overwhelming, if you're not comfortable with what has been covered in previous chapters.

This chapter contains a variety of techniques, from opacity and transparency issues, opacity masks and clipping masks, to some powerful features not covered elsewhere, such as multiple-object, shaped blends.

TRANSPARENCY

Although the artboard may look white, Illustrator treats it as transparent. To visually distinguish the transparent areas from the non-transparent ones, choose View > Show Transparency Grid. Change the size and colors of the transparency grid in the File > Document Setup dialog. You can enable Simulate Colored Paper if you'll be printing on a colored stock (click on the top swatch next to Grid Size to open the color picker and select a "paper" color). Both Transparency Grid and paper color are non-printing attributes that are only visible in on-screen preview once you click OK to exit the dialog.

The term *transparency* refers to any blending mode other than Normal and to any opacity setting that is less than 100%. opacity masks or effects, such as Feather or Drop Shadow, use these settings as well. As a result, when you apply opacity masks or certain effects, you're using Illustrator's transparency features.

Opacity and blending modes

To reduce opacity, select or target an object, layer, or group in the Layers panel, then choose a blending mode or reduce the Opacity slider in the Transparency panel. You can also reveal Transparency panel controls for a selected object by clicking Opacity in the Appearance or

Control panels. As it's called "Opacity" (and not "Transparency"), an object or group is completely opaque when Opacity is 100%, and invisible when Opacity is 0%.

Blending modes control how the colors of objects, groups, or layers interact with one another. Blending modes will yield different results in RGB and CMYK. As in Photoshop, the blending modes show no effect when they're over the *transparent* artboard. To see the effect of blending modes, you need to add a color-filled or white-filled element behind your transparent object or group.

From left to right: a building by Chris Leavens; the building with a rectangle in front (filled with a black-to-white linear gradient); and the building with the gradient applied as an opacity mask

OPACITY MASKS

With an opacity mask, you can use the dark and light areas of one object (the mask) to mark transparent areas of other objects. Black areas of the mask will create transparent areas in the artwork it masks; white areas of the mask leave corresponding areas of the artwork opaque and visible; and gray values create a range of transparency. (This works exactly like Photoshop *layer masks*.)

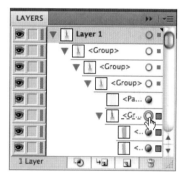

Objects being masked by an opacity mask are indicated by a dashed line in the Layers panel

To create an opacity mask, position one object or group you want to use as the mask in front of the artwork you want to mask. Select both the artwork and the masking object. (To mask a layer, first target the layer in the Layers panel.) Finally, choose Make Opacity Mask from the Transparency panel menu. The topmost object or group automatically becomes the opacity mask.

You may want to start with an empty mask and draw into it—in effect, painting your objects into visibility. To create an empty mask, start by targeting a single object, group, or layer. Since the default behavior of new opacity masks is clipping (with a black background), you'll need to turn off the "New Opacity Masks Are Clipping" option in the Transparency panel menu. If you don't do this, and your targeted artwork disappears when you first create the empty mask, simply enable the Clip checkbox in the Transparency panel. This creates an empty mask and puts you in mask-editing mode; the Layers panel changes to show the <Opacity Mask>. Next, click in the right thumbnail area. Use your drawing and editing tools to create

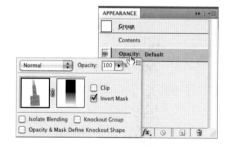

The Transparency panel displays by choosing Window > Transparency or by clicking the underlined word *Opacity* for a selected object in the Appearance or Control panel; here focused on the opacity mask for the building at top

When you click the opacity mask thumbnail in the Transparency panel, the Layers panel displays only the objects within the opacity mask. This is indicated by the Layers panel tab name; try to keep the Layers, Transparency, and Appearance panels open when editing opacity masks.

your mask. (For instance, if you create an object filled with a gradient, you'll see your artwork through the dark areas of the gradient.) While the <Opacity Mask> thumbnail is selected, you won't be able to select or edit anything else in your document because Illustrator puts you into an isolated mask-editing mode. To exit this mask-editing mode, you must click the artwork thumbnail in the Transparency panel (the artwork thumbnail is on the left; the opacity mask is on the right).

A few hints can help you with opacity masks. First, opacity masks are converted to grayscale, behind the scenes, when a mask is created (even though the opacity mask thumbnail still appears in color). The gray values between white and black simply determine how opaque or transparent the masked object is—light areas of the mask will be more opaque, and dark areas will be more transparent. In addition, if you select Invert Mask, you'll reverse the effect of dark and light values on the opacity—dark areas of the mask will be more opaque, and light areas will be more transparent. To identify which elements have been masked by an opacity mask, look for the dashed underline in the Layers panel.

The link icon in the Transparency panel indicates that the position of the opacity mask stays associated with the position of the object, group, or layer it is masking. Unlinking allows you to move the artwork without moving the mask. The content of the mask can be selected and edited just like any other object. You can transform or apply a blending mode and/or an opacity percentage to each individual object within the mask.

Precisely targeting and editing transparency

You can apply transparency to so many levels of a document that it can be a challenge to keep track of where you've applied it. For example, you can apply a blending mode to a path, then group it with several other objects and apply an opacity level to that group or to the layer that contains the group. To quickly and precisely locate and edit any transparent object, use the Layers, Appearance, and Transparency panels together. This is especially useful when you want to identify and edit the transparency of specific objects after using the Flattener Preview panel (covered in the next section) to see how current transparency settings will affect flattened output.

Remember that a gradient-filled circle in the Layers panel indicates that transparency is applied to an object, group, or layer, and an underlined name indicates that an opacity mask is applied. If the Appearance panel is open, it gives you access to the appearance details for the targeted object. Clicking the word Opacity in the Appearance panel (or the Control panel) displays detailed transparency settings for the targeted object. If you targeted an opacity mask, clicking the opacity mask thumbnail in the Transparency panel makes the Layers and Appearance panels provide information about the opacity mask.

BLENDS

Although gradients and mesh allow you to transition from one color to another, blends give you a way to "morph" one object's shape and/or color into another. You can create blends between multiple objects, and even blend gradients, symbols, compound paths such as letters, or even Point type objects. Because blends are *live*, you can edit the key objects' shape, color, size, location, or rotation, and the resulting *in-between* objects will automatically update. You can also distribute a blend along a custom path (see details later in this chapter).

The simplest way to create a blend is to select the objects you wish to blend and choose Object > Blend > Make (⌘-Option-B/Ctrl-Alt-B). The number of steps you'll have in between each object is based on either the default options for the tool or the last settings of the Blend Options. To later adjust settings on an existing blend: select the blend, then double-click the Blend tool (or choose Objects > Blend > Blend Options).

Another way to create blends between individual paths is to *point map* using the Blend tool. In the past, the Blend tool was used to achieve smooth transitions between

Isolating blending & knockout

Choose Show Options from the Transparency panel pop-up menu to control how transparency is applied to groups and multiple objects. You get different effects depending on whether you select individual objects, target groups, or enable/disable Isolate Blending and/or Knockout Group. If you enable Isolate Blending for a selected group, then the transparency settings of the objects inside the group only affect how those objects interact with each other, and transparency isn't applied to objects underneath the group. With a group or layer targeted, the Knockout Group option will keep individual objects of a group or layer from applying their transparency settings to each other where they overlap; for this reason, Illustrator automatically enables the Knockout Group option for all newly created blends. See the "Opacity&Blending.ai" ReadMe on the **WOW! DVD** for examples.

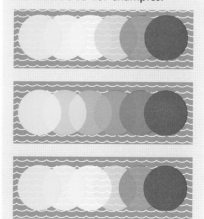

PostScript output devices and file formats such as EPS can only reproduce transparent artwork in "flattened" form. Illustrator's flattening process is applied temporarily if you print, and permanently if you save in a format that doesn't support transparency natively (transparency was first introduced in Illustrator 9). Flattening occurs when areas of transparent overlap are converted into opaque pieces that look the same. Some of your objects may be split into many separate objects, while others may be rasterized. For more details, search Illustrator Help for "print production guide transparency" to access "Adobe Applications: A Print Production Guide."

What you can do with blends

Once you're done tweaking your blend, you can also:

- Reverse the direction of a blend, with Object > Blend > Reverse Front to Back. Or reverse the order of objects on a spine by choosing Object > Blend > Reverse Spine.
- Release blends (Object > Blend > Release) removes blends, leaving key objects and spines.
  Hint: Select > Select All releases multiple blends simultaneously.
- Choose Object > Blend > Expand to turn a blend into a group of separate, editable objects.

blended objects. Now that it's been modified, however, it's probably best to use it for special morphing or twirling effects. To use the *point map* technique, begin by clicking on an anchor point of one object, and then on an anchor point of another object. Continue clicking on anchor points of any object you want to include in the blend. You can also click anywhere on the path of an object to achieve random blending effects.

When a blend first appears, it's selected and grouped. If you Undo immediately, the blend will be deleted, but your source objects remain selected so you can blend again. To modify a key object before or after making a blend, Direct-Select the key object first, then use any editing tool (including the Pencil, Smooth, and Path Eraser tools) to make your changes.

Blend Options

To specify options as you blend, use the Blend tool (see the "point map" directions in the previous section) and press the Option/Alt key as you click the second point. In Blend Options you can change settings before making the blend. To adjust options on a completed blend, select it and double-click the Blend tool (or Object > Blend > Blend Options). Opening Blend Options without a blend selected sets the default for creating blends *in this work session*— these options reset each time you restart the program:

- **Specified Steps** specifies the number of steps between each pair of key objects (the limit is 1000). Using fewer steps results in clearly distinguishable objects; a larger number of steps results in an almost airbrushed effect.
- **Specified Distance** places a specified distance between the objects of the blend.
- **Smooth Color** automatically calculates the ideal number of steps between key objects in a blend, in order to achieve the smoothest color transition. If objects are the same color, or are gradients or patterns, this option equally distributes the objects within the blend, based on their size.
- **Orientation** determines how the individual blend objects rotate as they follow the path's curves. Align to Page (the

default, first icon) prevents objects from rotating as they're distributed along the path's curve (objects stay "upright" as they blend along the curve). Align to Path allows blend objects to rotate as they follow along the path.

Blends along a path

There are two ways to make blends follow a curved path. The first way is to use the Direct Selection tool to select the *spine* of a blend (the path automatically created by the blend) and then use the Add/Delete Anchor Point tools, or any of the following tools, to curve or edit the path: the Direct Selection, Lasso, Convert Anchor Point, Pencil, Smooth, or even the Path Eraser tool. As you edit the spine of the blend, Illustrator automatically redraws the blend objects to align to the edited spine.

Secondly, you can also replace the spine with a customized path. Select both the customized path and the blend, and choose Object > Blend > Replace Spine. This command moves the blend to its new spine.

You can also blend between pairs of grouped objects. If you're not getting the results you expect, try creating your first set of objects and grouping them (⌘-G/Ctrl-G). Now copy and paste a duplicate set (or Option/Alt and drag to create a copy of your group). Select the two sets of grouped objects and blend by choosing Specified Steps as the blend option. Once the objects are blended, you can rotate and scale them, and use the Direct Selection tool to edit the objects or the spine. (To experiment with a pair of grouped blends in this way, find the figures at right on the **WOW! DVD** as "AaronMcGarry-blends.ai.")

CLIPPING MASKS

All of the objects involved in a mask are organized in one of two ways depending on how you choose to make your mask. One method collects all selected objects into a group. The other method allows you to keep your layer structure and uses the master "container" layer (see the Layers panel illustrations, next page). With any kind of clipping mask, the topmost object of that group is the

AARON McGARRY

The ripening tomatoes on a vine image above, was created using a variety of blends: the smooth color option for the vine, and groups of objects blended into each other with Specified Steps and a custom **S** *curve "spine" (see Aaron McGarry's explanation on the* **WOW! DVD***).*

To insert objects into a blend

Group-Select a key object and Option-drag/Alt-drag to insert a new key object (the blend will reflow). You can also insert new objects by entering isolation mode (see previous chapter) or by dragging them into the blend in the Layers panel.

Choose Clipping Mask >Make from the Object menu, or use the Make/Release Clipping Mask icon on the Layers panel (right)

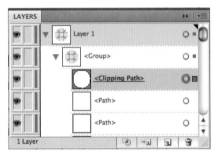

Choosing Object >Clipping Mask >Make puts all of the masked objects into a group with the clipping path at the top of the group

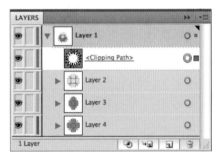

Clicking the Make/Release Clipping Mask icon at the bottom of the panel turns the first item within the highlighted group or layer into a clipping path, without creating a new group

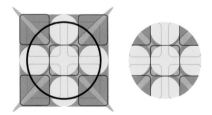

Before masking (left), the black-stroked circle is positioned as the topmost object in the stacking order, so it will become the clipping path when the clipping mask is created (right)

clipping path; this clips (hides) portions of the other objects in the group that extend beyond the clipping mask boundaries, leaving only the parts within these boundaries visible. Regardless of the attributes assigned to this top object, once you create the mask, it becomes an unfilled and unstroked clipping path (but keep reading to see how you can apply a stroke and fill to the new clipping path!).

In the Layers panel, there are two indicators of an active clipping mask. First, your <u><Clipping Path></u> will be underlined and will remain underlined even if you rename it. Second, with an active clipping mask, you'll see dotted lines, instead of the standard solid lines, between the clipped items in the Layers panel.

To make a clipping mask from an object, you must first create that object. Only a single path can be used as a clipping mask, which means that complex shapes or multiple paths must be combined into a single "compound path" before being used as a mask (using Object > Compound Path > Make). Make sure your path or compound path is above the objects to be clipped, then create the clipping mask using one of two options. Use either the Make/Release Clipping Mask icon on the Layers panel, or the Object > Clipping Mask > Make command. Each has its inherent advantages and disadvantages. The Object menu command gathers all the objects into a new group as it masks, allowing you to have multiple masked objects within a layer. It also gives you the ability to freely move masked objects within a layer structure without breaking the mask. However, if you have a carefully planned layer structure, it will be lost when everything is grouped. In contrast, the Layers panel command maintains your layer structure as it masks, but you can't have separately masked objects within a layer without building sublayers or grouping them first. This makes it difficult to move masked objects as a unit.

After you've created a clipping mask, you can edit the masking object, and the objects within the mask, using the Lasso, Direct Selection, or any other path-editing tools. When you're using the Selection tools on masks created using the Object menu, a recent enhancement to object clipping masks prevents you from inadvertently selecting hidden parts of the masked objects.

To move your clipped object (path and contents) simply select it with the Selection tool and move it. If you wish to select, move, or edit the clipping path or the contents independently, then you have a few options. If neither is selected, you can simply click on the clipping path or contents with the Direct Selection or Group Selection tool to edit or move that path or selection. If any portion of the mask or contents is already selected, you can click the Edit Clipping Path or Edit Contents buttons in the Control panel to focus on which portion will be selected and can be edited.

You also can now edit your clipping group in isolation mode. To isolate the entire clipping <Group>, double-click on any portion of it with the Selection tool; this dims all other objects on your artboard. You can now use the Control panel buttons to edit the path or contents, or use the Direct Selection and Group Selection tools.

You can also enter isolation mode via the Layers panel. Highlight the <Clipping Path> or any of the paths within the <Group> and choose Enter Isolation Mode from the Layers panel pop-up menu. Once in isolation mode you can freely edit or move the paths without affecting any other objects. If you are in isolation mode with one of the objects within the mask, you can even add additional objects within that grouping. To exit, double-click on the artboard (outside of the clipping group), or choose Exit Isolation Mode from the Layers panel pop-up menu.

Yet another way that you can determine which portion of your clipping group you wish to edit is by choosing Object > Clipping Mask > Edit Mask (or Object > Clipping Mask > Edit Content).

Once you have a clipping group and the mask has been created, you can then add a stroke (it will appear as if it's in front of all masked objects) and/or fill (it appears as if it's behind all masked objects). In addition, once the mask has been made, in the Layers panel you can even

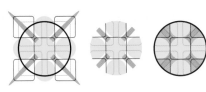

You can add a stroke and fill to a mask. The middle figure shows an unstroked mask; the right figure shows a dark blue stroke and a light blue fill added to the clipping mask.

Multiple artboard masks

Since layers are common to multiple artboards, if you make a mask using the Layer panel method, that mask will apply across multiple artboards. In order for artwork on other artboards to be seen, it must be above or below the layers being masked.

Figuring out if it's a mask

- <Clipping Path> in the Layers panel will be underlined if it's a mask (even if you've renamed it), and the background color for the icon will be gray.
- If Object > Clipping Mask > Release is enabled it means a mask is affecting your selection.
- An *opacity mask* has a dotted underline in the Layers panel.
- Select > Object > Clipping Masks can help you find masks within a document as long as they aren't inside linked files.

Collect in New Layer

To collect selected layers into one "master layer," Shift-click or ⌘-click/Ctrl-click multiple layers and choose Collect in New Layer from the Layers menu.

move the clipping path lower in the stacking order of the group or container and still keep its masking effect.

Masking technique #1: The Object menu command

The simplest way to create masks for objects is using the Object menu command. Use this method when you want to confine the clipping mask to a specific object or group of objects that need to be easily duplicated or relocated. Since this method modifies your layer structure, don't use it if you need to maintain objects on specific layers.

As before, start by creating an object or compound object that will become your clipping mask. Make sure that it's the topmost object, then select it and *all* the objects you want to be masked (this topmost object will become the mask). Now, choose Object > Clipping Mask > Make. When you use this method, all the objects, including the new clipping path, will move to the layer that contains your topmost object and will be collected into a new <Group>. This will restrict the masking effect to only those objects within the group; you can easily use the Selection tool to select the entire clipping group. If you expand the <Group> in the Layers panel (by clicking the expansion triangle), you'll be able to move objects into or out of the clipping group, or move objects up or down within the group to change the stacking order. (Don't miss the Tip "Magical clipping path" at right.)

When working with masks created using the Object menu, clipped objects are now truly hidden when clipped by a mask; you can no longer accidentally select the clipped portion of an object outside of the mask.

Masking technique #2: The Layers panel options

To mask unwanted areas of art within a *container* (meaning any group, sublayer, or layer), first create an object to use as your mask—make sure it's the topmost object in your container. Next, highlight that object's *container* and click the Make/Release Clipping Mask icon on the Layers panel. The result: The topmost object, *within* the highlighted container, becomes the clipping path, and all elements within that container extending beyond the clipping path are hidden (for details on using complex objects as a mask, see the section "Using type, or compound paths or shapes as a mask" below).

Once you've created a clipping mask, you can move objects up or down within the container (layer, sublayer, or group) to change the stacking order. However, if you move items outside of the clipping mask container, they will no longer be masked. Moving the clipping path itself outside of its container releases the mask completely.

Mask button

If you use File > Place to place an image, when the placed image is selected, you can instantly create a clipping path for the image by clicking the Mask button in the Control panel. However, masking is not immediately apparent because the clipping path has the same dimensions as the placed image's bounding box. Make sure the Edit Clipping Path button (in the Control panel) is enabled and then adjust the clipping path to shape the mask that is "cropping" your image.

Using type, or compound paths or shapes as a mask

You can use editable type as a mask to give the appearance that the type is filled with any image or group of objects. Select the type and the image or objects with which you want to fill the text. Make sure the type is on top, then choose Object > Clipping Mask > Make.

To use separate type characters as a single clipping mask, you have to first make them into a compound shape or compound path. You can make a compound shape from either outlined or live (i.e., non-outlined) text. You can make a compound path only from outlined text (not live text). Once you've made a compound path or shape out of separate type elements, you can use it as a mask.

Mask error message

If you get the message, "Selection cannot contain objects within different groups unless the entire group is selected," cut or copy your selected objects (to remove them from the group), then Paste in Front. Now you can to apply Object > Clipping Mask > Make.

When a placed image is selected, the Mask button appears in the Control panel

Pasting objects into a mask

To paste cut or copied objects into a clipping mask, make sure Paste Remembers Layers is off (in the Layers panel menu), then select an object within the mask and use Paste in Front or Back to place the copied object within the mask. You can also create or paste objects while in isolation mode.

Magical clipping path

Once an object is a clipping path, move it anywhere *within* its layer or group in the Layers panel—it still maintains its masking effect!

Left: The clipping mask (outlined in blue) above the floral illustration was created as 7 separate objects (6 petals and 1 center circle) and then united into a single compound path (using Object > Compound Path). Right: positioned on top of other objects, then used as a clipping mask.

Roping in Paths

Using Masks and Pathfinders for Shapes

Overview: *Create and organize layers, place a scanned sketch, and draw shapes; draw paths for the rope, outline their strokes, feather their fills, and draw masks; make a compound path, duplicate it, and reshape it.*

Hamann's scan of the pencil sketch he made from the photographs he took of himself

Hamann's Layers panel

HAMANN

When *Angels on Earth* magazine needed an online illustration featuring a heroic angel saving a woman from drowning, illustrator Brad Hamann responded with layering, masks, and pathfinder tools in "Angel in the Rapids."

1 Scanning a sketch, organizing layers, and drawing shapes. Hamann began by drawing and scanning a pencil sketch and placing it in Illustrator on a template layer.

Hamann's design called for layering so that artwork like the tubes and rope appeared in front of or behind other artwork. He created layers in the Layers panel based on visual hierarchy. To outline the angel against the rest of the image, Hamann created a blue outline of the angel, then a white one. To do this he copied the head and body objects, then used Paste in Back, and then applied Pathfinder > Unite. Giving this new shape a blue stroke and fill, he copied it, used Paste in Back, and then gave this duplicate outline a white fill and a wider white stroke.

2 Making and masking the rope. Hamann created the rope in sections, drawing paths between objects for the tubes and hands. He smoothed the curvature of the ropes by adjusting direction lines with the Direct Selection tool. To give the selected rope paths a dark blue edge with a light fill, he first changed the paths to a 4-pt, dark blue stroke. Next Hamann chose Object > Path > Outline Stroke and changed the stroke to 1 pt and the fill to orange. Finally, to add a subtle highlight to the rope, Hamann chose Effect > Stylize > Inner Glow and in the dialog entered 24 for Opacity and 0.03 inches for Blur, and clicked OK.

Where each rope section was cut off by another object, Hamann masked the rope by the edge of the other objects' strokes. He decided that drawing the masks by hand would be precise enough for the resolution of a web graphic. To mask the rope where it joined the fist, for example, Hamann drew a shape with the Pen tool that loosely surrounded the rope except for where the rope was cut off by the fist. For that area, he drew the path of the masking shape by hand along the edge of the fist's blue stroke. Finally, he selected the masking shape and the rope and chose Object > Clipping Mask > Make.

3 Drawing the tube. For the tube draped over the angel's left arm, Hamann drew a yellow-filled path for the tube's outer edge and another path for the tube's center hole. He selected both objects and chose Object > Compound Path > Make. To form shadows, he copied the compound path and used Paste in Front, then filled this duplicate with a darker yellow. With the duplicate still selected, Hamann used the Scissors tool to make two cuts on the right side of the outer edge, then selected and deleted the outer left edge of the compound path. Next, he used the Pen tool to redraw the shadow path between the two open points. When he completed the path, he filled it with a darker yellow and then chose Effect > Stylize > Feather, changed the feather radius to 0.05, and clicked OK. Hamann finished by drawing highlight shapes and pasting another duplicate of the tube in front, changing its fill to None and stroke to dark blue.

2

On the left, the paths for two sections of rope; on the right, the paths after choosing Object > Path > Outline Stroke, filling them with orange, and then applying Inner Glow to the fills

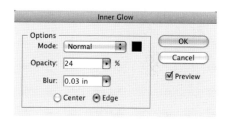

The mask drawn as a green-stroked path

The Inner Glow dialog

3

On the left, the drawn compound path; on the right, the compound path filled with yellow

On the left, a copy of the compound path pasted in front of the yellow tube; in the middle, the compound path cut on the right side; on the right, the finished shape filled with dark yellow

The Feather dialog

Floating Type

Type Objects with Transparency & Effects

Overview: *Create an area type object, key in text; add a new fill attribute in the Appearance panel; convert the fill to a shape; change transparency and add an effect.*

Top, the Selection tool (at right, selected); bottom, the Type tool in the Toolbox (right, selected)

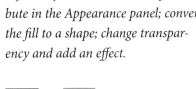

The type object after clicking with the Selection tool (the background photograph has been hidden in this view)

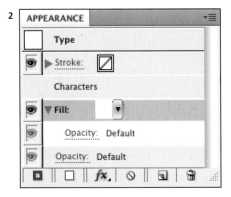

The Appearance panel after selecting the fill attribute and applying white to it

Using the Convert to Shape effect, you can create an area type object with transparency and effects that will save you from making and manipulating two objects (a type object and a rectangle with transparency and effects below it). For a virtual guide to Capitol Reef National Park, Steven Gordon created a transparent area type object with a hard-edged drop shadow that provided information for each of the park's most popular hiking trails.

1 Making the area type object. Start by selecting the Type tool, dragging it to create an area type object, and then typing your text. When you have finished typing, click on the Selection tool (the solid arrow icon) in the Tools panel. This deselects the text characters while selecting the type object, preparing the object (rather than the characters) for editing in the next step.

2 Creating a new fill and converting to a shape. Open the Appearance panel and select the Add New Fill icon at the bottom of the panel menu. Drag the new Fill attribute below Characters in the panel. The Fill attribute will be automatically deselected when you move it in the panel so you'll need to click on it again to select it. Next, apply a light color to it (Gordon chose white from the Swatches panel). Now click the panel's Add New Effect and choose Convert to Shape > Rectangle from the pop-up menu. In the Shape Options dialog, control the size of the rectangle around your type object by modifying the two Relative options (Extra Width and Extra Height).

3 Adjusting transparency and adding a drop shadow effect. Gordon designed each trail information box to incorporate transparency and a drop shadow, so its text would float above, but not obscure, the background photograph. To adjust the transparency of the object you converted in the previous step, first ensure that the type object's Fill or Rectangle attribute is selected in the Appearance panel. (If either attribute is not selected, then the transparency changes you're about to make will also affect the text characters.) Click on the Opacity attribute and in the Transparency panel adjust the transparency slider, or enter a value.

Instead of creating a soft drop shadow, Gordon opted to make a hard-edged shadow. To create this shadow, make sure the Fill attribute is still selected in the Appearance panel. Click the Add New Effect icon and choose Stylize > Drop Shadow. In the Drop Shadow dialog set Color to black, Blur to 0, and then adjust the X Offset and Y Offset sliders so the shadow is positioned as far down and to the right as you wish.

4 Editing the area type object. As you continue working, you may decide to resize the type object you originally created when you dragged with the Type tool. (This is different from editing the Shape Options dialog values to change the size of the transparent rectangle around the type object, as you did previously.) To resize the object, choose the Direct Selection tool and click on the edge of the type object you want to resize, then drag the side of the object inward to make it smaller, or outward to enlarge it. Because the transparent drop shadow shape was formed using the Convert to Shape effect, it is "live" and will automatically resize as you resize the type object.

Similarly, if you edit the text by adding or deleting words, the type object will resize, causing your transparent drop shadow shape to resize automatically.

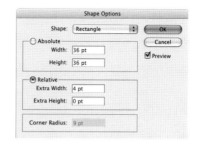

The Shape Options dialog with the Relative options edited

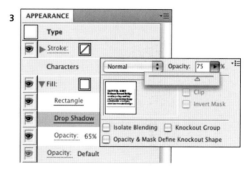

Left, the Appearance panel with the transparency attribute selected; right, the Transparency panel

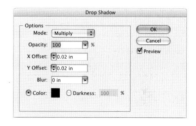

The Drop Shadow dialog

4

The Direct Selection cursor when it nears the edge of an area type object

Getting an edge

To help click on the edge of a type object rather than on the type itself, make sure Smart Guides are enabled in the View menu and Object Highlighting is enabled in the Illustrator > Preferences > Smart Guides dialog.

Adding Highlights

Using Transparency to Create Highlights

Overview: *Create highlights in objects for the interior of the cell using the Blend tool; stack them and lower opacity; create highlights with gradients for other objects and reduce opacity; create a bright lens flare.*

1

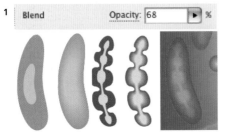

After creating an object by blending a light object with a darker, same-shaped object to represent a highlight, transparency further blends the "lit" object (mitochondrion) into its surroundings

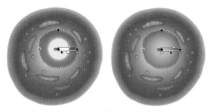

Adjusting the radial gradient adjusts the size and edge of the highlight, while transparency settings adjust the final blend into another object

2

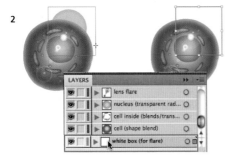

The Lens Flare tool needs a non-transparent background to reach maximum brightness

Adding transparency to blended or gradient-filled objects, or conversely, eliminating transparency beneath a lens flare, gives you a great deal of versatility when constructing believable highlights.

1 Using multiple techniques for blending colors in order to simulate natural highlighting. When Gary Ferster wanted to illustrate a living cell, he chose various methods for constructing blended highlights. For the mitochondrion (pinkish objects), he used the Blend tool to create two initial shapes, one very light, and one the "local" color. When blended smoothly, this method created soft highlights. He then stacked one blended object over the other and reduced the opacity in each, in order to make them appear to be part of the cell. For the small bubbles (lysosomes) and nucleus in the cell, however, Ferster used simple radial gradients with a very light center gradating to the local color of the object. By adjusting the gradient stops, he could make highlights bigger or smaller, with sharper or more feathered edges, and then adjust opacity to blend these objects into the cell.

2 Using the Lens Flare tool for maximum highlighting. Nothing suggests a powerful light source quite like a lens flare, but Ferster had observed that using the Lens Flare tool over a transparent background creates a dulled, gray flare. A simple solution was to draw a solid white rectangle, at least as big as the flare, behind all the objects. The part of the lens flare that extended beyond the cell became white, disappearing into the background entirely.

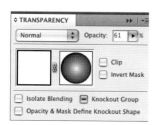

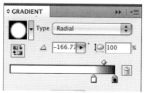

BEAUREGARD

Christiane Beauregard

Christiane Beauregard created this illustration as a "prequel" version to a commissioned piece she would later submit to her client. To create the glows around some of her stars and flowers, she used opacity masks, a technique that gives her the control she needs over each object, and also scales readily when she copies the object. For the stars, she drew a circle filled with solid white to blend with the background, and placed it behind a star. She used the White, Black Radial gradient in the opacity mask to make the "glow" partially transparent over most of its range, and reduced layer Opacity to soften the glow even more. She used the same technique for the glowing flower centers, but adjusted the Radial gradient in the opacity mask to ensure that most of the flower retained full opacity, and the glow was restricted to just the outer edge. For more about making and using opacity masks, see Beauregard's "Opacity Masks 101" lesson following this gallery.

Opacity Masks 101

Transparency Masks for Blending Objects

Overview: *Create a simple mask and apply it to an object; refine transparency by adding controlled masking with a precise opacity mask; choose opacity mask options.*

Drawing the object that will become the glow around the match, and the gradient-filled object that will become the object's opacity mask

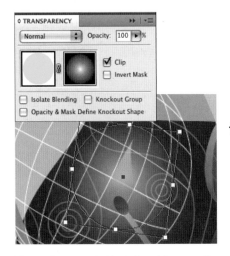

The semitransparent object after adding a gradient-filled opacity mask

Christiane Beauregard's illustrations often depend upon the intertwining and overlapping of objects to convey connections between ideas and elements. She frequently uses transparency to express those connections in a direct, visual manner, and depends upon opacity masks to control more precisely the extent of the transparency than the Opacity setting allows. In "Global Warming," Beauregard used a series of opacity masks to immerse her objects in their surroundings.

1 Creating and applying an opacity mask. Beauregard expressed one aspect of global warming by showing her subject holding a match to the globe. To create the glow, she first drew a circle filled with a yellow-orange. Next she drew a circle directly on top and fully covering the first circle so that transparency would carry to the very edges of the glow. She filled it with the White, Black Radial gradient. She selected both circles, opened the Transparency panel's pop-up menu, and chose Make Opacity Mask. This automatically placed the top object (the gradient-filled circle) in the right thumbnail pane to make the mask. The glow is fully visible where the mask is white, transparent where it's gray, and invisible where it's black. You can use colored artwork for the masking object, but the mask only uses the luminosity values of the hues.

2 Combining transparency with a precisely constructed opacity mask. For several objects, Beauregard used both transparency (to blend objects with the objects below), and an opacity mask for localized, typically gradated transparency. She created the effect of the fish's tail fading into the water by drawing a separate object filled with white for the tip of the tail. So that the mask would align precisely with its path, she copied the tail path and used Paste in Front (⌘-F/Ctrl-F) to create the mask object. This time she filled the mask with the first (default) Linear Gradient, using the Gradient tool to adjust it so that it faded to black at the tip. With both objects selected, she chose Make Opacity Mask to place the gradient-filled path into the Transparency panel's mask pane. She could further adjust the opacity of the masked object using the Opacity slider in the Transparency panel, or even toggle the mask on and off by Shift-clicking the mask pane.

3 Clipping and non-clipping masks. Because Beauregard's masks typically are either contoured to the objects they mask, or are larger than the object, she doesn't normally bother to alter the default setting of New Opacity Masks Are Clipping, since clipping will not clip off any portion of the masked object. If the masking object is the exact same size or larger, and in the same position, a clipping mask affects transparency only. If the mask is smaller than the object being masked, enabling the option will clip the object. At any time, she can change a mask's clipping behavior with the Clip checkbox, and choose to invert the mask then as well, if an object is inadvertently being clipped or the transparency needs to be reversed.

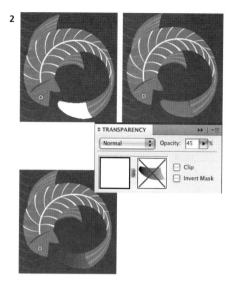

2

Original object, copied and pasted into mask; mask disabled (above right); and enabled (below), with object's Opacity lowered

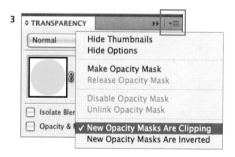

3

Choosing default settings for creating opacity masks through the Transparency panel pop-up menu

Objects that make masks

Opacity masks can be made from any artwork, whether comprised of a single object or several. These objects can be distorted, filtered, stroked, or otherwise manipulated like any normal object. They can even have their own opacity masks. However, only the luminosity values of the masking object will determine the masked object's transparency.

Simple Masking

Applying the Basics of Clipping Masks

Advanced Technique

Overview: *Create a clipping mask; gather and order objects to clip; use the mask to clip multiple objects; use a mask to clip another mask.*

Above are the three objects to be used, first the image, next the text, and topmost is the board

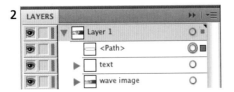

The Layers panel showing the correct stacking order of the objects before masking

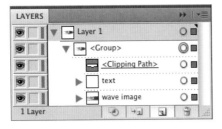

The Layers panel showing the objects <Group> after applying the clipping mask

The surfboard uses two clipping masks: the text is used to clip the image and then the board clips the text.

This custom surfboard design was created by San Diego based illustrator Aaron McGarry, who finds much of his work inspired by a life tailored to the beach communities and industries of southern California.

1 Preparing the elements for masking. Create the objects that you'll use as a clipping path, and collect the objects that you'll be masking within the clipping path. McGarry created a surfboard outline using the Pen tool. He next painted a wave in Photoshop, then in Illustrator he chose File > Place, selected the image, disabled Template, and clicked OK. With the Type tool, McGarry created text on top of his placed image, with white fill and no stroke. He chose the Earth (normal) font because he felt it was a modern, fresh typeface with enough weight to show an image through the characters if he later wanted to use the text as a clipping mask. To create a slightly "edgier" feel, he rotated the text using the bounding box.

2 Positioning the objects and applying the mask. Position the object you'll be using as a clipping path within the Layers panel, as the topmost object above the objects it will mask. With the surfboard above his image and text McGarry selected them all and chose Object > Clipping Mask > Make (⌘-7/Ctrl-7); this placed all the objects in a clipping group (on one layer), with the type and image being masked by the surfboard <Clipping Path>.

For a variation of the surfboard, McGarry masked the image with the text first; selecting text and image he applied ⌘-7/Ctrl-7. Next selecting this new clipping group, the surfboard path, and the yellow background he applied ⌘-7/ Ctrl-7. He created finishing details (edges) for both surfboards using blends with transparency.

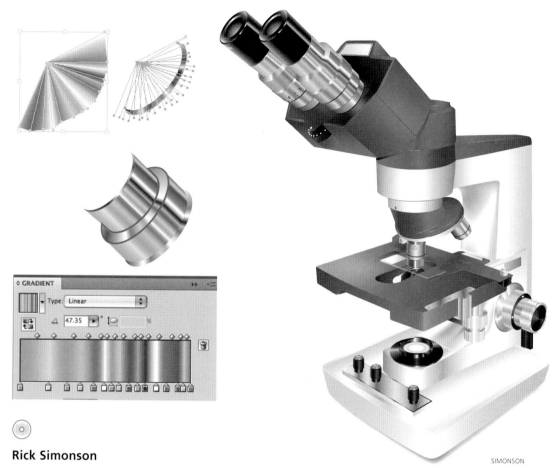

SIMONSON

Rick Simonson

For his remarkable feat of photorealism with this illustration of a microscope, Rick Simonson used blends and gradients to mimic reflections in metal. To make some of the metal sections that reflected multiple colors, he began by drawing with the Line tool. After drawing a line, he selected one end with the Direct Selection tool and left the other anchor point unselected. He dragged on the selected point, adding the Option/Alt key to duplicate the line in the start of a fan shape—the unselected anchor remaining in place. He repeated adding new lines at varying distances from each other, and coloring them, until he had enough lines to equal all the color changes in the reflection. He then selected all the lines and chose the Blend tool with Smooth Color selected in the tool's options. With the keyboard shortcut ⌘-Option-B/Ctrl-Alt-B, he created a blend object from the lines. Next Simonson drew the object he required for a part of the microscope on top of his newly blended object. With both objects selected, he chose Object > Clipping Mask > Make (⌘-7/Ctrl-7). For other complex reflections, Simonson created gradients with multiple color stops that colored the objects to match up with those made from the blends.

Blending Elements

Using Transparency to Blend and Unify

Advanced Technique

Overview: *Prepare images in Photoshop to integrate in Illustrator; use Multiply and opacity masks to blend; make backgrounds transparent.*

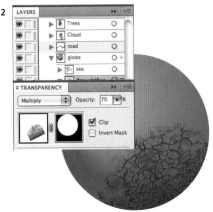

Using a photo or hand drawing for texture, prepared in Photoshop for use in Illustrator—here two are shown with Photoshop's Transparency grid, while the fire is completely opaque

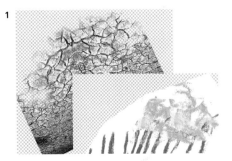

A gradient-filled globe with a grayscale photo, and using the Blending Mode to Multiply, and an opacity mask to add texture

JENNINGS

When David Jennings was hired to make an illustration about environmental issues for Climate Concern UK, he wanted to use contrasting textures to highlight negative influences on the global climate. He used Photoshop for some of the textural elements, but because most of the details would be vector, he used Illustrator for blending all the objects, raster and vector, into one coherent whole.

1 Preparing images to place in Illustrator. Jennings began the project by using pastels on paper to hand-draw smoke, clouds, trees, and fire. He scanned these into Photoshop and adjusted color. He also adjusted a grayscale image of cracked earth that, once blended with a globe in Illustrator, would depict drought. With these files ready and saved as PSD images, he turned to Illustrator.

2 Using Multiply, Opacity Mask, and reduced opacity to blend textures and add shading. Now in Illustrator, Jennings drew a circle for the planet, filled it with a brown radial gradient, and copied the circle to the clipboard. He then chose File > Place to bring in the earth texture, then scaled and rotated it. He then used the Transparency panel to fit the texture into the circle. First he changed the Normal blending mode to Multiply, allowing only the values of the texture darker than the gradient to appear. He then created a transparency mask by double-clicking the blank "mask" spot to the right of the texture icon, used ⌘-F/Ctrl-F (Paste in Front) to paste the copied circle in place, changed the fill to white, and reduced the opacity (Clip should be enabled, Invert Mask disabled). To exit mask mode, he double-clicked the texture icon.

Using mainly the Pen tool, Jennings then began drawing manmade and solid natural elements—the cars and planes, the factory and housing, the human and polar bear. To create shading he added darker objects on top of the originals, switching the Blending Mode to Multiply and/or changing Opacity in the Transparency panel to alter the appearance of the objects below. If he needed the shading to be even darker than the color he had already chosen, he used Multiply to deepen the colors. If the color was a bit too dark, he lowered the opacity. To create the shadow for the factory, he not only used Multiply to deepen the colors below his shadow shape, but he also chose Gaussian Blur as a Live Effect to add even more transparency and softness to the shadow's edges.

3 Making transparent backgrounds for Photoshop

images. Jennings now needed to add the textured, natural elements he had prepared in Photoshop. He knew that Multiply mode drops out the white backgrounds often imported with raster images, so he placed the cloud, trees, and smoke images, scaled and transformed them to fit, and then selected Multiply to merge them seamlessly with the objects below. For the fire, however, Jennings needed both transparency within the fire image itself and opacity when he placed it over the tree layer. If he used Multiply, then the fire, being lighter than the trees, would seem to disappear. In this instance, Jennings painted a transparency mask for the fire in Photoshop, which Illustrator recognized and preserved upon import. (See the *Creatively Combining Apps* chapter for lessons with Photoshop.)

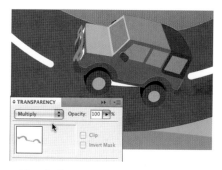

Adding shading with an object in Multiply mode

Adjusting Opacity to precisely determine degree of shading and depth

Using Blending Mode > Multiply and also applying Effect > Blur > Gaussian Blur, creates transparent shadows

3

Trees and tree trunks set to Multiply drop their white background against the globe, but the lighter-colored fire requires transparency painted into a mask in Photoshop

GLITSCHKA

Von R. Glitschka

Von Glitschka begins his pattern-making process by creating a very precise pencil sketch to place as a Template layer. On a layer above the placed sketch, he used the Rectangle tool to draw a square to define the pattern repeat area. From the View menu, Glitschka enabled Snap to Point and Smart Guides. Using both the Pen and Ellipse tools, Glitschka drew the main pattern. Although he followed his template very closely, Smart Guides ensured exact placement of his paths. Glitschka refined the curve of the paths with the aid of an Illustrator plug-in, Xtream Path (CValley Software, demo on the **WOW! DVD**). And to complete the main pattern elements he applied Pathfinder commands to the closed paths (Unite, Minus Front, and Intersect). To place repeating elements in perfect registration (such as the large flower at the top) Glitschka relied on Option-dragging/Alt-dragging a copy of the element along with the square, using Snap to

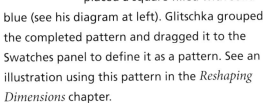

Point to guide in the alignment. At this point Glitschka could have defined his pattern by simply placing an unstroked, unfilled, unrotated copy of the tile bounding square behind the other elements. In preparing the patterns for his book and DVD (see Gallery opposite), he minimizes changes that can be made to his patterns by trimming off parts of each object that extend beyond the pattern. (To do this, he selects one object at a time with a copy of the square and clicks Intersect Pathfinder.) To complete this pattern, Glitschka filled the elements with a 40% tint of blue. He next rotated a copy of these pattern elements 90°, and changed these to a white fill with 20% transparency. Underneath both pattern squares he placed a square filled with solid blue (see his diagram at left). Glitschka grouped the completed pattern and dragged it to the Swatches panel to define it as a pattern. See an illustration using this pattern in the *Reshaping Dimensions* chapter.

Psychotronic

Graphic Bloom

Single Cell

Grate Expectations

Funkus

Scorn Thistle

Alien Cells

Frillicious

Greener

Von R. Glitschka

Shown above is just a small sample of unique patterns from Von R. Glitschka's latest book and DVD entitled, *Drip.Dot.Swirl. 94 incredible patterns for design and illustration* (How Publishing). Using similar techniques described on the oppo-site page (with some variation such as applying blending modes or effects to a layer), Glitschka created editable patterns in a wide range of styles. See www.vonsterbooks.com for details about the book.

Warping Blends

Creating and Warping 3D Blends

Advanced Technique

Overview: *Draw lines with the Pen or Pencil tools; create a blend from the lines then expand the blend; modify with the Warp and Eraser tools; extrude as a 3D object.*

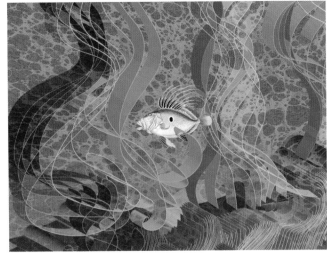

Drawing the eight lines that will become key objects in the blend

Blend produced by selecting the Object > Blend > Make command

Blend Options dialog with the Spacing menu set to 30 steps

Blend produced after increasing the Spacing menu steps to 30

Transparency & blends

To make part of your blend transparent, select one of the blend's key objects, open the Transparency panel and set its opacity to 0%.

Inspiring her students at the Community College of Baltimore County, artist and instructor Dedree Drees likes to bend the rules of graphic design and Illustrator techniques. In her undersea vignette "The Dory," Drees creates intricate blends that she warps and twirls and then extrudes as 3D coral and seaweed.

1 Creating, then expanding blends. Drees began her complex 3D blend by drawing eight lines using the Pencil tool. Each line served as a key object in the blend, marking a transition of shape, position, and color. When you're drawing the key object lines, be sure to experiment with the shape and color of each line and the distance between the lines. You can draw as many lines as you like, but the resulting blend may be complex and slow your computer when you apply 3D effects later.

To create the blend, Drees selected the lines and chose Object > Blend > Make. With the blend selected, double-click the Blend tool (or use Object > Blend > Blend Options) to open the Blend Options dialog. From the dialog's Spacing menu, select Specified Steps and key in a value to control the speed or smoothness of the blend. Drees used 30 steps for her blend. When you're satisfied with the look of the blend, select Object > Blend > Expand to expand the blend to a group of lines.

2 Using the Warp, Twirl, and Eraser tools. With the blend expanded, Drees turned to the Warp tool to reshape the expanded blend. Double-click the tool to display the Warp Tool Options and then set the Width and Height to 100 pt and Intensity to 20%. Now click inside or outside the blend and drag with your mouse or stylus. Where you click inside or outside of the blend will govern how much of the object will morph as you drag the Warp tool.

Like Drees, you can sculpt your blend further by using the Twirl tool (click and hold down the Warp tool icon in the Tools panel to display its companion tools) to create wave crests and tight curves. To begin, double-click the Twirl tool to access the Twirl Tool Options dialog. Make sure you set a low number for Intensity (Drees used 20%) and for the Twirl Rate (a positive number twirls counter-clockwise while a negative number twirls clockwise). Try the companion tools to Warp and Twirl to see what effect they have on your blend; the Wrinkle tool, for example, creases and crinkles a blend's smooth lines.

Drees finished fine-tuning her blend by using the Eraser tool on the edges. You can modulate the shape and size of the Eraser tool by double-clicking the Eraser tool icon and resetting some of the default values.

3 Extruding the blend. Before applying the 3D effect, you'll need to simplify your blend by reducing the number of points your computer has to process. To do this, select Object > Path > Simplify. Now extrude the blend by opening the Appearance panel and clicking on the *fx* icon at the bottom of the panel. From the pop-up menu, select 3D > Extrude & Bevel. Enable the Preview checkbox in the 3D Extrude & Bevel Options dialog so you can see how the default settings, and any changes you make to them, affect the look of your blend.

To finish the illustration, Drees saved the blend as a Photoshop file (File > Export > Photoshop), which she opened in Photoshop and layered with other elements. (See the gallery in the *Reshaping Dimensions* chapter for more about Drees's techniques with blends and 3D.)

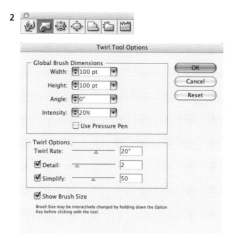

The Warp tool panel above and the Twirl Tool Options dialog below

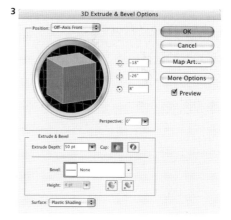

The blend after being expanded and then modified with the Twirl and Eraser tools

The 3D Extrude & Bevel Options dialog (above) and the finished 3D object (below)

Moonlighting

Using Transparency for Glows & Highlights

Advanced Technique

Overview: *Create a Radial gradient with transparency for a circular object; use the Blend tool with a duplicate object to create a circular or oval blend with transparency; create a glow or highlight for a non-circular object.*

GUSMAN JOLY

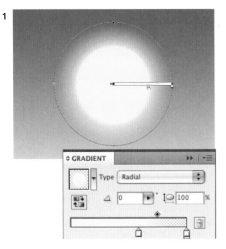

Using the Gradient tool with either the Gradient Annotator (top) or Gradient panel (bottom) to create a gradient with transparency

Because the glowing moon is circular in Annie Gusman Joly's "Solo-Flight" illustration about growing up an identical twin, it could be created by using either a radial gradient or a shaped blend. The key to making a gradient or blend work against any background is to use transparency for the edge of the object that touches the background.

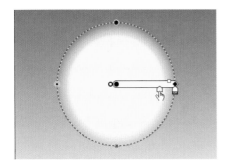

Drag the color stop for the inner object toward the transparent stop to make the object larger; drag the diamond to alter the size of the glow

1 **Creating a glow from a Radial gradient.** With the object selected, click on it once with the Gradient tool to fill with the last-used or default gradient, and, if necessary, change the type in the Gradient panel to Radial. Either in the Gradient panel or with the aid of the Gradient Annotator, double-click on each color stop and choose the same color for them. Reduce the opacity for the stop that represents the outer edge to 0%; drag the opposite color stop inward to make the solid part of the object bigger and more solid, and adjust the Gradient slider between them (the diamond shape on the top of the gradient bar) to create a larger or smaller amount of feather (or "glow").

2 Creating a glow for a circular object from an object blend. With a pale yellow Fill color, choose a stroke of None, and draw a circle (Shift-drag with the Ellipse tool). With Smart Guides on (View menu), move your cursor over the circle until you see the word "center," hold down Option/Alt, and Shift-drag out a new, smaller circle. Set the Opacity of the larger circle to 0%. Select both circles and choose Object > Blend > Make (⌘-Option-B/Ctrl-Alt-B); then double-click the Blend tool in the toolbox to adjust the steps. For this example, somewhere between 20 and 30 steps makes a very glowing moon.

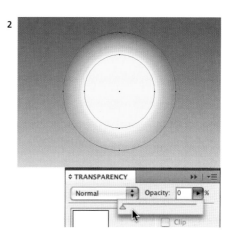

Creating a blend between two circles with one set to 0% Opacity.

3 Shaping a glow with a blend made from non-circular objects. When you don't have a circle or oval path, only a blend can "shape" the glow evenly around the object. So that the glowing object can be placed over any background, we'll continue to create the glow with transparency. Create your first object—here, a crescent moon filled with pale yellow and no stroke. Many asymmetrical shapes don't scale easily relative to the original's boundaries, so with your object selected, choose Object > Path > Offset Path. Enable Preview and use a negative number for a smaller object. Select the larger object and, in the Transparency panel, set the Opacity to 0%. Now select both paths and choose Object > Blend > Make. If you haven't already created a blend with the Specified Steps or Specified Distance Spacing option in your current working session, Illustrator might use Smooth Color. Smooth Color doesn't create a glow, but rings the inner crescent moon with a lighter color. To get the glow, double-click on the Blend tool to open the dialog and choose Specified Steps for the Spacing option. Around 25 steps should create a decent glow. If necessary, adjust the offset, miter, and path edges until the blend is smooth and glowing.

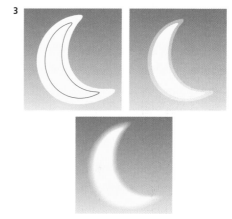

Creating the second object with Offset Path (top left) and using Object > Blend > Make; the default Smooth Color doesn't blend (top right), but switching to Specified Steps creates the glow

This shaped-blend method can also be used for making any shape or size of highlight for any object. By creating the highlight as a separate object, you gain the advantage of being able to change the object's color later without having to reconstruct the object and the blend.

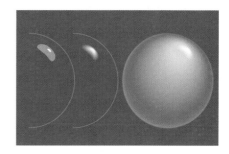

Creating a highlight using a shaped blend with one opaque and one transparent object

Creating Depth
Gradients Add Dimension in Space

Advanced Technique

Overview: *Create paths with solid colors for basic shaping; substitute shaped and transparent gradients for solid fills to add realism; add live effects to further blend gradients for added depth.*

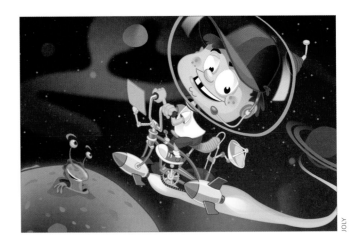

1

Paths ready to be filled with solid color

Paths filled with solid color, using a range of values for each hue that a gradient would later express

2

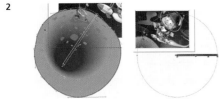

Creating objects that extend beyond the picture frame to hold a radial gradient, or even moving the gradient itself beyond the boundaries for subtle realism

Dave Joly creates illustrations for both printed pieces and animation. When he created "Biker Kid in Space," he made extensive use of Illustrator's gradient capabilities, such as elliptical gradients (with an aspect ratio of less than 100%), or full circle; and transparency, for greater realism and more depth than a flat illustration can convey. He also added Gaussian Blur and Outer Glow effects to some of his gradient-filled objects to further enhance the illusion of deep space.

1 Establishing color for all the objects. After sketching on paper, Joly began his artwork in Illustrator with a line drawing of his main subject. He organized the elements by placing all the paths for the boy's hat, for instance, on one layer, and then filled the paths with solid colors. He prepared for the gradient fills in advance by filling the paths with several closely-related colors, the better to see if the overall lighting and illusion of depth was working, and to establish the range of values that the gradients would need to encompass for the different objects.

2 Creating gradients for light and depth. Once Joly had drawn the background and subject paths, and established general color and tonal values, he began to construct the gradients that would blend the colors smoothly. When creating the gradients, Joly found it helpful to see the "big" picture—the planets and space itself that extended beyond the picture frame. He mocked up the entire planet, seen in the foreground, before applying a radial gradient to shape the sphere. For deep space, he centered one radial gradient completely off the page. As a result, subtle gradations created a realistic transition between light and shadow in his objects.

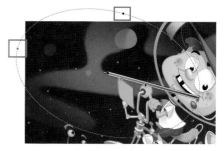

For the nebula swirling in the background, Joly used Illustrator's ability to alter the aspect ratio of a radial gradient to make it elliptical. This helped color the swirling gases, bending their appearance without creating another planet-like shape. With the Gradient tool selected (G), he applied the Radial gradient to the nebula, grabbed the solid black circle at the top of the Radial gradient, and pulled it down to form an oval. He dragged on the circle with a black dot in the center to size the gradient, and used the arrow endpoint of the Gradient Annotator to rotate the angle of the gradient. He also used the Gradient Annotator to interactively position the color stops.

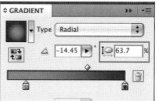

Transforming the aspect ratio of the gradient from circular to elliptical, and using another anchor to size the gradient

Joly made extensive use of transparency in his gradients, notably to blend the rocket flares and create the illusion of their trails disappearing into space, and for the shadows and highlights in the space kid's shirt and helmet. He used the same color for each stop, but reduced the opacity for one stop to nothing (0). He then moved the gradient slider (the diamond above the gradient bar) to control how abruptly the gradient switched from fully opaque to fully transparent.

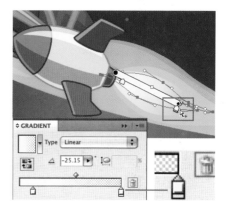

Adding transparency to gradients, indicated on the Gradient Annotator or panel by a hollow rectangle added to the bottom of the color stop

3 Using live effects for the final touches. Although the gradients themselves provided most of the form and depth in his objects, Joly clicked the *fx* icon in the Appearance panel to add live effects to some of them in order to further enhance lighting and a sense of the objects receding into space. Joly added a Gaussian Blur effect to several background elements, as well as to the highlights on the helmet, to add depth and to blend the helmet highlight more completely. Joly added a Glow effect around the planet, increasing the light in the radial gradient, bringing it further into the foreground.

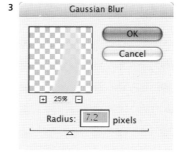

Adding a Gaussian Blur effect to a gradient that uses transparency for shaping, thus increasing the illusion of an object receding

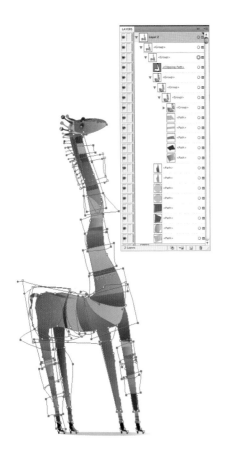

BEAUREGARD

Christiane Beauregard

Christiane Beauregard relies on Illustrator's clipping masks to provide her with the maximum flexibility when creating the intricate patterns in the giraffes, palms, and snake. In order to easily edit the individual objects that fit precisely into these curvilinear shapes, Beauregard first created her objects by very loosely and roughly following the intended outline. She allowed the objects to overlap, using their stacking order in the Layers panel to help delineate the interior edges. Throughout the development of the illustration, she could adjust where each object met another, because the objects weren't "cut to fit." The clipping masks then hid all the extraneous, outside portions of her layered objects, giving her palms, snake, and giraffes their final form. By clicking the Edit Clipping Path or Edit Contents icon in the Control panel, she could hide the clipped objects to edit just the clipping path, or reveal the objects to edit them. Using clipping masks, she retained both the vector edge of her objects, and the ability to edit again at any time in the future. Her use of gradients with several objects provided additional complexity and dimension, and she used opacity masks to soften the edges of the clouds and shadows.

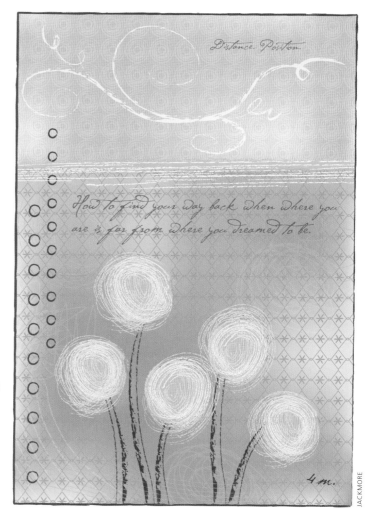

Lisa Jackmore

Lisa Jackmore combined layers of patterns, brushes, and gradient mesh, to create texture in this interpretation of a page in her sketchbook. For each gradient mesh background, she filled a rectangle with a solid fill and added mesh points with the Mesh tool. Jackmore kept most of the mesh points near the edges of the rectangle, and filled them with a light color to achieve a faded appearance. She created two patterns to layer above the mesh. For the circle pattern, she drew several concentric circles with the Ellipse tool, grouped them, and applied the Pencil Art brush. She selected the Twirl tool, and while holding Option-Shift/Alt-Shift, she click-dragged on the artboard, and sized the diameter of the Twirl to fit over the circles. Then she clicked on the circles with the Twirl tool until she was happy with the amount of twirl. She grouped the objects and dragged them to the Swatches panel. To make the diamond pattern, Jackmore used a combination of Rectangle, Ellipse, and Rotate tools. She then grouped the objects and dragged them to the

Swatches panel. Jackmore colored the pattern the same base color as the gradient mesh background so the pattern disappears in the dark areas. She then added more details to the background, and made the flowers with custom brushes she created. (For more about brushes see the *Expressive Strokes* chapter.) Jackmore also used several default brushes from the Artistic_ChalkCharcoalPencil library. Finally, she created a clipping mask to contain the brush marks that extended beyond the rectangle.

"Red Indian"
Copyright © 2009 Chris Nielsen

NIELSEN

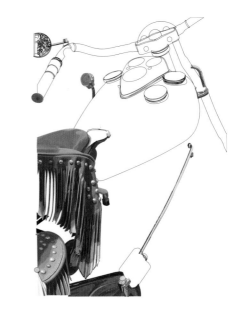

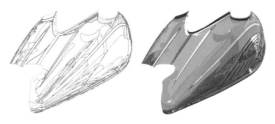

Chris Nielsen

When Chris Nielsen spotted a classic *Indian* motorcycle, fully restored, he wanted to illustrate it with his signature photorealistic technique. He knew his basic 8 MP digital point-and-shoot camera would capture enough detail, but with other bikes parked right next to the *Indian*, getting the reference shot at all was a major undertaking. Once he brought it into Illustrator, he used the same methods described on the opposite page, relying on the Pen tool to draw progressively smaller details, and the Pathfinder panel with the Divide command to create the areas representing every nuance of the bike and its reflections. He worked on a section at a time,

starting with less detailed areas, and bringing each to near completion before moving to the next area. Nielsen would often zoom to a comfortable 300% or so to work on fine details, but rarely more than that. In this manner, he always managed to keep an eye on the way the area he was working on was affecting the image as a whole. Color started with the photo itself, but Nielsen didn't rely upon the photo to produce the most accurate and pleasing tones. He used his artist's eye to adjust colors until the right hues and values were represented. When completed, Nielsen's *Indian* brought to life a rare, vintage motorcycle for everyone to enjoy.

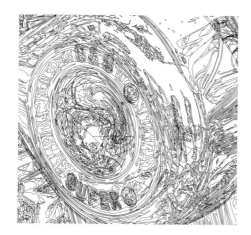

"Super Stock"

Copyright © 2005 Chris Nielsen

NIELSEN

Chris Nielsen

Chris Nielsen created another stunning image using the same drawing technique described on the opposite page. Nielsen likes to begin drawing an area of the photograph that contains a large object, such as a gas tank, or big pipe. Working over a template layer that contained his original photograph, he first drew the outline of a large object with the Pen tool. Then he drew paths for each area where the color value changed within that object. He selected the paths and clicked the Divide Pathfinder icon. He continued in this manner until there were enough shapes to define the object. This was a particularly challenging motorcycle to draw because there are only slight variations in one overall color. Nielsen filled each individual object with a custom color chosen from the Swatches panel. In all of his motorcycle illustrations, the reflection of Nielsen taking the photograph is visible—here it's shown in the magnified detail on the left.

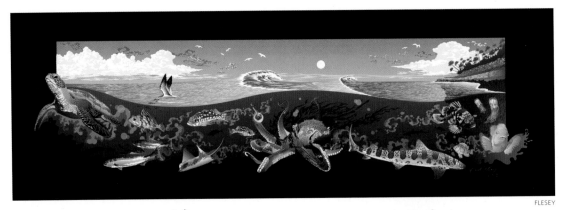

FLESEY

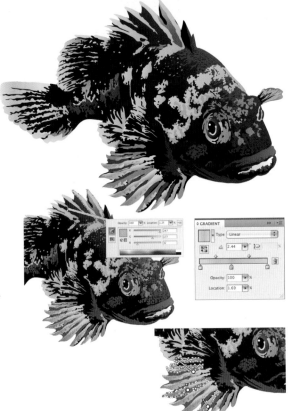

Erick Flesey

Erick Flesey captures the essence of underwater life in his imaginative illustrations filled with subtle gradients (creating this very large illustration for the San Diego Oceans Foundation). He begins his drawings by roughly shaping the animal or plant he wants to illustrate, then creates a highly detailed image using the Pencil tool, which preserves the natural, hand-drawn appearance that complements his subjects. After creating some basic gradients, Flesey begins to apply them to his objects using the updated Gradient tool with the Gradient Annotator toggled on (⌘-Option-G/Ctrl-Alt-G). Now he can quickly edit a gradient without taking his eyes off his artwork, and at the same time easily select several gradients that must work together and see that their angles correspond to the direction of the objects and the lighting. For example, the curved structure of the fin, while delineated in separate objects, is now easy to visualize and maintain by interactively dragging

with his cursor when the Rotate icon appears at the arrow end of the Gradient Annotator. Reducing Layer Opacity with the gradient-filled objects increases the appearance of depth and consistent lighting across the image. (See a larger version of this at www.erickflesey.com.)

WINDER

Darren A. Winder/daw Design

To create a city seen through fog on a rainy night in "Darkness Falls," Darren Winder (Daz) used transparency in gradient mesh objects, feathered objects, and symbols, as well as blend modes and some glow effects. Daz created both the black background and the moon from gradient mesh, using transparency and glow effects for the moon. To construct the moon's larger halo in the mist, he drew a freeform shape behind the moon with the Pen tool, chose Effects > Feather, then copied and pasted it in front of the first halo object, scaling it smaller. He made the street lamps in a similar fashion, but created a blend in steps between two street lamps to get the intermediate lamps. He enhanced the blurry appearance of the lamps by duplicating them, pasting behind, then nudging the copies down and over a pixel or two, and lowering opacity. Daz also used blended steps to create the tower floors,

adding clipping masks in some places to hide portions behind other buildings. He created the illusion of solid objects (people, etc.) lost in the fog with the Pen tool using various gray fills, also feathered. He built a symbol for the raindrops that included a feather and reduced opacity, then dragged it into the Symbols panel. He used the Symbol Sprayer, Shifter, Sizer, and Screener tools to quickly create a few symbol sets of raindrops all over. Finally, Daz created a large rectangle—filled with dark blue and set to Soft Light, which enhanced contrast—to cover the image. He reduced the opacity to tint the entire image a cool, rainy color.

GUSMAN JOLY

Annie Gusman Joly

Transparency can be created with Blending Modes that interact with the layers beneath, forming new colors based on the type of Blending Mode used. Artist Annie Gusman Joly uses them here to create a complex pattern of shadows. In this tropical forest, light filters through the leaves and flowers to fall on the ground beneath the white bird's feet. To create the random and overlapping patterns, Joly first fills a large object on one layer with a solid blue. After drawing the path for the shadows on

the layer above, she fills it with blue and sets the Blending Mode to Multiply. If the shadow color is too dark, she reduces the layer Opacity to increase the shadow layer's transparency. She uses the same technique for the shadow beneath her three-toed sloth.

HUBIG

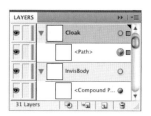 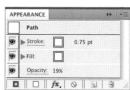

Dan Hubig

In this Illustration for *California Magazine*, Dan Hubig first combined blends, gradients, and transparency in Illustrator, and then enhanced his image in Photoshop with Blurs, Brushes, and Adjustment layers. Hubig used Transparency to render the cloak and torso only partially opaque, which kept his options open for expressing invisibility in Photoshop. He created his "cloak of invisibility" in Illustrator with a white Fill and Stroke and an opacity of only

19%, then duplicated it with a Stroke and no Fill to a new layer on top. By planning ahead, he would be able to reduce the cloak's visibility to zero, if he chose, but maintain that important outline. For one version, Hubig also made the man's torso completely invisible, but for the final version, he retained a hint of opacity. To learn more about how Hubig creates his illustrations, see the "Planning Ahead" lesson in the *Creatively Combining Apps* chapter.

Jean Aubé

For his "Nuit de Terreur" poster, Jean Aubé began by using the Pen tool to trace the outline of a photograph he took of a friend. He added a gradient fill and applied Effect > Stylize > Outer Glow. For the overall lighting, he created a background with a radial gradient, positioning the center between the hands. He then drew a circle for the moon. He made a tiny blue circle to represent a star and saved it as a symbol. Using the Symbol Sprayer, he sprayed the "stars" on two layers for depth. He expanded the symbols in order to delete unwanted extras. He set "Nuit de Terreur" as a block of type,

then converted the type to outlines. Aubé chose Object > Envelope Distort > Make with Mesh to distort the type. He set the other blocks of type separately. On a layer behind the stars and type he created spooky swirls by drawing many ovals, and then used Pathfinder operations on the ovals until he had broken them down to strands. He selected and deleted portions of the strands that remained. Finally he arranged, grouped, and filled them with a single linear gradient. He made the ovals appear ghostly by placing them in Overlay Mode and applying Outer Glow to them.

Chris Nielsen

Chris Nielsen has trained his artistic eye to recognize subtle shifts of color within a photograph and translate them into a striking image using layers of filled paths. Nielsen first placed an original photograph in a bottom layer to trace upon. He worked on one small section at a time, such as the eye in the detail to the right. With the Pen tool he made paths (no fill, with a black stroke) and traced the areas of primary color he saw in the photograph. He chose the darkest value first (dark blue or black), then on another layer, he drew the objects with progressively lighter values (a lighter blue, red, gray, etc.). He continued building layers of paths until the area was completely covered. He moved throughout the image this way until the portrait was finished. When all of the paths were drawn he began to fill them with color. Nielsen chose the Eyedropper tool, pressed and held the ⌘/Ctrl key to switch to the Direct Selection tool, and selected an object to color. Then he toggled back to the Eyedropper tool by releasing the ⌘/Ctrl key and sampled a color from the photograph. He toggled between the Direct Selection tool and the Eyedropper tool until the paths were filled. Most of the time, Nielsen liked the sampled colors, but if not, he would tweak the color using the sliders in the Color panel. Once all

▲ NIELSEN

Copyright © 2006 Chris Nielsen

of the paths were filled with color, Nielsen hid the template layer. He saw gaps of white in his drawing where the paths didn't quite meet or overlap. To fill these gaps, he made a large object that covered the area, filled it with a dark color, and placed it on the bottom-most layer.

COCKS

Joel Cocks

When Adobe commissioned Joel Cocks to create a piece that showcased new Illustrator features (and included in the Sample Art folder buried inside the Cool Extras folder installed with Illustrator), he created "Crowd," a piece that contrasts our individuality with our shared humanity. He began with a sketch of the central figure that he traced with the Blob Brush. Every new part of the figure was placed on a separate layer, allowing him to blend each layer's opacity to enhance the illusion of seeing our inner likeness and outer character at the same time. He used the Bristle Brush to soften many of the edges created by the Blob Brush. Cocks created the rest of the figures in a similar fashion, and used the Bristle Brush extensively on the background. Finally, he added a texture image he created, using Multiply for the blending mode and reducing its opacity. Look for a complete explanation of how he made this image on the **WOW DVD!** (or in your Cool Extras folder).

8

Creatively Combining Apps

Creatively Combining Apps

This chapter showcases some of the ways you can use Illustrator together with other programs. The connections between Photoshop or Flash and Illustrator make sharing work between these programs easy, while Illustrator connections to programs like Flash Catalyst are built in. But moving files between programs isn't without limitations, and the following pages address many of the decisions you will have to make when working with other programs.

LINKING VS. EMBEDDING IN ILLUSTRATOR

The major choice you'll need to make when placing art in Illustrator is whether to *link* or *embed* the file. When you link a file, you don't actually include the artwork in the Illustrator file. Instead a copy of the artwork acts as a placeholder, while the image remains in a separate file. Linking leaves the file editable in the original program, making it easy to update when the original is changed. Not only are .ai files with linked images smaller than those with embedded images, but linking permits you to link the same file several times in your document without increasing the file size for each instance. The Links panel keeps track of all the raster images used in your document, regardless of whether they were created within Illustrator, opened, or introduced via the Place command. Just remember that you have to include the separate, linked files if you move the .ai file to another computer.

When you embed artwork, you're actually including it in the file, which can sometimes be helpful even though the file size increases. Although it's trickier to update an embedded file in the original program, embedding is the answer if you need to be positive an image is included in the document—because you might need to edit it in Illustrator or retain its transparency, or if there's a danger the linked file won't travel with the document when sending it to a client or press, so they may require that you embed it, not link.

Placing a file using the Link option

MOVING ILLUSTRATOR FILES TO OTHER PROGRAMS

When moving artwork from Illustrator to other programs, you must decide which objects in your artwork you want to remain as vectors, if possible, and which you can allow to become rasterized. What you'll be able to do with your Illustrator artwork in that other program depends both on how you prepare your Illustrator files as well as the strengths and limitations of the program into which you'll be moving your artwork. Parameters that you might be able to control include moving only selected objects or the entire file; bringing Illustrator files in as paths, styled vectors, or rasters; and bringing in images flat or with layers.

Copy and Paste/Drag and Drop

- **You may be able to preserve the vector format** if the receiving program supports PostScript drag and drop behavior. In order for this to work, make certain that the AICB (Adobe Illustrator Clipboard) is enabled in Preferences > File Handling & Clipboard.

- **Your artwork will likely be automatically rasterized** at the resolution that you have specified in most raster-based programs when you copy and paste, or drag and drop Illustrator art into it.

- **Photoshop enjoys a special relationship with Illustrator** (see "Illustrator & Adobe Photoshop" in the next section), and you can often choose to create either vector or raster objects with Copy and Paste or Drag and Drop between the programs.

Save vs. Export

- **Save options in the File menu:** Save and Save As (for Illustrator and other vector formats), Save for Web & Devices, Save for Microsoft Office, and Save As Template.

- **Export formats, including raster and Flash:** Know which file formats your other application supports (e.g., Flash prefers you save in .ai format!) and the type of information (vector, raster, layers, paths) you want to bring from Illustrator into the other program to determine which format to choose.

When EPS is *not* recommended

If the application you're working in can place or open native .ai, native PSD, or PDF 1.4 or later formats, it's better to use those than the old standard EPS, which cannot preserve layers, transparency, and other features.

So you think it's linked?

Flattening transparency (Object menu) of a linked image automatically embeds the image. In addition to increasing the file size, you can no longer update the link.

Getting it into Illustrator

From most programs, and on most platforms, you can Save As, or Print and Save As a PDF document. Illustrator will open any PDF document (if there are multiple pages, it will ask you which one you want). Your objects and text might be broken up, but everything should be in there.

✓ Illustrator CS5
Legacy Formats
Illustrator CS4
Illustrator CS3
Illustrator CS2
Illustrator CS
Illustrator 10
Illustrator 9
Illustrator 8
Illustrator 3
Japanese Illustrator 3

After choosing Adobe Illustrator Document, the Version pop-up choices give you access to CS5 and legacy formats; save multiple artboards as individual files in CS5 format, instead of having to choose a legacy format for that option

ILLUSTRATOR & ADOBE PHOTOSHOP

There are many options for moving artwork between Illustrator and Photoshop—and you can control whether you want to maintain vector data, rasterize in part or whole, or whether to maintain layers. The rules for working with layers and paths between Illustrator and Photoshop are complex and often have unexpected results.

Illustrator to Photoshop: Smart Objects

To retain vector data and the ability to edit the original art, use Smart Objects. Illustrator art brought in as a vector Smart Object can be scaled, rotated, or warped without loss of data, and when you edit one instance of a Smart Object, Photoshop will automatically update all instances of that Smart Object. You can still modify the Smart Object in Photoshop using Adjustment layers and Smart Filters.

- **To Create Photoshop Smart Objects from Illustrator data,** copy/paste to open the Paste dialog and choose Smart Object. Or create a Smart Object automatically by dragging and dropping or choosing File > Place.
- **To edit an Illustrator Smart Object,** double-click on its thumbnail in Photoshop's Layers panel to automatically launch Illustrator and open a working copy of your artwork. Edit and save in Illustrator, and the Smart Object automatically updates in Photoshop.
- **To replace a Smart Object file with a different file on disk,** choose Layer > Smart Objects > Replace Content. This means you can use Smart Objects as placeholders for content you place in Photoshop later.

Illustrator to Photoshop: Pixels, Paths, and Layers

- **To create a pixel image, path, or Shape layer,** copy and paste an object, selecting from among these in the Paste dialog that opens.
- **To preserve layers and keep text editable,** place the text on a top-level layer, not a sublayer, and choose Export to save the file in "Photoshop (psd)" format. The other vector objects are rasterized, but text stays editable. You

can even use Illustrator's anti-aliasing options—None, Sharp, Crisp, Strong—which are comparable to Photoshop's text options and supported by it.

- **To reliably export compound shapes to Photoshop,** place your compound shape on a top-level layer. Also avoid using strokes, because Photoshop can't retain the stroke, and may not even be able to retain the compound shape with some types of strokes.

Photoshop to Illustrator

- **To keep text live,** in Photoshop place text layers at the top of the layer stack, and save the file in PSD format. In Illustrator, choose File > Open (or File > Place with the Link checkbox disabled), and in the Photoshop Import Options dialog, enable Convert to Layers.
- **To link a file, rather than embed it,** choose File > Place and enable the Link (File > Open has no link options).
- **When linking a file,** you will be able to relink, or edit the original, and have the link update reflect your modifications, but you can't import PSD or TIFF layers.
- **When embedding a file,** you can import text layers and keep them live, with image layers flattened in a separate layer, but you can't edit the PSD or TIFF file and have it reflected in the Illustrator file by relinking or updating.
- **To import Photoshop layers,** in Photoshop be sure the layers are normal image or fill layers. Illustrator doesn't understand Adjustment layers and will flatten all the non-text layers in a file if it encounters an Adjustment layer. If necessary, merge an Adjustment layer with the layer it's modifying before saving the PSD or TIFF file. When using Place or Open, enable the Convert to Layers option.
- **In order to be able to preserve the results of a layer mask** that has been modified using Photoshop's Masks panel, you must apply the mask to the layer in Photoshop when converting to layers. Otherwise, when you import the PSD layers into Illustrator, Illustrator can't read the Masks panel settings and will apply the unmodified mask to the layer (which it rasterizes) before it imports it, eliminating any Density or Feather settings.

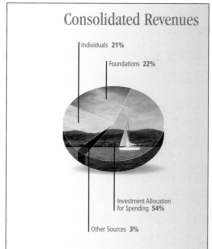

For an annual report of the environmental organization Scenic Hudson, Adam Z. Lein used Microsoft Excel's Chart Wizard to turn data into a pie chart, and then tilt in a perspective view. Lein used the Acrobat PDF maker to create a PDF of the graph. When he opened the PDF in Illustrator, the graph retained the vector objects as vectors. He completed the styling of the chart in Illustrator, incorporating images of New York's Hudson Valley using clipping masks and gradients (see the Color Transitions and Mastering Complexity chapters for more about masks and gradients)

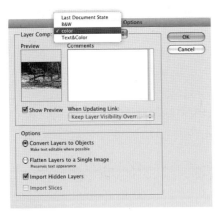

In this example of placing a layered PSD file saved from Photoshop, conversion options are enabled, a Layer Comp can be chosen, and the "When Updating Link" options are disabled, either because the Link checkbox was disabled in the Place dialog, or because File > Open, which doesn't allow linking, was chosen

Meaningfully naming your layer comps will help you determine which one to choose in Illustrator

Illustrator layers in InDesign

To control the layer visibility of an Illustrator file in InDesign, when you choose Place, enable "Show Import Options," or select a file you've already placed in InDesign and choose Object > Object Layer Options. In the Object Layer Options dialog, click an Eye icon to hide or show any layer. At the bottom of the dialog you can choose whether to update layer visibility settings for a linked Illustrator file when the link is updated.

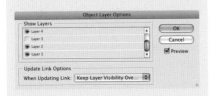

ILLUSTRATOR & ADOBE INDESIGN

- **To preserve transparency when you copy and paste** artwork from Illustrator into InDesign, leave both PDF and AICB enabled in Illustrator's File Handling and Clipboard preferences. In InDesign's Clipboard Handling preferences, enable "Prefer PDF When Pasting."

- **To paste an Illustrator file that you can edit in InDesign,** firstly, it can't contain transparency (even from effects). Then disable the Prefer PDF preference in InDesign. Objects are grouped, but they can be ungrouped and then edited with InDesign tools and effects.

- **To paste paths so they can be edited in InDesign** (they'll lose appearances such as gradients or graphic styles), choose Preserve Paths instead of Preserve Appearance and Overprints in Illustrator Clipboard preferences.

- **To Place artwork (linking it rather than embedding),** save your Illustrator file with the Create PDF Compatible File option enabled (it's on by default). InDesign, as well as other programs, recognizes and previews only the PDF portion of the file.

- **To control how an Illustrator file imports,** enable Show Import Options in the Place dialog. If you're placing an Illustrator file containing multiple artboards, InDesign lets you select which artboard to import; the Layers tab lets you control visibility of top-level Illustrator layers.

ILLUSTRATOR, PDF, AND ADOBE ACROBAT

Acrobat's Portable Document Format (PDF) lets you transfer files between different operating systems and applications. And when you open a version of an Illustrator document that's newer than the version of the program that you have, you actually are opening the PDF portion of the .ai file.

When you choose the Adobe Illustrator format, in the File > Save As dialog, keep the "Create PDF Compatible File" option enabled so Acrobat (and earlier versions of Illustrator) can open an .ai file.

- **To have access to the full set of PDF options,** choose "Adobe PDF (pdf)" from the Save As format pop-up and click Save, which opens the Adobe PDF Options dialog; then choose from among the full range of PDF options, such as Optimize for Fast Web View.

- **To save your layered Illustrator files as layered Acrobat files,** enable the "Create Acrobat Layers From Top-Level Layers" option in the Adobe PDF Options dialog. **Note:** *Illustrator can open many kinds of PDF files made by other applications, but can only open one page at a time. Also, text in the PDF will be broken up into multiple text lines when opened in Illustrator.*

ILLUSTRATOR & 3D PROGRAMS

In addition to Illustrator's 3D effects (see the *Reshaping Dimensions* chapter) you can also import Illustrator paths into 3D programs to use as outlines and extrusion paths. Once you import a path, you can transform it into a 3D object. Photoshop's Repoussé feature can work with any closed path whether pasted as pixels, path, or Shape layer. Autodesk Maya, Strata's 3D StudioPro, SketchUp!, and LightWave 3D are just a few of the many full-featured 3D programs that you can use in combination with Illustrator.

WEB GRAPHICS

This section looks at some of the complexities of creating web graphics for modern displays. Adobe has worked to eliminate obstacles between Illustrator and web programs such as Flash, but some of its features can produce large files that result in long load times, or features that don't scale to large and small displays.

Document profiles and templates, such as Flex Skins, were designed to optimize your design for the web from the start. If you choose the Web, Mobile and Devices, or Flash Catalyst document profiles when creating a new document, most of the settings—including setting resolution, RGB color mode, pixels for ruler units, and enabling Align to Pixel Grid—are geared for screen display.

- **Use multiple artboards;** these are a great aid for sharing resources when you need to maintain a look, but on vastly different scales. Save for Web lets you export only

Finding 3D information

To learn more about using Illustrator to create 3D artwork, see the *Reshaping Dimensions* chapter, and check out the excerpt on the **WOW! DVD** from Mordy Golding's *Real World Illustrator CS5.*

Pixel Preview

While Illustrator's default preview is optimized for print, choosing View > Pixel Preview will allow you to see your art as it would appear when displayed on the web or on a digital screen. Pixel Preview will show the effects of anti-aliasing, which often will affect the visual appearance of your art.
—*Mordy Golding*

Using the Pixel Preview grid

The Pixel Preview grid automatically shows up when you zoom to 600% or greater with Show Pixel Grid, enabled by default in Preferences.

Anti-alias & Save for Web

If you use Save for Web & Devices, choose Type Optimized on the Image Size tab to preserve character-level anti-aliasing choices.

Creating separate objects on their own top-level layers and saving them as symbols allows for importing them into Flash, where they can be assembled on the Flash Stage and motion-tweened to create the animation.

the *active* artboard, but your file will have all your assets in one place.

- **To prevent colors from being altered when working for print and display,** work in CMYK (the more limited color space), and then convert a copy of your file to RGB.
- **To assist in creating bold graphics,** turn on Pixel Preview to see how the anti-aliasing is affecting each object.
- **To keep sharp-edged objects crisp and prevent unnecessary anti-aliasing** wherever Illustrator paths line up with the pixel grid, enable Align to Pixel Grid in the Transform panel (if it's not enabled by default because you chose a Web or Flash Catalyst document profile).

From Illustrator to Flash

Because Flash and Illustrator objects are both vector-based, you can create just about any artwork intended for a Flash project inside Illustrator. If you own both programs, you can copy and paste or drag and drop between Illustrator and Flash. To get the best results in Flash, save your artwork as Illustrator (.ai) format and choose to import to the Flash Stage or Library. Note that if you save an .ai file and import it to Flash, you'll need to have top-level layers (not the sublayers automatically created by Illustrator's Release to Layers). Manually select all of the sublayers in Illustrator and drag them up to become top-level layers. Here are some strategies for maximizing the quality and usefulness of your Illustrator files in Flash:

- **Use Illustrator symbols for objects that you intend to place multiple times,** instead of using multiple copies of the original art. Symbols can reduce the size of any files that you export from Illustrator for Flash.
- **To modify symbols while keeping the file size small,** select them and apply Effects from the *fx* menu of the Appearance panel. Flash imports only one instance of a symbol no matter how many different instances have effects applied (although the effects may not stay live). Don't use the Symbol Stainer, Screener, or Styler on your symbols; using these tools will result in a larger SWF file with many unique symbols.

- **Gradients with more than eight stops, and all mesh objects, are rasterized.** Use gradients with fewer than eight stops if you want them to remain gradients in Flash. Flash retains transparency in gradients (called Alpha).

- **To create a Flash frame from each Illustrator layer,** export as an SWF file and choose Export Layers to SWF frames.

- **When exporting SWF files,** switch between Preserve Appearance and Preserve Editability and check the Optimized view to discover if anything has changed.

- **To control the way a symbol transforms,** set a registration point in Illustrator; it will be effective in both Illustrator and Flash. Use the registration point to precisely position and transform symbols relative to the artboard coordinates before exporting them to Flash. The registration point "anchors" the symbol to that point for transformations. When editing symbols in isolation mode, the registration point's x,y location is always 0,0, and can't be changed using the ruler.

Designing for expanded web access

Illustrator's vector features make it well-suited to designing websites and applications that scale easily and adapt to different screen sizes, such as cell phones and other web-enabled, handheld devices. If your target market includes Flash Lite–enabled devices, the Adobe Device Central application can help you work to those device specifications. Device Central is a full-fledged program with features beyond the scope of this book, but following are a few tips for using it with Illustrator:

- **To use Device Central to start a new document for selected devices,** click "Mobile and Devices Document" on the Welcome Screen (Help menu), or choose File > Device Central and click on the Create button.

- **To install selected device emulators** from the Adobe site to your own hard drive for use offline, when online select a device in the Browse workspace of the Device Library, and drag it to the Test Devices panel, where you can create your own sets of devices.

Use Anti-alias options for type

Illustrator permits each text frame to take on its own anti-alias setting. With your type object selected, choose an anti-alias option such as "Strong" from the Character panel (show Options). Vary your choice for web display depending upon the font used and the size you will use to display it, so your anti-alias settings keep your type from becoming blurry.

Symbols and guides

When aligning a symbol to an object or guide, be aware that its content, not just its bounding box, can snap to align with objects and guides. Choose this option from the Transform panel menu, and turn on Smart Guides to assist you.

9-slice scaling in Illustrator

Enable 9-slice scaling on symbols to allow you to protect outside areas of a symbol, such as its corners, from becoming distorted when transformed in Illustrator.

Use .ai for Flash

The best way to bring artwork into Adobe Flash Professional is to save a native Illustrator (.ai) file, which you can then import to your stage. Saving in .ai will preserve groups, layers, symbols, instance names, its registration point, and even certain live effects, such as drop shadows.—*Andrew Dashwood*

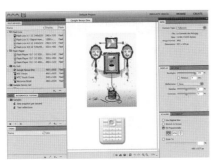

Using Device Central to emulate the appearance of an image on a selected device

The Illustrator document title bar displaying information that a Flash Catalyst component is being edited; clicking Done or Cancel returns the artwork to Catalyst

MICHAEL CRESSY

Round-trip editing showing the Flash Catalyst project dimmed, with the selected button on its own layer (not dimmed)

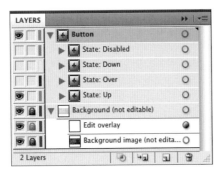

Illustrator layers control visibility for the component being edited and the screenshot Flash Catalyst makes of the project; turn off the "Edit overlay" sublayer's visibility to see the Background without screening

- **To create a document the right size for your selected device(s),** click on the Create workspace, select a size that best suits your device(s), click the Create button, and Illustrator will open with an artboard set to that size.

- **To preview your Illustrator file on a selected device** in the Emulate workspace, use Save for Web & Devices, and click on the Device Central button.

- **To review how a Flash Lite–enabled device responds** under a variety of conditions, choose the Emulate workspace. Select various emulator settings and operate a mock-up of the selected device's interface.

- **To automate testing on several different devices** in order to check that your project works on all of them, run test scripts and review the log that automatically opens when the script finishes running.

- **Use the Tasks panel to distribute your project files** to other devices. You can choose to send to a Bluetooth device, a mounted drive, or to an FTP server.

Flash Catalyst for web design

Flash Catalyst is an application that helps designers using Illustrator, Photoshop, or Fireworks (using the FXG file format) to create interactive websites and applications without having to write code for all the interface elements. When round-trip editing a Catalyst object between Flash Catalyst and Illustrator, the Document window displays Done and Cancel commands for Catalyst. Flash Catalyst also allows the designer to edit a component (such as a button's different states) against a screenshot of the developing Flash Catalyst project. Following are some tips for working between Illustrator and Flash Catalyst:

- **To start a Flash Catalyst project inside Illustrator,** create as many components as desired, keeping them on separate layers for easy editing, then save as either an Illustrator .ai file, or in the Flash exchange format FXG.

- **To easily identify the various parts of a website or application interface,** name your layers and individual graphics with identifying names while inside Illustrator. These will be carried into your Catalyst project.

- **Copy/Paste to get an Illustrator graphic into an open Catalyst project** without having to save a separate file.
- **Let Catalyst create the component states,** such as button states, rather than creating them as separate objects in Illustrator. You can edit the appearance of the objects for each state later on with round-trip editing from Catalyst to Illustrator.
- **To see a component you're editing in Illustrator within its environment** without the screenshot overlay dimming all the other elements, unlock the background screenshot layer, then unlock and turn off the visibility of the Overlay layer. This makes the background appear in its normal state.

CREATING ANIMATION WITH LAYERS

You can use Illustrator layers to design a sequence for an animation, or export it to another program for further manipulation. You can also place the parts of objects you want to animate on top-level layers, instead of a sequence.

- **To create layers so each object (or layer) can be manipulated/animated separately** in another program, such as After Effects, choose Release to Layers (Sequence).
- **To create the animation in Illustrator before exporting it** (similar to onion-skinning), choose the Build option; the bottom layer's object gets placed on every layer, with the next object placed on every layer except the first layer, and so on, until all the objects are placed on the top layer and the animation sequence is complete.
- **To animate your layers and objects in other applications** such as Flash and After Effects, which have sophisticated animation toolsets and can import Illustrator files directly, save in the .ai format.
- **To create a composition to import into After Effects,** use the Video & Film Document Profile. This creates two artboards—one large artboard that serves as a "scratch" area on which you can place objects for later use in After Effects, and one sized for your chosen video format. To retain each artboard and the layers, create a multi-layered file and save with Create PDF Compatible File enabled.

Animate with Graphic Symbols

If you use Illustrator layers to create an animation that doesn't need to be tweened in Flash, try importing the layers as keyframes in a Graphic Symbol. The animation is complete as soon as you insert a frame on the Timeline for every keyframe (Illustrator layer)

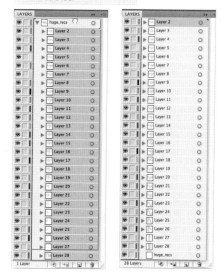

With the containing layer selected, choosing Release to Layers (Build), then moving the sublayers out of the containing layer—from a very large animation by Terry Lush

Exporting animations to SWF

To export a simple sequence created from layers for animations that don't need further work, or to work with a legacy version of Macromedia Flash, choose the SWF format. Be aware that exporting as SWF may break your artwork into many simple objects, even if you had them made into Flash Movie Clips.

Garden Slicing

Designing a Web Page in Illustrator

THE GARDENS AT MADISON

Like a colorful friend, these gardens will surprise and delight you. Come spend a day and make a friend for life.

hours tickets tours info

what's blooming now

special events classes gifts

donations membership volunteering

GORDON / CARTAGRAM, LLC

Illustrator & Web

Overview: *Set up a document for web page design; use layers to structure artwork for pages; create guides for artwork positioning; save an image of a page; slice artwork to save an HTML file or sliced image files.*

1

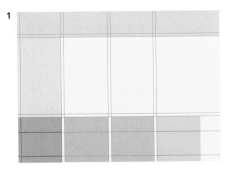

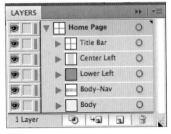

Gordon started the website by creating a 700 by 500 pixel file; he then created color-filled rectangles to represent areas of the home page and subsequent pages that would be filled with images and text, using layers to help organize

Limiting objects to artboard...

To limit the objects that will be exported to those within the current artboard, when using Save for Web & Device make sure that Clip to Artboard is enabled in the Image Size tab, or use Object > Slice > Clip to Artboard.

—*Jean-Claude Tremblay*

If you're comfortable designing and drawing in Illustrator, why go elsewhere to design your web pages? Steven Gordon used Illustrator to design and preview web pages, create comps for client approval, and slice and optimize artwork for use in his web software.

1 Setting up your document. To start designing your website, create a new document using File > New. From the New Document Profile menu select Web, and then choose one of the default sizes from the Size menu or enter your own custom size. Because your artwork will be exported in a bitmap format like GIF or JPEG, consider turning on pixel preview (View > Pixel Preview). With pixel preview you can see the anti-aliasing of your artwork as if it were rasterized, and can therefore make any adjustments if necessary. Set up the various regions of your website using colored rectangles on separate layers (for layers help, see the chapter *Your Creative Workspace*).

2 Structuring pages with layers and adding artwork.
Continue to let the Layers panel help you design and organize the content of the pages in your website. Gordon set up the full layer structure for his website, creating a master layer for each of the website's five pages; then within each layer were separate sublayers for the type, artwork, and images that would be on that particular page.

Next, to help you align and constrain artwork, create a grid (Preferences > Guides & Grid) or create a set of guides using View > Show Rulers (⌘-R/Ctrl-R), dragging guides into the artboard from the rulers, and positioning them precisely using the Control or Transform panels (be sure View > Guides > Lock Guides is not enabled). Now you're ready to create the content of each web page.

3 Saving an image and slices. You can now save an image of each page to serve as a template for your web software. Simply hide all layers except the master layer, and its sublayers represent a web page. Then select File > Export and choose a file format compatible with your web software. Another option is to export the text, artwork, and images as image slices so that you can use them in your web software to build the finished pages. Use artwork selections, guides, or the Slice tool to divide a layer's artwork into slices. You can use non-contiguous objects for slicing: Illustrator will add empty slices to fill in any gaps between objects. To begin, select an object (if the slice will be a masked image, click on the clipping mask, not the image, with the Group Selection tool). Then choose Object > Slice > Create from Selection. Repeat these steps until you've created all of the slices you need. If you want to remove a slice, select and delete; or in the Layers panel, drag its name (<Slice>) to the panel's Trash icon.

When you've finished slicing your artwork, you can save the slices as text and images. Choose File > Save for Web and Devices; in the dialog, click on the Slice Select tool and click one of the slices. Pick the settings that you want to use for saving that selected slice. For the flower images, Gordon chose JPEG as the file format and enabled Optimized to make the file sizes smaller. After clicking on Save, he then entered a file name for the HTML file (which automatically became the root name of each of the sliced image files) and made sure that HTML and Images were selected in the Format pop-up menu. Gordon continued the website development by opening the HTML file in his web software.

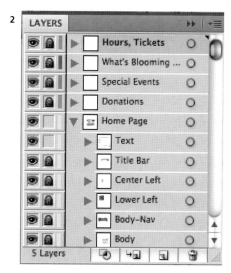

The layer structure for the web page design, showing the various pages as master layers and the sublayers as elements within the Home Page

The numbered slices created after using the Object > Slice > Create from Selection command

216 colors, or millions?

The palette of 216 non-dithered, web-safe colors was designed for text and graphics displaying on 8-bit monitors. But how many people are restricted to 8-bit color anymore? Not many. Most computers are now equipped with 24- or 32-bit video boards, rendering web-safe colors unnecessary, so you can choose from millions of colors, not just 216.

Ready for Flash

Creatng an Animation from Layers

Illustrator & Flash

Overview: *Draw the subject in different positions, using blends to create intermediate positions on duplicates; group and move each complete instance to its own layer; import layers as keyframes into Flash, creating a graphic symbol for the sequence.*

GRACE

To create an animation of a running dog, Laurie Grace used Eadweard Muybridge's early photographic sequences of animal locomotion for inspiration. In an RGB document, she created several instances of a dog in different positions using blends, and used Illustrator layers to import the animation into Flash, keeping their top-level layers intact. By creating a graphic symbol in Flash from the .ai file, she tied it to the Timeline and could convert each layer to a keyframe in the Flash animation.

1

Starting with a sketch of the main movements of a running dog

Redrawing the dogs, refining their forms

After blending and before expanding the blend to add a new limb to the dog in the middle

2

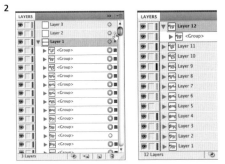

Moving each group (dog) to its own layer, above left, so the groups can be aligned and the layers imported as keyframes in Flash

1 Drawing the dogs. Grace used the Blob Brush to loosely sketch a few instances of the dog in running positions. She used the layer as a template and redrew the dogs on a new layer with the Pen tool. She added an intermediate duplicate between each original for a smoother animation, and then deleted one leg or other part she wanted to reposition from the duplicate dog in the middle. She selected that part on each of the originals and created a one-step blend between them, then chose Object > Blend > Expand. The blended object gave her a good idea of the intermediate positions required, even if she had to redraw some of the parts on the duplicate dog in the middle. Once she had all the dogs drawn, she filled them with color and used a 2-point oval brushstroke to outline them.

2 Grouping and placing on layers for Flash. The next steps required that Grace select and group the paths for each dog. She would need each dog to be a separate group in order to align them all later. She then added 11 more layers (one for each dog), selected all the dogs, and de-selected the first dog by Shift-clicking on it. She dragged the small colored square in the Layers panel to the layer above, (moving all except the first dog to the second layer), and repeated the Shift-click to deselect one dog at a time, moving the rest to the layer above, until all 12 groups were distributed among the 12 layers. With all the dogs selected, she clicked on Horizontal Align Center and Vertical Align Bottom in the Control panel. She moved the aligned dogs to the center of her artboards, and saved the file in Illustrator (.ai) format.

3 Creating the animation in Flash. Grace created a new document in Flash, and chose Insert > New Symbol to create an empty graphic symbol named dog_running (Flash would automatically convert the .ai file to the symbol on import). Graphic symbols sync with the main Timeline, and don't have interactive controls, but they do keep file size down. With the empty graphic symbol still open, she chose File > Import > Import to Stage and chose her .ai file. She kept all the layers selected in the Flash Import dialog, and chose Convert Layers to Keyframes. When she clicked OK, Flash automatically placed the first key-frame of the running dog graphic symbol on the stage, still in the edit symbol isolation mode. She could see that all 12 keyframes were there, but in order to configure the animation on the Timeline, she needed to click back on "Scene." She next dragged the symbol into the Scene, showing only the first keyframe within frame one. To create the right number of Timeline frames (12) to display each keyframe, she Control-clicked/Right-clicked on the twelfth frame in the Timeline and chose Insert Frame. Grace then slowed down the frame rate (fps) at the bottom of the Timeline (from 24 to 12). She tested the animation inside Flash by pressing the Enter/Return key and choosing Control > Loop Playback. Finally, she used Export to create a Flash movie in SWF format (see the animation at: http://lauriegrace.com/wowdogs.htm).

Adding an empty Graphic symbol to Flash's library, so that the .ai file could be added as a symbol to the Library when imported to the Stage

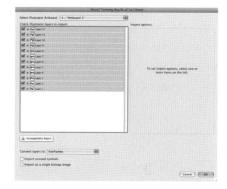

Keeping enabled the layers of the .ai file to import (or disabling some if desired), and choosing how to convert them (to Flash layers, keyframes, or flattened to a single Flash layer)

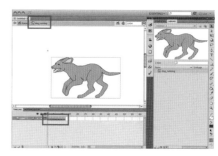

The layered .ai file opens on the stage in isolation mode with the Graphic symbol in the library, ready to be edited—all 12 Illustrator top-level layers convert to keyframes

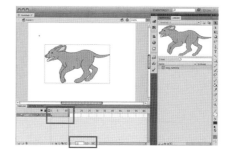

Dragging the graphic symbol to the stage, inserting frames, and changing the frame rate

Symbols to Flash

Turning Objects into Flash-ready Symbols

Illustrator & Flash

Overview: *Draw characters using discrete objects for each part which the animation will be constructed from; save objects as symbols; import the saved .ai file to a Flash library.*

The assembled snowbunny and carrot that would
be animated in Flash

The working parts on the artboard that are later
assembled in Flash as an animation

When designing a Flash animation, Kevan Atteberry uses Illustrator's advanced vector capabilities for preparing a "morgue" of parts, and converts those parts to symbols for easy import into Flash. There Atteberry assembles his scene and his characters, creating the final animation for SWF output. He created an animation to send to friends as his Christmas greeting e-card using a snowbunny who finds a Christmas carrot.

1 Creating characters and splitting artwork into parts for animating. In order for his snowbunny and candy carrot to have "moving" parts, Atteberry drew each part that might be animated with custom artbrushes. By starting off with parts even before planning the animation, he ensured that he would have the maximum "play" to all their features when it came time to create with motion. The snowbunny and carrot were designed with unarticulated separate parts. He planned to use Flash's transforming tools to generate motion "tweens." However, had he needed a leg to bend in the middle, for instance, he could have drawn a path stroked with his artbrush in a start and ending position, and used an object blend in steps to generate in-between positions. (See the *Mastering Complexity* chapter for details on creating object blends.)

2 Converting the separate parts to symbols. Having placed his objects on named layers, the next step to an animation was for Atteberry to select each part that he planned to animate in Flash, or parts of the scene he simply felt more comfortable drawing in Illustrator, and turn it into a Flash-compatible symbol. Since the panels are now "spring-loaded," he was able to simply hover over the icon with the object he was dragging until the panel popped open to receive it, which automatically opened the Symbols Options dialog. There he could give each symbol a descriptive name and designate it as either a Movie Clip or a Graphic. He could also have used the keyboard shortcut F8, or, if he'd wanted to keep that panel open during this process, he could click on the New Symbol icon in the Symbols panel (Option-click/Alt-click to skip the dialog). He kept the Movie Clip designation because Atteberry planned to animate most, if not all, of the symbols he imported. If he only wanted a symbol that would remain static in the scene, he could have chosen Graphic instead, but it wasn't really necessary to change the default for one or two symbols, since Flash lets you change the designation for a symbol at any time. Enable Guides for 9-slice scaling when Movie Clip is chosen and you want to create an interface element, such as a button, later on. Atteberry left that disabled. And finally, he could choose to save his symbols with a Flash registration point. This is the "transform" point that anchors an object being rotated or scaled, for instance, in the animation. This registration point, too, can be modified in Flash later on.

3 Importing Illustrator symbols to a Flash library. Once Atteberry had saved the Illustrator file, he opened Flash, began a new document, and chose File > Import > Import to Library. He browsed to his Illustrator file, and when the Import (file) to Library dialog opened, he checked that all the layers for the objects were enabled, he enabled "Import unused symbols" (just in case an object was left off the artboard), and accepted Flash's suggestion for handling an object that was not compatible with Flash. From this point on Atteberry was set to construct his scene and animate his characters using his Illustrator symbols.

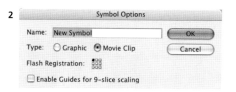

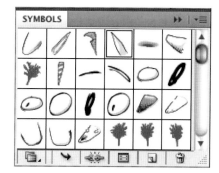

Checking out all the options for exporting symbols that are ready to go inside Flash

Everything that needs to be animated in Flash becomes a symbol

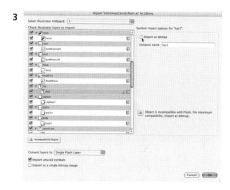

The Import to Library dialog in Flash

The Flash Library containing all the file's assets; here, previewing a symbol

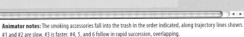

Laurie Wigham

Illustrator & Flash

Using Illustrator, Laurie Wigham created the art for the Flash animation, "The Last Draw," a web-based application designed to help people stop smoking, (produced by Health Promotion Services, Inc., funded by the National Heart, Lung and Blood Institute). To make the lines simple and expressive, Wigham drew the characters and other objects with the Pen tool. To create a relaxed and casual look, she drew open-ended unfilled paths, using a thick black stroke with a rounded end cap and corners (Window > Stroke). Beneath the outlines she created unstroked solid-colored objects, deliberately misaligned with the strokes to produce a loose, cut-paper look. Wigham created a collection of drawings that would provide a library of symbols for the animator to later assemble in Flash. She drew each character with different

positions and facial expressions, and included a collection of separate body parts and props that could move independently. She assembled all the drawings needed for each tutorial unit in a single file, positioned on a "stage," framed by the navigation and play controls of the website and browser. Each master layer in the file contained all the elements for a key frame within the animation, as well as motion paths and detailed instructions for the animator.

WIGHAM / Health Promotion Services, Inc.

DEL VECHIO

Gustavo Del Vechio
Illustrator & Photoshop

When Gustavo Del Vechio wanted an illustration to go along with his humanistic interpretation of an urban development project, he decided to make it appear as if the designer could make a real city rise up from his pencil-and-paper drawing. He contrasted the flat paper with the dimensional illustration, and the illustration with the full three-dimensionality of a photograph; then lit the whole to place the designer under a drafting lamp. He made the background from a simple rectangle filled with a white to black radial gradient. He filled another rectangle with white and used Effect > Scribble on black-filled objects to create very flat-looking hatch marks representing the urban area. Del Vechio then linked the photos of each hand to a separate layer, adding

Effect > Drop Shadow to one with a positive X value, and to the other with a negative X value, maintaining the illusion of radial light from above. Finally he added the completed illustration from his project for the urban development proposal. He had used 3D Studio Max for the initial structures, hand-traced the rendering, and later turned it into a Live Paint group to complete the colorful illustration (see his lesson in the *Rethinking Construction* chapter). Having placed his buildings in a designer's environment, his final illustration demonstrated what goes into creating a city, from the artist's initial concept to a three-dimensional reality.

Ready to Export

Exporting Options for Layers to Photoshop

Illustrator & Photoshop

Overview: *Organize objects on layers that Photoshop can understand; use Export to Photoshop (psd) or Copy/ Paste as Smart Object for editing layers in Photoshop; add texture or run other filters as Smart Filters.*

Each brush objects is listed in the Layers panel as a <Path> with a filled target icon (see the chapter Your Creative Workspace *for help with targeting)*

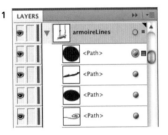

Upon Export to Photoshop, each object stroked with a brush in Illustrator becomes a layer within a Layer Group in Photoshop

If Knockout Group is enabled in Illustrator's Transparency panel (see the Mastering Complexity *chapter intro for more about the Transparency panel) sublayers become one layer in Photoshop*

ATTEBERRY

When Kevan Atteberry wants to add finishing touches to his illustrations in Photoshop, he has several options for preparing and exporting his artwork from Illustrator. Shown above is a detail from his "Frankie Stein" series, where Atteberry uses Illustrator's ability to write Photoshop layers when exporting to the PSD format, as well as Photoshop's ability to paste selected and copied objects directly as Smart Objects. Exporting layers as PSD layers is the quickest method for adding texture or other raster effects in Photoshop. To use Transform on the object (scale, rotate, etc.), Atteberry copies and pastes it from Illustrator as a Smart Object, which preserves the underlying vector for Photoshop to work with. (For the full illustration, see the "Frankie Stein" gallery following this.)

1 Organizing and rasterizing the layers in Illustrator for export as Photoshop PSD. When Illustrator writes layers for a Photoshop file, it attempts to maintain the layer structure, including all the sublayers. But some types of objects, such as those created with brushes, blends, symbols, or envelopes, generate an unmanageable number of extra sublayers. Two important steps in Illustrator can prevent this from becoming a nuisance in Photoshop. First, Atteberry collects all paths that make up a given object into a named layer. This might be a sublayer of a layer that contains more of a subject, such as the "MUM-layers" containing a "mumsDress" layer. This is just like organizing your hard drive in miniature, making it easy to quickly identify what objects the layers contain. Next, he targets the sublayers, opens the Transparency panel and enables Knockout Group (you may need to expand panel options). To extend our example, "mumsDress" now becomes a single, rasterized layer in Photoshop, but is still separate from "mumsHair," and both are contained in a Layer Group called "MUMlayers." Photoshop now can preserve Illustrator's file structure and layer names, without creating too many nested groups.

Well-named layers and enabling Knockout Group keeps layers manageable in Photoshop

2 Using Smart Objects and Smart Filters. Although any layer or Layer Group can be converted to a Smart Object inside Photoshop, Atteberry copies and pastes Smart Objects directly from Illustrator when he wants to Transform or Warp them. After importing and merging layers as described above, he goes back to Illustrator, selects and copies an object—such as Mum's hand—that he wants to fine-tune in the final version in Photoshop. With the object copied to the Clipboard, he returns to Photoshop and chooses Paste. A dialog pops up with options, and he chooses Smart Object. Once the Smart Object is in the right position both in the image and in the stack of layers, he hits Return/Enter to accept it. He then can delete the rasterized layer he had exported earlier, if it doesn't contain other paths. The new layer will always link to the vector file for transforming (so the art won't degrade the way pixel-based artwork would) and for editing in Illustrator.

If he doesn't need to transform an object, but wants to add texture inside Photoshop using a filter, instead of copying and pasting from Illustrator again, Atteberry converts the layer to a Smart Object from within Photoshop. Now he can run a Smart Filter on the Smart Object layer (in our example, mumsDress). This allows him to reopen the filter dialog at any time, change settings, delete or add filters, etc., all without altering the original object.

2

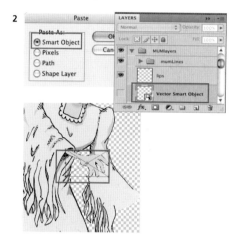

Pasting an object into Photoshop as a Smart Object in order to Transform the object without pixel degradation (blurring)

The dress before adding texture in Photoshop—and after, running Texturizer as a Smart Filter

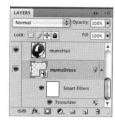

After choosing Filter > Convert for Smart Filters, a Smart Object layer protects the original pixels and any filter becomes editable

ATTEBERRY

Kevan Atteberry

Illustrator & Photoshop

For his "Frankie Stein" series of illustrated children's books, Atteberry uses Illustrator to create the basic illustration, and then moves into Photoshop to add textures and special effects. He carefully constructs his layers in Illustrator to make sure that he can work freely and easily in Photoshop, taking advantage of Photoshop's unique way of creating original artwork. In this illustration (spread over two pages), he prepared his Illustrator layers to use filters, Layer Styles, and Photoshop's soft, feathered brushes. He did this by ensuring the elements that would receive the same treatment in Photoshop were kept on different layers from other elements. See the "Ready to Export" lesson earlier in this chapter for more about layer organization.

ATTEBERRY

Kevan Atteberry
Illustrator & Photoshop

Once Atteberry has imported his descriptively-named Illustrator layers to become rasterized Photoshop layers, he depends upon Photoshop's ability to add texture with filters and images, blending it seamlessly into the objects he drew in Illustrator. He makes extensive use of Photoshop's natural soft, feathery brushes to add shadows and highlights to his characters and their environment. He even paints entirely new characters, such as the ghost (opposite page), using soft brushes and building it up gradually with multiple layers set to varying opacities, giving it its ethereal, ghostly quality. Adjustment layers are added to tweak color. The final results of his multi-layered approach achieve his unique blend of the real and the imaginary.

Planning Ahead

Working Between Illustrator & Photoshop

Illustrator & Photoshop
Advanced Technique

Overview: *Plan ahead for export to Photoshop with layer organization; group or separate some objects on layers based on the Photoshop technique you will use; make a registration rectangle for precise placement.*

HUBIG

1

The Illustrator file before export to Photoshop

LAYERS

			PatientTieViolinParts	○
		▶	DentistCuffPatientShirtViolinEdge	○
		▶	DentistFacePatientLegs	○
		▶	DentistID	○
		▶	DentistUnderID	○
		▶	**BlueCloud**	○

28 Layers

Keeping overlapping objects on separate layers, making it easier in Photoshop to add texture and effects to objects without making selections

When Dan Hubig creates an illustration like "Soothing Nervous Patients," above, he relies upon both Illustrator and Photoshop to get the job done efficiently and quickly. Consequently, he constructs his files in Illustrator with Photoshop's strengths and weaknesses in mind. Because the two programs have very different features, even when those features share the same name (such as brushes), Hubig organizes his objects so their Photoshop layers will allow him complete flexibility and ease in creating the finishing touches. And by setting his layers to flatten sublayers on export, he reduces the RAM requirements of his large files and shortens the time it takes Illustrator to create the Photoshop file.

1 Planning ahead. The main rule Hubig has when organizing his layers is that overlapping objects he will work on in Photoshop *do not* reside on the same layer. As long as they are on separate layers when exported to Photoshop, he'll be able to lock transparency (which acts like a mask limiting a tool to actual pixels), clip an Adjustment layer so it affects only that object, etc.—all without having to make tedious selections inside Photoshop. By constructing his layer organization this way, rather than grouping by subject (such as the Dentist on one main layer, with its parts as sublayers), he can rasterize all the sublayers, so Photo-shop doesn't import them as nested Groups when he uses Knockout Group to export the blends he likes to use (see the lesson "Ready to Export" for a full description of this method). The trade-off, however, is that if Hubig doesn't pay careful attention to naming the layers, once they're in Photoshop, his layer organization may not always be as "intuitive" as it would be if grouped according to subject matter.

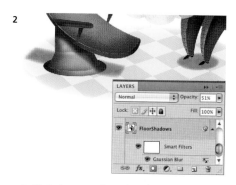

In Photoshop, creating a Smart Object to apply a Smart Filter on two Illustrator objects placed on one layer, and reducing opacity for both at the same time

2 Preparing artwork for finishing in Photoshop. Aware of the Photoshop techniques he plans to use, Hubig is also able to save time by putting objects that will receive the same treatment in Photoshop on the same layer. If you look at the two floor shadows in the illustration, you can see they both have Gaussian Blurs and reduced opacity. By creating them on a single Illustrator layer, Hubig is able to apply the blur and change the layer opacity in Photoshop just once for both objects. On the other hand, by keeping the blue cloud on a separate layer, Hubig is able to make changes even though it overlaps other objects visually. He can adjust the cloud's opacity, and by locking the layer's transparency he can loosely apply a brush with a broad "Scattering" (set in the Brushes panel), knowing his paint won't spill onto other objects.

Locking just the transparency in a layer to limit the effect of a tool or command to just the pixels—essentially, "auto-masking" the object

3 Bringing new objects into Photoshop with a registration rectangle. Although Hubig typically eyeballs the placement of objects in Photoshop, you might have a need for precision when moving objects into Photoshop. Make sure your artboard and image sizes in Photoshop are the same. Then, to achieve precise registration, create an unstroked, unfilled rectangle on the top layer (to select easily) that is the same size as the artboard. Select both the object(s) and the registration rectangle, and copy and paste them as pixels in Photoshop. This positions your new art precisely where it belongs with respect to earlier artwork, and on its own layer. Finally, drag the artwork layer into position among the other layers, if necessary.

3

Creating a registration rectangle with no stroke, no fill, and selecting both it and an object to paste as pixels in Photoshop for precise alignment with existing artwork

McGARRY

Aaron McGarry
Illustrator & Photoshop

To create this urban portrait, Aaron McGarry used the combined strengths of Illustrator and Photoshop. He began in Illustrator by placing original photos as template layers, and hand-tracing over them into another layer using the Pen, Rectangle, Ellipse, and Type tools. To simulate metal on the various components, he filled the objects with gradients from the Metals library (Window > Swatch Libraries > Gradients > Metals). Since each of the main objects represented a different depth, he next selected each main grouping of objects and applied separate drop shadows (Effect > Stylize > Drop Shadow). With the objects complete and assembled on various layers, he hid the template layer (see inset). Placing a photograph of a wall as a background layer (below the objects), McGarry then exported the file to Photoshop, preserving the layers. In Photoshop he created the illusion of a glass cover on the meter by placing a photo of the sky. Then, using the Warp command (Edit > Transform > Warp), he warped the photo to the roundness of the meter face. He next added a layer mask to the photo layer and used a gradient (Black, White) to fade the lower part of the photo, blending it in with the background image and adjusting the opacity to simulate the reflective, transparent quality of curved glass. For the finishing touches he used a variety of Photoshop's Brush tools, as well as the Eraser and Smudge tool (all with varying opacity), to paint the rust, stains, and grime, thereby creating a grittier look.

SHOGLOW

Lisa Shoglow
Illustrator & Photoshop

When Lisa Shoglow created this CD cover for a spiritual singer and Jewish educator, she was mindful that the artwork should have an ethereal quality that evoked a strong spiritual sense, yet also reflected the singer's passion for education. Knowing that the words were of equal import as the feeling the image would express, Shoglow first created the words in Illustrator, to be sure the text maintained legibility after adding them to her Photoshop image. In Photoshop, Shoglow made adjustments to her original photograph with Hue and Saturation and also applied several filters in varying degrees (Filter > Distort). In Illustrator, she embellished the word T'Fillah with calligraphic flourishes drawn with the Brush tool using a pressure-sensitive tablet. In the Brushes panel she clicked on a default 10-pt Round Calligraphy Brush and double-clicked to open the Options dialog. Shoglow changed the Diameter to 3 pt, then set the Roundness and Diameter to Pressure and clicked OK. She selected the word and its calligraphic flourish, chose the Shear tool, and stretched it to the desired angle. She placed (File > Place) the Illustrator text into Photoshop on separate layers above the image. She applied one or more filters to the words (such as Shear and Twirl), and she applied Gaussian Blur to the Hebrew text until they all mimicked the movement in the Photoshop image.

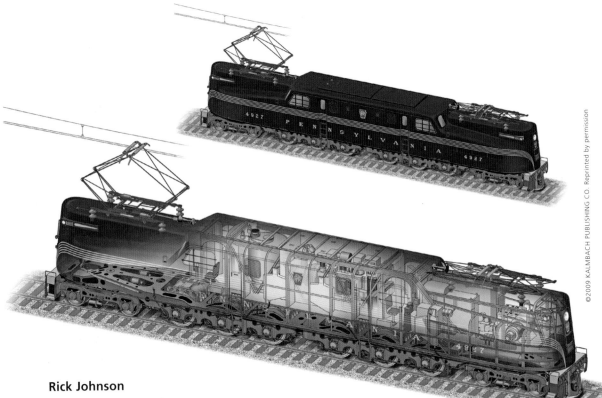

Rick Johnson

CADtools & Photoshop

Rick Johnson illustrated this GG1 electric locomotive, most of which were built in the late 1930s for the Pennsylvania Railroad by General Electric, for *Classic Trains* magazine using blueprints, photographs, and field notes. One might be tempted to draw this using Illustrator's perspective tools, but Johnson needed this drawing to be as technically accurate as possible. He began by drawing everything precisely to scale in "flat" orthographic top, front, and side views, in Illustrator using HotDoor's CADtools plug-in (find a CADtools demo on the **WOW! DVD**). Then, also using CADtools, Johnson projected those surfaces to their respective trimetric angles. With the help of custom-angle Smart Guides (set to 39°, –12°, 90° in Preferences>Smart Guides), he aligned the pieces to

their appropriate X, Y, and Z axis. He divided the art into 76 layers based on logical groups (e.g., tracks and power trucks, underframe, interior components, skeleton, and shell). He then exported the art to a layered Photoshop (psd) file, and in Photoshop he adjusted the coloring, contouring, and shading. He used layer masks to reveal the most (and most interesting) interior detail while still showing the outside form of this classic locomotive, which meant sometimes ghosting several layers at once. Since he had already drawn the entire locomotive from the inside out, the ClassicTrains.com Web site was able to repurpose the art, so visitors could disassemble the locomotive, peeling away a layer at a time.

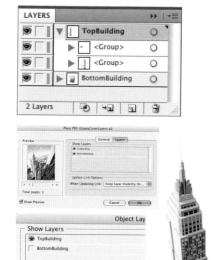

ZAPPY, HEFT

Michel Zappy (illustration) & Mimi Heft (design)

Illustrator & InDesign

When Mimi Heft from Peachpit Press saw Michel Zappy's New York illustration, she thought it would be perfect for the cover of the *Adobe Illustrator CS4* **WOW!** *Book*—if only the Empire State Building could enhance the illusion of depth by being placed in front of the first **W**. In order to keep most of the image beneath the type, Zappy duplicated a portion of the Empire State Building to a second layer. He then fit his artboard precisely to the size needed for the book cover, saved it as an .ai file with PDF compatibility enabled, and handed it over to Heft. She placed the artwork in InDesign's Place PDF dialog (enable Show Import Options in the Place dialog), setting the Crop option to Media to ensure the crop would be the exact size of the artboard (important in the next steps for registration of the artwork layers). Still in the Place PDF dialog, she made sure that both layers would be placed and visible, and clicked OK. Back in InDesign, she duplicated the image by dragging its icon on top of the Create New Layer icon in the Layers panel. She now had two layers and two complete images in perfect registration. Selecting the second layer image, she chose Object > Object Layer Options. Here she turned off the background layer, leaving only the Empire State Building visible on that layer. Finally, Heft added a text layer between the other two and inserted the text for the cover.

Eliot Bergman

Autodesk Maya & Photoshop

When the Japanese camping outfitter, A & F Country, asked Eliot Bergman to design a line of T-shirts with a camping theme, he turned to Illustrator, Maya, and Photoshop to produce the graphic realism he desired. Using Illustrator for its precision and ease in drawing, Bergman drew the paths that would shape his 3D models in Maya. For "Fresh," he drew a profile for the coffee pot he would later revolve in Maya, and he drew paths for the handle and spout. Bergman imported these paths into Maya using the "Create Adobe Illustrator object" command, where he assembled the coffeepot and generated the materials that gave it its speckled, metallic appearance. He created the type in Illustrator using Type Warp, and then assembled all the elements in Photoshop for the final touches, including the soft shadows.

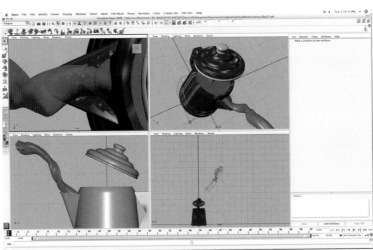

Eliot Bergman

Autodesk Maya & Photoshop

Continuing with his assignment for camping goods outfitter A & F Country, Eliot Bergman chose another icon of camping: the kerosene lantern. Again he began the process in Illustrator by drawing a profile for the lantern he would revolve using the 3D program, Maya. He also drew the lantern's handle, but the rest of the fittings he added in Maya with basic primitives. After rendering the lantern and creating the same appearance for the type in Illustrator he had used with "Fresh," he brought the various elements into Photoshop for the final assembly. Bergman created soft glows with brushes and blending modes, and created a soft shadow from a duplicate of the lantern filled with black, set to Multiply and a very low opacity. This ensured that the shadow, as with "Fresh," would show against light fabrics, while the glow would shine brightly against dark.

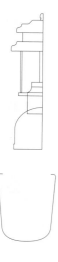

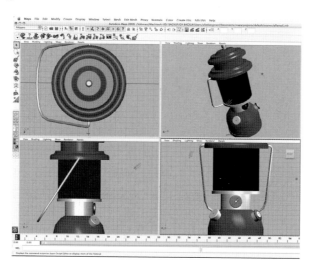

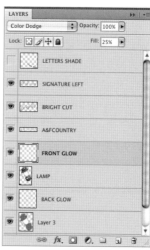

JOLY & RIDDLE

Dave Joly & Mic Riddle

Illustrator, Flash, & Cinema 4D

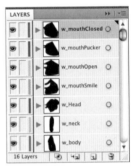

When Dave Joly and Mic Riddle collaborated on the "Trick or Treat" movie, they produced a unique mix of 2D and 3D artwork, using everything from Flash to Maxon's Cinema 4D, to After Effects, to Apple's Final Cut Pro, and it all started with Illustrator. To begin the 2D animation, they drew all the parts in an Illustrator file that they would use for a segment. Every part was placed on its own layer. So, for example, the man and woman seen here were created with separate heads, bodies, and expressions—each change in position on its own layer. They only needed B&W in Illustrator; the color would come from other programs. Once all the parts were finished, they could choose either to create and name symbols in Illustrator for later importing into a Flash library, or they could save the file and import it to the Flash stage (which is what they did for this scene). They chose to have Flash convert all the layers as Flash layers, which preserved Illustrator's layer names and organization. After animating the husband and wife talking, they were ready to export their 2D Illustrator art as a QuickTime file with an alpha channel (to create transparency around the animated characters), and from there take it into Cinema 4D to become a "texture" for a 3D type of "material" that controls how the 3D models appear. Eventually, with the aid of other programs, such as After Effects and Final Cut Pro, this 2D segment became incorporated into the rest of the movie.

RIDDLE & JOLY

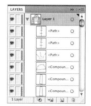

Mic Riddle & Dave Joly

Illustrator, Cinema 4D, & After Effects

Still working on their "Trick or Treat" movie, Mic Riddle and Dave Joly created the 3D scenes for the animation. Again, they often began inside Illustrator. Most 3D programs are able to import Illustrator paths and use them as the start for creating an extruded or lathed object, such as the doorway and clock shown here, both of which have dimension. It's these surfaces that, once lit in Cinema 4D or another 3D application, cast and receive shadows that convince us the objects are no longer flat illustrations. And just as they created a layer for each 2D part they intended to animate in Flash, they drew each "object" on its own layer that would be extruded in Cinema 4D, making extensive use of compound paths to represent both a solid dimensional surface and a hole for windows, or the cavity for a clock's pendulum. They added more animation and camera movements, color, texture, and pattern, then rendered their movie "scenes" to be imported into After Effects. They used After Effects both for features that were easier to produce there, and to save some time tweaking a scene by not jumping back and forth between programs. Finally, files were collected in Final Cut Pro, where they added sound and performed final edits, and saved as a .mov file (find a low-res version of the animation on the **WOW! DVD**).

Finishing Touches

Adding Scenic Entourage Elements & Using Photoshop for Lighting Effects

MARIC

Illustrator, Painter, Go Media, & Photoshop

Overview: *Place a photo sky as the background; add entourage elements; create lighting effects in Photoshop.*

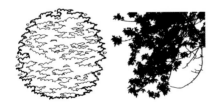

1

Sky background image created in Corel Painter

Go Media's bush and "foreground" tree vector entourage elements

To complete his architectural rendering created with Illustrator's perspective grid, Pete Maric inserted a photo background, added scenic "entourage" elements, and manually created lighting effects in Photoshop.

1 Replacing the sky background image and importing entourage elements. Maric decided to change the mood of the illustration by replacing the background sky image to reflect a dusk setting. In Illustrator, Maric created a new bottom layer and chose File>Place to choose a JPG of a sunset that he photographed and transformed with Corel Painter. Maric relies heavily on a library of entourage elements (cars, people, trees, bushes, etc.) to add interest to his illustrations. After importing a couple of his own trees, Maric opened Go Media's Architectural Elements Vector Pack and chose a bush and a foreground tree detail to copy and paste into his rendering. He sampled the grass color with the Eyedropper tool, then filled each bush with that color by holding Option/Alt and clicking. To populate the scene he duplicated each bush individually by holding Option/Alt while dragging it into place, using the bounding box to scale when needed.

The illustration with all entourage added

2 Creating lighting effects in Photoshop. In Photoshop, he rasterized the Illustrator file using File > Open, enabled the Constrain Proportions setting and set the Resolution to 300 pixels/inch. In order to help focus the image on the architecture, he darkened the corners by adding a blue solid rectangle layer, set the transparency to Multiply, created a layer mask, and applied a radial gradient to the center of the mask. Maric then manually created mood lighting effects by overlaying another series of gradient-filled layers on top of the image. He created the gradients by sampling color from his image using Photoshop's Eyedropper tool. He created the gradients on separate layers, then he painted on one layer, added layer masks as necessary to each of them, adjusted the layer opacity, and applied different blending modes.

The light effect layers created in Photoshop

3 Adding realistic reflections to the windows and simulating interior artificial lighting. To create a reflection in the windows, Maric used Photoshop's Pen tool to create an accurate selection inside the windows. He then opened a photo, selected and copied it to the clipboard, and pasted it into the window selection using Edit > Paste Special > Paste Into. To integrate the reflection photograph into the overall look of the illustration, he applied Gaussian Blur and Watercolor effects to it. To create an interior light glow effect, Maric added an additional 50px feather to the window selection using Select > Modify > Feather, created a new layer, filled it with a light yellow color, and reduced the layer opacity. For added interest and to mimic hotspots from interior lights, he created a new layer, used the Elliptical Marquee tool to select a small circular area within the windows, feathered the selection by 10px, and filled the selection with the same color used for the glow layer. To duplicate the highlight, he held Option/Alt and click-dragged it into place. He continued to duplicate the highlights for most of the front windows.

The window reflections photograph shown pasted inside the window selection

Window glow and highlights in Photoshop

Artists

Anil Ahuja
Adobe Systems
I-1A, Sec-25A
Noida UP-201301
INDIA
+91-9810566779
ahuja@adobe.com

Susan E. Alderman

Ted Alspach
ted@bezier.com
www.bezier.com

Kevan Atteberry
P.O. Box 40188
Bellevue, WA 98015-4188
206-550-6353
kevan@oddisgood.com
oddisgood.com

Jean Aubé
785 Versailles #302
Montréal Québec
CANADA
H3C 1Z5
jeanaube01@videotron.ca

Janaína Cesar de Oliveira
Baldacci
São Paulo City, São Paulo
Brasil
(011) 37910918, (011) 73687068
janacesar@gmail.com
jana@janabaldacci.com
www.janabaldacci.com

Christiane Beauregard
514-935-6794
c.beauregard@videotron.ca
www.christianebeauregard.
com

Eliot Bergman
12-1 Nishi-Gokencho,
Shinjuku-ku, Tokyo, 162-0812
Japan
212-693-2300
eliot@ebergman.com
www.ebergman.com

Dan Brown
79 Center Lane
Kensington, CT 06037
860-335-0480
drgn5ly@msn.com

Cinthia A. Burnett
cinabur@yahoo.com

Conrad Chavez
design@conradchavez.com
www.conradchavez.com

Kazimiera Cichowlaz
136 Texas Dr.
New Britain, CT 06052
860-224-9053

Scott Citron
112 W. 27th St., #700
scott@scottcitrondesign.com
scottcitrondesign.com

Sandee Cohen
33 Fifth Avenue, #10B
New York, NY 10003
212-677-7763
sandee@vectorbabe.com
www.vectorbabe.com

Mike Cressy
www.mikecressy.com

Jeanne Criscola
1477 Ridge Rd.
North Haven, CT 06473
203-248-4285
info@criscoladesign.com
www.criscoladesign.com
www.jeannecriscola.net

Michael Cronan
mpc@cronan.com
www.michaelcronan.com

Andrew Dashwood
info@adashwood.com
www.adashwood.com

Gustavo Del Vechio
Brazil
gustavodelvechio@gmail.com
www.gustavodelvechio.com.br

Dedree Drees
5307 Wayne Ave.
Baltimore, MD 21207
410-448-3317; 443-840-4423
dedreedrees@cavtel.net
ddreesart.wordpress.com

Elaine Drew
elaine-drew@comcast.net
www.elainedrew.com

Gary Ferster
10 Karen Drive
Tinton Falls, NJ 07753
732-922-8903
Fax: 732-922-8970
gferster@comcast.net
www.garyferster.com/

Erick Flesey
1405 Calle Goya
Oceanside, CA 92056
619-654-0090
fleseyman@yahoo.com
www.EricFlesey.com

Greg Geisler
512-619-3635
greg@raytracer.com
www.raytracer.com

Ian Giblin
408-448-2614
n.giblin@comcast.net

Nicole Gilbertie
ngilbertie@gmail.com

Von R. Glitschka
971-223-6143
von@glitschka.com
www.glitschka.com

Mordy Golding
Design Responsibly LLC
320 Leroy Avenue
Cedarhurst, NY 11516
info@designresponsibly.com
www.designresponsibly.com
www.mordy.com

Steven H. Gordon
Cartagram, LLC
136 Mill Creek Crossing
Madison, AL 35758
wow@cartagram.com
www.cartagram.com

Laurie Grace
laurie.grace@gmail.com
www.lauriegrace.com

Gusman, see Joly

Brad Hamann
Brad Hamann Illustration
& Design
brad@bradhamann
www.bradhamann.com

Pattie Belle Hastings
Ice House Press & Design
266 West Rock Ave.
New Haven, CT 06515
203-389-7334
http://pattiebellehastings.net

Dan Hubig
209 Mississippi St.
San Francisco, CA 94107
415-824-0838
dan@danhubig.com
www.danhubig.com

Gerard Huerta
Gerard Huerta Design, Inc.
54 Old Post Road
Southport, CT 06890
203-256-1625
gerard.huerta@sbcglobal.net
www.gerardhuerta.com

Lisa Jackmore
ljackmore@cox.net
13603 Bluestone Court
Clifton, VA 20124-2465
703-830-0985

Lance Jackson
Lax Syntax Design
www.noirture.com
www.lancejackson.net

David Jennings
7 Castleton Avenue
Romanby
Northallerton
North Yorkshire
DL78SU
UK
+44(0)1609 770795
+44(0)7754 796831
david@davidjennings.co.uk
www.davidjennings.co.uk

Mohammed Jogie
PO Box 44007, Linden
Gauteng Province 2104
South Africa
+27 (0) 82 655 2999

Rick Johnson
Graffix plug-ins
http://rj-graffix.com

Donal Jolley
10505 Wren Ridge Road
Johns Creek, GA 30022
770-751-0553
don@donaljolley.com
www.donaljolley.com

Annie Gusman Joly
860-928-1042
annie@picturedance.com
www.anniejoly.com

Dave Joly
860-928-1042
dave@picturedance.com
www.picturedance.com

Stephen Klema
69 Walnut St.
Winsted, CT 06098
stephen@stephenklema.com
sklema@txcc.comnet.edu
www.stephenklema.com

Chris Leavens
chris@unloosen.com
www.chrisleavens.com

Adam Z Lein
40 Morrow Ave., Apt 3HS
Scarsdale, NY 10583
914-437-9115
adamz@adamlein.com
www.adamlein.com

Emily Looper
56 Wickham's Fancy
Canton, CT 06019
lady_krile@yahoo.com

Terrance (Terry) Lush
PO Box 185143
Hamden, CT 06518
t.lush@tlush.net
www.tlush.net

Pete Maric
contact@petemaric.com
440-487-4205
contact@petemaric.com
www.petemaric.com

Greg Maxson
116 W. Florida Ave
Urbana, IL 61801
217-898-6560
gmaxti@sbcglobal.net
www.gregmaxson.com

Laura McCloskey

Aaron McGarry
aron@amcgarry.com
www.amcgarry.com

Nobuko Miyamoto
3-8 Matuba-cho
Tokorozawa-shi
Saitama-ken Japan/359-0044
04-2998-6631
venus@gol.com
venus.oracchi.com/

Yukio Miyamoto
Matubacho 3-8
Tokorozawasi
Saitama Prefecture/359-0044
+81-42-998-6631
yukio-m@ppp.bekkoame.ne.jp
www.bekkoame.ne.jp/
~yukio-m/intro

Laura Mottai
860-307-3084
Lauramottai@hotmail.com
www.lauramottai.com

Sebastian Murra Ramirez (mu!)
Ronda General Mitre 162
3ro - 2da, 08006
Barcelona, SPAIN
648726515
info@mu-illustration.com
www.mu-illustration.com

Stéphane Nahmani
sholby@sholby.net
www.sholby.net/

Gary Newman Design
2447 Burnside Rd
Sebastapol, CA 95472
gary@newmango.com
www.newmango.com

Chris D. Nielsen
6662 Timaru Circle
Cypress, CA 90630
714-323-1602
carartwork@ca.rr.com
chris@pentoolart.com
www.pentoolart.com

Ann Paidrick
ann.paidrick@ebypaidrick.com
www.ebypaidrick.com

Theresa Palmer
Meltdw@hotmail.com
meltdw.deviantart.com

Ellen Papciak-Rose
info@ellenpapciakrose.com
www.ellenpapciakrose.com

Laurent Pinabel
laurent@pinabel.com
pinabel.com

Federico Platon
Jose Mtnez. Velasco 8
Madrid 28007
91-573 2467
grafintek@gmail.com
www.grafintek.com

Shana Popyk
860-302-5716

Ryan Putnam
520 W. San Miguel St.
Colorado City, CO 80905
719-357-9730
ryan@rypearts.com
www.rypearts.com

Michael (Mic) Riddle
micrid3d@mac.com

Jessica Rosario
162 M Homestead St.
Manchester, CT 06042
860-713-8419
studio@jessicarosario.com
www.jessicarosario.com

Andrew Rudmann
Long Island, NY
andrew@rudmanndesign.com
www.rudmanndesign.com

Lisa Shoglow
64 Old Hyde Rd.
Weston, CT 06883
203-454-7977
LRShoglow@optonline.net

Rick Simonson
RLSimonson Studios
4010 Ave. R #G8
Kearney, NE 68847
rlsimonson@mac.com
www.RickLSimonson.com

Judy Stead
704- 877-5988
judy@judystead.com
www.judystead.com

Sharon Steuer
c/o Peachpit Press
1249 Eighth St.
Berkeley, CA 94710
www.ssteuer.com

Ilene Strizver
The Type Studio
Westport, CT
ilene@thetypestudio.com
www.thetypestudio.com
203-227-5929

Barbara Sudick
California State University
Dept. of Communication
Design
Chico, CA 95929
530-898-5028

Brenda Sutherland
345 Park Avenue
San Jose, CA 95124

Jack Tom
1042 Broad Street
Bridgeport CT 06604
203-579-0889
art2go2006@yahoo.com
www.jacktom.com

Jean-Claude Tremblay
Proficiografik
135 Boul. Champlain
Candiac, Québec J5R 3T1
CANADA
514-629-0949
info@proficiografik.com
www.proficiografik.com

Matthew Triompo
29 Hawthorne Dr.
Southington, CT 06489
860-426-0473
MattTri88@hotmail.com

David Turton
thegraphiclibrary.com

Hugh Whyte
Lehner & Whyte
8-10 South Fullerton Ave.
Montclair, NJ 07402
201-746-1335

Laurie Wigham
209 Mississippi Street
San Francisco, CA 94107
laurie@lauriewigham.com
lauriewigham.com

Darren Winder
Daw Design
darren@dawdesign.net
ww.dawdesign.com

Michel Zappy
6606 Drolet St.
Montréal, Québec H2S 2S8
CANADA
514-948-0477
michel.zappy@videotron.ca
www.michelzappy.com

Resources

1802
Pongo
Matteo Discardi
Piazza monte falterona 4
Milano, ITALY 20148
3471116116
info@1802.it
www.1802.it

Abneil Software Ltd.
*Andrew's Vector Plugins
Volume 4 (Multitoolbox +
Warping), Andrew's Vector
Plugins Volume 6 (Perspec-
tive), Andrew's Vector Plugins
Volume 26 (Linetool)*
UK
Andrew Buckle: 01622 688 375
support@graphicxtras.com
www.graphicxtras.com

Adobe Systems, Inc.
345 Park Avenue
San Jose CA 95110-2704
408-536-6000
info@adobe.com
www.adobe.com

Astute Graphics Limited
Phantasm CS Combined Trial
2 Bridge Street
Hereford HR4 9DF
ENGLAND
+44 (0) 1432 341073
enquiries@astutegraphics.com
www.astutegraphics.com

Avenza
MAPublisher®
124 Merton Street, Suite 400
Toronto, ON M4S 2Z2
CANADA
416-487-5116
sales@avenza.com
support@avenza.com
www.avenza.com

Code-Line
SneakPeek Pro, Art Files 2
6520 Platt Avenue, #711
West Hills, CA 91307
818-610-2228
softwaresales@code-line.com
techsupport@code-line.com
www.code-line.com

CValley, Inc
Xtream Path 1.4, FILTERiT 4.4
18552 MacArthur Blvd. Ste 375
Irvine, CA 92612
949-528-6617
info@cvalley.com
support@cvalley.com
www.cvalley.com

Design Tools Monthly
info@design-tools.com
WOW! readers get 3 free issues of
DTM from: www.design-tools.
com/ilcs5wow/

GoMedia
*Vector Set, Vector Pack,
Vector Sampler*
4507 Lorain Ave
Cleveland, OH 44102
216-939-0000
adam@gomedia.us
kim@gomedia.us
http://arsenal.gomedia.us/

Graffix
*Alien Palette CS3, Arrowheads
CS3, Concatenate CS3, Isometric
Line Tool CS3, Nudge Palette
CS3, Proof Block CS3, Select
Menu CS3, Square Up CS3,
Trackplan Tools CS3*
P.O. Box 373
Waukesha, WI 53187–0373
262-309-3452
sales@rj-graffix.com
support@rj-graffix.com
http://rj-graffix.com

Hot Door Inc.
CADtools
PO Box 5220
Laguna Beach, CA 92652
949-464-0300
orders@hotdoor.com
knock@hotdoor.com
www.hotdoor.com

Peachpit Press
**Real World Adobe Illustrator
CS5, Real World Photoshop
CS5, InDesign VQS, Painter
WOW!, Photoshop WOW!**
1249 Eighth Street
Berkeley, CA 94710
800-283-9444
ask@peachpit.com
www.peachpit.com

Premedia Systems
*Premedia Systems WOW Scripts
for Illustrator CS5*
P.O. Box 2767
Danville, CA 94526-7767
510-655-4454
info@premediasystems.com
support@premediasystems.com
www.premediasystems.com

Shinycore Software
Path Styler Pro
Compagnonsweg 28
8434 NW Waskemeer
THE NETHERLANDS
+31(0)516423637
sales@shinycore.com
support@shinycore.com
www.shinycore.com

Wacom
1311 Southeast Cardinal Court
Vancouver, WA 98683-9589
360-896-9833
www.wacom.com

Worker72a
*Scoop, SepPreview, QuickCarton,
PointControl, Zoom to Selection,
Select Effects, White Overprint
to Knockout, White Overprint
Detector, Tag72a, Bag72a,*
18535 Dixie Highway
Homewood, IL 60430
708-738-8441
info@worker72a.com
http://worker72a.com

Zevrix Solutions
ArtOptimizer
105 McCaul Street, Suite 301
Toronto, Ontario M5T 2X4
CANADA
416-217-0607
support@zevrix.com
http://zevrix.com

General Index

Blob Brush tool, *continued*
  applying, 89
  combining objects with, 61–62
  features introduced in CS4, xiii
  painting over part of letters
      with, 56
  refining pencil-and-paper
      sketch with, 76
  sketches for animation with,
      244
  sketches with, 230
  tracing with, 74–75
  using on Wacom tablet for
      freehand drawing, 77
bold fonts, 52
book cover design, 42–43
Break Link button, Control Panel,
    93
Bristle Brushes
  atmosphere and depth created
      with, 120
  loading and using, 79
  options in library, 112
  overview of, 91
  painting in layers with, 110–111
  pastel-like drawing created
      with, 113
  pressure, rotation, and tilt
      preferences, 98
  softening edges with, 230
  using with Art Pens, 95
  using with tablet or pen, 87
  what's new in Illustrator CS5,
      xiii
Brown, Dan, 116, 266
brushes. *see also* **by individual type**
  applying to letterforms, 54–55
  creating textures with, 221
  duplicating, 264–265
  mimicking traditional media,
      118
  modifying characteristics while
      working with, 111
  overview of, 89–91
  selecting, 117
  transparency used with, 190
  washes used with, 96–97
  working with, 91–92
Brushes library, 55, 117
Brushes panel
  dragging art to/from, 89
  New Brush option, 105
brushstrokes. *see also* **strokes**
  adding interest to, 98
  converting to/from basic
      strokes, 99

  dynamic variable-width strokes,
      86–89, 95–101
  effects added to, 115
  effects created with, 248
  transparency/opacity of, 96, 120
bullets, using star for, 56
Burnett, Cinthia A., 117, 266
Butt cap, end cap styles in Strokes
    panel, 88

C

CADtools plug-in, from HotDoor,
    258
Calligraphic brushes
  customizing, 97
  embellishing words with, 257
  fluid designs created with, 99
  graphic illustration of organic
      forms created with,
      116–117
  handwriting with, 55
  overview of, 89
  pressure, rotation, and tilt
      preferences, 98
  self-portrait created with, 114
  sizes and shapes of, 158
calligraphy
  Blob Brush tool and, 62
  creating shadows around, 177
  Eraser tool and, 60
  using brushes with washes,
      96–97
Chalk brushes, 119
Change to (Global/Artboard ruler)
    command, 4
Character panel
  adjusting offset of type from
      type path, 45–46
  capitalization options, 36
  font options, 50
  text formatting, 31
  tracking or kerning controls, 49
Character Styles panel, 31
characters
  applying styles to, 32
  changing shape and spacing
      of, 45
  entering with Type tool, 34
  special characters in Glyphs
      panel, 35
Charcoal brushes, 118
Chavez, Conrad, 5, 266
Cichowla, Kazimiera, 117, 266

Cinema 4D, from Maxon, 262–263
circles
  drawing, 71, 80
  drawing concentric, 221
  scaling, 80
  setting type on, 30
Citron, Scott, 40–41, 42–43, 266
Clear Appearance icon, 21
client files, storing related
    information in, 25
clipping masks
  applying, 208–209
  building and shading complex
      artwork, 82
  creating intricate patterns with,
      220
  Draw Inside mode and, 67
  Layers panel options, 198–199
  Mask button in Control panel,
      199
  Object menu command for, 198
  overview of, 195–198
  type, compound paths, or
      shapes used as masks,
      199
  vs. nonclipping masks, 207
clipping paths
  clipping masks and, 195–196
  maintaining masking effect
      anywhere within layer,
      199
CMKY
  blending modes and, 191
  process colors and, 123
  using Illustrator for web
      graphics and, 238
Cocks, Joel, 230
CodeLine, 269
Cohen, Sandee, 35, 40, 266
color groups
  applying, 136
  creating, 133
  creating with Kuler, 138–139
  creating with Live Color, 136
  creating/saving based on Color
      Guide, 134–135
  in Live Color, 129
  overview of, 123–124
  placing in Swatches panel, 152
Color Guide panel
  creating/saving color groups
      and, 134–135
  Edit Colors icon, 128
  mixing/matching colors,
      122–123

fonts
    with bold characteristics, 52
    opening files without correct
        fonts loaded, 35
    point sizes, 54
    san serif and serif options, 57
    selecting typefaces, 51
    setting font sizes, 50
    type outlines and, 33
    vs. outlines, 31
    Western Bullets WF, 56
formatting text, 31–32
four color process jobs, 123
Free Transform tool, 15
freehand files, opening/converting
    into multiple artboards,
    36
fx. *see also* effects
    accessing in Appearance panel,
        22, 58
    accessing Live Effects from, 162
    adding Live Effects to give sense
        of lighting and depth,
        219
    applying effects to brushstrokes,
        115
    choosing 3D effects, 165

G

galleries, in organization of this
    book, xvi
Gaps settings, Shape Builder tool,
    62
Gaussian Blur
    adding to background objects,
        219
    applying to words, 257
    creating reflection effect, 265
    creating shadow effect, 183
    Live Effects and, 211
    softening transitions, 177
Geisler, Greg, 56, 110, 114, 266
geographic features, on maps
    artwork, 26
geometric drawing, modified keys
    controlling, 60
Giblin, Ian, 65, 266
Gilbertie, Nicole, 116, 266
Gillespie, Cristen, x, xvii
GIS data, importing, 138
Glitschka, Von R., 124, 177, 212–
    213, 266
Global Adjust, color adjustment

sliders, 153
global process colors, 122–123
Global rulers, 4
glossary, on DVD accompanying
    this book, xvi
glow effects
    adding to appearance attribute
        set, 20
    creating, 205–206, 225
    creating from radial gradient,
        216
    Inner Glow. see Inner Glow
        effect
    Outer Glow. see Outer Glow
        effect
    for sense of lighting and depth,
        219
    transparency and, 216–217
Glyphs panel, type options in, 35
Golding, Mordy, xiii, xvii, 41, 107,
    149. 162, 163, 237, 266
GoMedia
    Architectural Elements Vector
        Pack, 264
    clip art from, xiii
    as resource, 269
Gordon, Steven, x, xii, xvii, 18, 20,
    26, 46–47, 138, 140, 144,
    202, 242, 266
Grace, Laurie, 244, 266
Gradient Annotator
    accessing, 126
    controlling fills with, 142–143
    creating gradients with, 159
    customizing gradients with, 147
    editing gradients with, 125–126
    rotating gradients with, 219, 224
Gradient Fill pop-up menu, 125
gradient meshes
    applying to backgrounds, 108
    converting gradients to, 146–
        147
    converting objects to, 157, 183
    creating textures with, 221
    overview of, 126–127
    using transparency with, xiii,
        154–155, 190, 225
    using with Live Color, 131
Gradient panel, 125
gradients
    applying to text title, 53
    black to white, 256
    blends compared with, 193
    color stops in, 209
    combining with blends and

transparency, 227
    complexity and dimension
        added with, 220
    converting to gradient meshes,
        126
    creating, 159
    editing and selecting, 224
    Eyedropper tool used with, 265
    filling objects with, 142–143
    filling rectangle with, 185
    filling square with, 180
    Flash and, 239
    glow effects created with,
        216–217
    grid objects converted to, 183
    light and depth added with,
        218–219
    from Metals library, 256
    within opacity masks, 179
    overview of, 124–126
    paper fold simulated with,
        144–145
    resetting defaults, 127
    reusing, 145
    transparency used with, 190
    unifying across several objects,
        143
Graffix, 269
Graham, Cheryl, 115
Graphic Styles
    applying to objects, groups, or
        layers, 9
    creating border with Boundary
        style, 41
    naming new style, 21
    saving and applying, 53
    saving effects settings as, 22–23
Graphic Symbol, 241
graphic tablets. *see also* Wacom
    tablet, 13
graphics, designating symbols as,
    247
grayscale
    adjustments, 210
    reducing colors to, 152–153
grids
    options for, 5
    Perspective grid. see Perspective
        grid
    positioning elliptical image
        with, 48
    Transparency Grid, 190
    workspace and, 4–5
Ground Level control point, in
    perspective drawings, 184

Group Selection option, of Direct
Selection tool, 51
groups
applying appearances to, 20–21
applying opacity, blend modes,
or transparency effects,
190
applying transparency to, 193
assigning style to, 21
blending between pairs of
grouped objects, 195
color groups. see color groups
Grunge Brush Vector Pack library,
120
guides
for 9-slice scaling, 247
aligning symbols to, 239
applying globally or to
individual artboards,
4–5
for artwork, 243
creating, 5
customizing, 43
for finding vanishing points,
184
for mesh objects, 154
positioning, 16–17
turning outlines into, 156

H

Habben, Douglas, 269
Hamann, Brad, 200, 266
handwriting, with Pencil tool, 55
Hard Light, Blending modes, 160
Harmony Rules, Adobe
creating/saving color groups
based on, 135
in Live Color, 129
for mixing/matching colors, 123
Hastings, Pattie Belle, xii, 267
headline, adding arc to, 52–53
Heft, Mimi, 259
help, accessing Illustrator Help, xvi
Hide/Show Edges, 5
hiding/viewing layers, 19
highlights
adding, 111, 204–205
Gaussian Blur effect used for,
219
simulating, 145
transparency used for, 216–217

Horizon Line control point, in
perspective drawings,
184, 187
Horizontal Align Center
aligning artwork, 245
in Control Panel, 16
Hot Door Inc.
CADtools plug-in, 258
as resource, 269
HTML files, 243
Hubig, Dan, 227, 254, 267
hue, adjusting in Photoshop, 257
Huerta, Gerard, 44–45, 267

I

Illustrator
combining apps with. see apps,
combining programs
with Illustrator
combining Photoshop with,
257–258
combining with Cinema 4D and
After Effects, 263
combining with Maxon Cinema
4D and Flash, 262
combining with Photoshop and
Maya, 260–261
creating Flash animations from
Illustrator layers,
244–245
features introduced in CS4, xiii
how to use this book, xiv–xvi
InDesign used with, 58
Web page design in, 242–243
what's new in CS5, xiii
working with EPS files from, 57
images
preparing in Photoshop, 210
resizing, 96
saving slices as, 243
importing
animation effects, 241
from Photoshop, 235
symbols to Flash library, 247
InDesign
page-layout program, 42
pasting text into, 234
using with Illustrator, 58, 236
Inner Glow effects
applying, 201
in Multiply mode, 177
in/out ports
Path type, 29

of text objects, 31
working with threaded text,
30–31
interlocking objects, creating with
Pathfinder panel and Live
Paint, 80–81
Internet. see Web
Intersect pathfinder command,
71, 212
introduction, in organization of
this book, xv
Invert Mask command, 192
isolation mode
editing clipping group in, 197
for managing objects, 6
restricting effect of Eraser tool,
60

J

Jackmore, Lisa, xi, xvii, 98–99,
106, 113, 146, 221, 267
Jackson, Lance, 76, 120, 267
Jennings, David, 210, 267
Jogie, Mohammed, 179, 267
Johnson, Rick, 258, 267, 269
Join styles
changing path look with, 55
in Strokes panel, 86
joining objects, 66–67
Jolley, Donal, 95, 267
Joly, Annie Gusman, 216, 226, 267
Joly, Dave, 142, 218, 262–263, 267
JPEG files
export options for artboards, 11
for image files, 243
saving sketch as, 74

K

kerning controls, for letter and
word spacing, 49, 51
keyframes, importing layers
into Flash as. see also
animations, 244
keystrokes, in WOW! glossary, xiv
Klema, Stephen, 16, 84, 116, 267
Knockout Groups
creating blends and, 193
exporting blends and, 255
managing layers in Photoshop,
251
Korn, Peg Maskell, xi, xvii

Selection tools, 63–64
Live Trace tool
    for rendering raster images into
        vector graphics, 64–65
    using Kuler themes with,
        140–141
Locate Layer option, in Layers
    panel menu, 19
Locate Object option, in Layers
    panel menu, 19
Lock/Unlock toggle
    color wheels, 130
    guides, 5, 16
    layers, 19
logos
    coloring interlocking objects
        on, 80
    creating for client, 40–41
    designing as part of company
        identity package, 39
    digitizing, 12–13
    selecting typeface for, 51
Looper, Emily, 117, 267
luminosity option, blending
    modes, 56
Lush, Terrance, 11, 267

M

Mac computers
    shortcuts and keystrokes for, xiv
    user competence and, xiii
Mac computers, turning
    Application Frame on/
    off, 2
Make with Top Object, options for
    distorting text, 52–53
making ends meet, strokes, 88–89
mapping
    artwork onto objects, 168–169,
        179
    compared with warps, 169
maps
    creating with terrain image, 47
    geographic features on, 26
    organizing layers and sublayers
        for, 18–19
    using paths to label curving
        features of, 46
MAPublisher, from Avenza, 138
Maric, Pete, xi, xvii, 186, 264, 267
Mask button, in Control panel,
    199

masks. *see also* clipping masks
    creating glow effects using, 205
    opacity masks. see opacity
        masks
    for rope shape, 200–201
    using Layers panel options,
        198–199
    using Object menu command,
        198
master layers
    collecting layers into, 198
    hiding/viewing, 19
    organizing into nested
        hierarchy, 19, 26
    targeting, 22–23
Maxon's Cinema 4D, 262–263
Maxson, Greg, xvii, 104, 267
Maya, from Autodesk, 260–261
McCloskey, Laura, 116, 267
McGarry, Aaron, xi, xvii, 102, 184,
    208, 256, 267
Measure tool, copying art between
    artboards, 11
measurement, setting units of, 4
Mesh tool
    creating textures with, 221
    deleting mesh points from
        warps or envelopes,
        162
    editing meshes, 147
meshes. *see also* gradient meshes
    blends compared with, 193
    converting gradients to, 146–
        147
    mesh points, 126, 162
    options for distorting text,
        52–53
Metals library, 256
Microsoft Office, moving objects
    to/from, 235
midtones, adding to artwork, 111
Minus Front pathfinder command,
    71, 80–81, 212
Miter joins, end cap styles in
    Strokes panel, 88
Miyamoto, Nobuko, 103, 267
Miyamoto, Yukio, 103, 159, 267
modified keys, controlling
    geometric drawing, 60
monochromatic color, 152
Motion Tweens, in Flash, 246
Mottai, Laura, 117, 267
mouse, drawing with, 13
Move/Copy Artwork with
    Artboard, 11, 39, 40

movie clips, designating symbols
    as, 247
multiple artboards. see artboards,
    multiple
Multiply mode
    blending modes, 145, 211, 226,
        230
    Inner Glow options in, 177
    Outer Glow options in, 177
Murra Ramirez, Sebastian (mu!),
    160, 267

N

Nahmani, Stephane, 7
naming conventions
    artboards, 10
    layers, 18
    styles, 21
navigating, through artboard
    layers, 11
nested layers, 18–19
New Art Has Basic Appearance
    setting, xv, 167
New Artboard button, 10
New Brush option, 105
New Color Group icon, 15, 124
New Document Profiles
    saving artboard configurations,
        10
    working with documents, 4
    working with Web documents,
        242
New Layer icon, 5, 93–94
New Symbol icon, 109
New Window, options for viewing
    artboards, 10
Nielsen, Chris, xvii, 222–223, 229,
    267
Normal drawing mode, 67

O

object management
    Appearance panel for, 8–9
    copy and paste techniques, 7–8
    isolation mode, 6
    overview of, 5–6
    selection and targeting
        techniques, 7
Object menu command, 198
objects
    applying appearances to, 20–21

object, *continued*
changing to gradient meshes, 157
combining, 86
composition process for, 14–15
constructing. see constructing objects
defining as guides, 5
drawing and filling, 146
envelopes as. see envelopes
interlocking, 80–81
making masks from, 207
mapping artwork onto, 168–169, 179
preparing for masks, 208
resizing, 203
saving as symbols, 246
type objects, 34–35
using ready-made, 13
wrapping text around, 31
Office, moving objects to/from Microsoft Office, 235
Offset paths. *see also* **Baseline Shift,** 217
one-point perspective view, 180–181
opacity masks
combining transparency with, 207
creating and applying, 206–207
glow effects using, 205
gradients within, 179
identifying, 198
overview of, 191–192
softening transitions with, 220
opacity settings. see transparency/opacity settings
Opacity slider, in Transparency panel, 190, 207
OpenType, 35
Options of Selected Object, in Brush panel menu, 92
orientation, of blends, 194–195
Outer Glow effects
applying, 228
in Multiply mode, 177
overview of, 47
simulating shadows with, 145
Outline mode, using isolation mode as alternative to, 6
outlines
converting type to, 32–33, 45, 54, 56, 228
filling with color, 158
Outline Stroke options, 201
turning into guides, 156

ovals, creating with Ellipse tool, 102
overlapping art
across multiple artboards, 11
Art Brushes and, 88
coloring with Live Paint, 80
overlay option, blending modes, 56, 228
overrides, avoiding text formatting overrides, 31

P

page-layout programs, 42
Paidrick, Ann, 131, 154, 156, 157, 267
paint bucket, using Shape Builder as, 63
Paint Strokes, enabling/disabling, 73
Paintbrush tool
applying Bristle Brush stroke, 112
customizing, 97
preferences, 116
Painter, from Corel, 264
Palmer, Theresa, 117, 267
panels. *see also* **by individual type**
clustering frequently used, 2
for creating/manipulating type, 28
hiding/viewing, 2
setting up, xv
tips for arranging, 3
for working with color, 122
Pantone color, 40
Papciak-Rose, Ellen, 58, 152, 267
Paragraph panel, 31
Paragraph Styles panel, 31–32
paragraphs, applying styles to, 32
paste. see copy and paste
Paste in Back command, 7–8, 79
Paste in Front command, 7–8, 71, 79, 207
Paste in Place command, 7–8
Paste on All Artboards command, 7–8
Paste Remembers Layers, 9
Path Eraser tool, 61
Path type
creating labels, 49
creating paths and adding type to, 44–45

labeling curving features on maps, 46
overview of, 29–30
setting on curve, 48–49
type objects and, 34
working with threaded text, 30–31
Pathfinder panel, 69, 80–81
Pathfinders
applying to closed paths, 212
constructing paths using, 70–71
Divide command, 222–223
Minus command. see Minus Front pathfinder command
Unite command. see Unite pathfinder command
paths
blends along, 195
building layers of, 229
clipping masks and, 196
compound paths vs. compound shapes, 67
constructing using Pathfinders, 70–71
creating and adding type to, 44–45
creating with brushes, 54–55
editing in InDesign, 236
filling with solid color, 218
labeling curving features on maps, 46
modifying with Blob Brush tool, 61
moving objects from Illustrator to Photoshop, 234–235
protecting from Eraser tool, 60–61
Simplify command, 66
Pattern Brushes
adding detail with, 104–105
creating, 90
making new brush, 105
overview of, 90–91
posters created with, 118
use in necklace design, 103
patterns
fills, 4
for repeating elements, 212–213
PDF (Portable Document Format)
Create PDF Compatible File, 232
creating multi-page PDF, 40–41
moving other program files into Illustrator, 233

Scissors tool
    cutting arc with, 17
    cutting paths with, 44
    making curved path with,
        48–49
Screen, blending modes, 173
Scribble effect, 249
scripts
    adding and editing colors,
        138–139
    Colorizer script, 78
Select Object Behind, 7
selection indicators, 7
selection techniques
    for clipping masks, 199
    Live Paint tools and, 73
    for managing objects, 7
Selection tool
    moving clipping masks with,
        197
    scaling type with, 28–29
serif fonts, 57
shading
    adding with Blob Brush tool, 83
    applying to 3D effects, 167–168
shadows
    adding custom blurred shadow
        to type, 54
    adding to artwork, 111
    creating, 158
    paths for, 81
    simulating, 145
    transparent, 211
    using around calligraphy, 177
Shape Builder tool
    combining objects into shapes,
        13
    constructing objects with,
        62–63, 78–79
    preparing objects for use with
        Draw Inside mode,
        82–83
    shaving time in constructing
        illustrations, 84
    what's new in Illustrator CS5,
        xiii
shapes
    clipping masks, 199
    compound paths vs. compound
        shapes, 67
    drawing, 200
    exporting compound shapes to
        Photoshop, 235
    sketching and scanning, 44
sharing artboards and libraries, 39

Shear filter, applying to words, 257
Shinycore Software, 269
Shoglow, Lisa, 257, 268
shortcuts, in WOW! glossary, xiv
Show Transparency Guide, View
    menu, 190
Simonson, Rick, 109, 209, 268
Simplify command, paths, 66
Simulate Colored Paper option,
    190
Single-line composer, dealing with
    line breaks, 33
sketches
    applying perspective to, 186–
        187
    basic to complex in composition
        process, 14–15
    basing perspective drawings
        on, 188
    creating with Blob Brush tool,
        230
    placing as template, 110
    refining pencil-and-paper
        sketch with Blob
        Brush, 76
    scanning, 96, 174, 200
    of shapes, 44
    tracing, 74–75
slices
    for 9-slice scaling, 247
    of image files, 243
Small Caps option, Character
    panel, 36
Smart Filters, in Photoshop, 251
Smart Guides
    activating, 17
    aligning rectangles with, 80
    creating circular shapes, 217
    creating repeating patterns, 212
    for custom angles, 258
    enabling/disabling, 5, 162, 203
    using with Pen tool in drawing
        line art, 72
Smart Objects, in Photoshop, 234,
    251
Smooth Color option, Blend tool,
    209, 217
Smooth tool, accessing from Blob
    Brush, 61
smoothing color, in blends, 194
smoothing lines, 13
Snap to Point
    creating repeating pattern, 212
    moving objects to guide or
        anchor points, 60

Soft Light, blending modes, 141
software, on DVD accompanying
    this book, xiii
solid filled objects, transforming
    into gradient meshes, 126
spine, in curving blends along a
    path, 195
Splash brushes, 119
spot colors
    applying with Live Color,
        148–149
    selecting, 40
    types of solid fills, 122–123
stacking order, of attributes, 9
stacking panels, 3
Star tool, 84
stars, using ready-made objects in
    building logo, 13
Stead, Judy, 86, 268
Steuer, Sharon, (book author), x,
    xii–xiii, xviii, 78, 96, 268
Stretch Between Guides option,
    Art Brushes, 90
Stretch to Fit, 103
Strizver, Ilene, 36, 268
Stroke Weight menu, 47
strokes. see also brushstrokes
    adding to type objects, 34
    appearance of stroked text, 34
    brushes and, 89–91
    control settings, 89–90
    creating multi-stroked lines, 21
    duplicating, 8
    increasing weight of, 58
    making ends meet, 88–89
    making labels standout on
        maps, 47
    opening panel for, 9
    overview of, 84
    resizing, 66
    retaining interior strokes in
        drawings, 62
    transparency with, 190
    types of Symbolism tool, 94
    varying width of, 88–91, 95–101
    working with brushes, 91–92
    working with symbols, 92–94
Strokes panel
    control settings, 87–88
    dynamic variable-width strokes,
        86–89, 95–101
    end cap styles in, 88
    opening panels in Appearance
        panel, 9

Web
    designing for expanded access
        on, 239–240
    Flash Catalyst used for web
        design, 240–241
    using Illustrator for web
        graphics, 237–238
    web-safe colors, 243
    working with Web documents,
        242

Web page, designing in Illustrator,
    242–243

web slices, Photoshop and TIFF
    files and, 234

White, Black Radial gradient,
    205–206

Whyte, Hugh, 134, 268

Width Point Edit dialog, 87

Width tool
    adding depth and variance to
        brushstrokes, 100
    Stretch Between Guides option,
        90
    varying width of strokes, 86–89,
        95–101

Wigham, Laurie, 22, 248, 268

Winder, Darren A., xvii, 225, 268

Window menu, accessing panels
    from, xv

windows, options for viewing
    images, 10

Windows computers
    shortcuts and keystrokes for, xiv
    user competence and, xiii

wireframes, using for positioning,
    174–175

word spacing
    maintaining when converting
        type to outlines, 33
    warping type and, 49

Worker72a, 269

workspaces
    New Document Profiles, 4
    organizing, 2–3
    rulers, guides, and grids, 4–5
    tips for arranging panels, 3

wrap objects, 31

wrapping text
    Area type and, 28–29
    around objects, 31

X

x-axis. *see also* **coordinates, of axes,**
    165

Xtream Path, from CVally
    Software, 212

Y

y-axis. *see also* **coordinates, of axes,**
    165–166

Z

Zappy, Michel, 259, 268

z-axis. *see also* **coordinates, of axes,**
    165

ZenLessons folder, on DVD
    accompanying this book,
    xii

Zevrix Solutions, 269

Zig Zag, Distort & Transform
    option, 173

zoom
    commands affecting active
        artboard, 11
    for drawing smooth lines, 55
    before tracing, 65
    working on detail and, 222

Windows WOW! Glossary

and essential Adobe Illustrator shortcuts

Ctrl **Alt**	Ctrl always refers to the Ctrl (Control) key Alt always refers to the Alt key
Marquee	With any Selection tool, click-drag over object(s) to select
Toggle	Menu selection acts as a switch; choose once turns it on, choosing again turns it off
Contextual menu	Right-click to access contextual menus
Group	Ctrl-G to group objects together onto one layer
Copy, Cut, Paste, Undo	Ctrl-C, Ctrl-X, Ctrl-V, Ctrl-Z
Select All, Deselect	Ctrl-A, Ctrl-Shift-A
Paste Remembers Layers	With Paste Remembers Layers on (from the Layers panel menu), pasting from the Clipboard places objects on the same layers that they were on originally; if you don't have the layers, Paste Remembers Layers will make the layers for you
Paste in Front	Use Ctrl-F to paste objects on the Clipboard directly in front of selected objects, and in exact registration from where it was cut (if nothing is selected, it pastes in front of current layer with Paste Remembers Layers off)
Paste in Back	Use Ctrl-B to paste objects on the Clipboard directly in back of selected objects, and in exact registration from where it was cut (if nothing is selected, it pastes in back of current layer with Paste Remembers Layers off)
Toggle rulers on/off	Ctrl-R
***fx* menu**	From the Appearance panel, click the *fx* icon to access effects
Select contiguous	Hold Shift while selecting to select contiguous layers, swatches, etc.
Select non-contiguous	Hold Ctrl while selecting to select contiguous layers, swatches, etc.
Toggle Smart Guides on/off	Ctrl-U
Turn objects into guides	Ctrl-5
Turn guides back into objects	Ctrl-Alt-5 (you must select the guide first; if guides are locked, you must unlock them first from the contextual menu or from the View > Guides submenu)
⊙	Find related files or artwork in that chapter's folder on the **WOW! DVD**
Illustrator Help	Access ***Illustrator Help*** from the Help menu

Windows Finger Dance

from **The Zen of Illustrator**, *to help you learn, to "think in Illustrator"**

Object Creation	*Hold down keys until AFTER mouse button is released.*
⇧ Shift	Constrains objects horizontally, vertically, or proportionally.
Alt	Objects will be drawn from centers.
Alt click	Opens dialog boxes with transformation tools.
[spacebar]	Spacebar turns cursor into the grabber Hand
Ctrl [spacebar]	Turns cursor into the Zoom-in tool. Click or marquee around an area to Zoom in.
Ctrl Alt [spacebar]	Turns cursor into the Zoom-out tool. Click to Zoom out.
Caps lock	Turns your cursor into a cross-hair.

Object Selection	*Watch your cursor to see that you've pressed the correct keys.*
Ctrl	The current tool becomes the last chosen Selection tool.
Ctrl Alt	The current tool becomes the Group Selection tool to select entire object. Click again to select next level of grouping. To move selection release Option key, then Grab.
Ctrl Tab	Toggles whether Direct Selection or regular Selection tool is accessed by the Ctrl key.
⇧ Shift click	Toggles whether an object, path, or point is selected or deselected.
⇧ Shift click	With Direct Selection tool, click on or marquee around an object, path, or point to toggle selection/deselection. **Note:** *Clicking inside a filled object may select the entire object.*
⇧ Shift click	Clicking on, or marqueeing over objects with Selection tool or Group Selection tool, toggles selection/deselection (Group Selection tool chooses objects within a group).

Object Transformation	*Hold down keys until AFTER mouse button is released.*
⇧ Shift	Constrains transformation proportionally, vertically, and horizontally.
Alt	Leaves the original object and transforms a copy.
Ctrl Z	Undo. Use Shift-Ctrl-Z for Redo.